# The Career Adventure

## Your Guide to Personal Assessment, Career Exploration, and Decision Making

### CANADIAN EDITION

Susan M. Johnston
Sinclair Community College

Sandra Moniz-Lecce
Kwantlen University College

PEARSON

Prentice
Hall

Toronto

Library and Archives Canada Cataloguing in Publication

Johnston, Susan M.
    The career adventure : your guide to personal assessment, career
exploration, and decision making / Susan M. Johnston. — Canadian ed.

Includes bibliographical references and index.
ISBN 0-13-127459-7

    1. Vocational guidance.  2. Job hunting.  I. Moniz-Lecce, Sandy II. Title.

HF5381.J66 2006          650.14          C2004-906090-2

ISBN 0-13-127459-7

Vice President, Editorial Director: Michael J. Young
Executive Editor: Dave Ward
Signing Representative: Carmen Batsford
Marketing Manager: Toivo Pajo
Associate Editor: Jon Maxfield
Production Editor: Kevin Leung
Copy Editor: Linda Cahill
Proofreader: Susan Marshall
Production Coordinator: Janis Raisen
Manufacturing Coordinator: Susan Johnson
Page Layout: Heidi Palfrey
Art Director: Mary Opper
Cover Design: Jennifer Stimson
Cover Image: Miguel S. Salmeron/Gettyimages

13 14 15  CP 14 13 12

Printed and bound in Canada.

# Contents

## 11  Continuing the Adventure: Your Lifelong Journey   188

## Appendix   193

Sample Résumés and Cover Letters

# Dedication

To my husband, Jack, and my sons, Charlie, Mitch, and Russ ... My deepest gratitude for your love and support. SMJ

To my husband, Joey, and my daughter, Julia, who give my life journey meaning. SM-L

# Preface

Choosing a career is an exciting process of self-discovery. It draws you out into the world to explore occupations and make decisions that will result in insight, growth, and reward. This journey is most fulfilling when undertaken with a belief in yourself, a willingness to risk, and a sense of humour! The adventure does not end when an occupation is chosen—your career is always a work in progress and continues to change as the adventurer grows and changes.

The most important resource in any career adventure is you—the person who explores new vistas and makes the career choice. *The Career Adventure: Your Guide to Personal Assessment, Career Exploration, and Decision Making*, First Canadian Edition, is designed to actively engage readers in planning the future of their careers. The exercises and activities found throughout the book make the adventure an interactive one; you are encouraged to consider thoughtfully each step of the journey, building confidence as you see your decisions yield results.

The book is divided into three parts. Part I, "Self-Awareness: Learning about Yourself," focuses on self-knowledge and discovery. Readers explore career dreams, motivations, values, life stages, abilities and skills, personality, and interests. Examining these areas begins the process of discernment that is critical to making meaningful career decisions.

Part II, "Occupational Research: Learning about the World of Work," guides you through the labour market and future job trends and investigates government resources and other publications useful for obtaining research and information on occupations. Important discussions about networking, acquiring experience, finding appropriate education and training programs, and making effective career decisions, accompanied by practical exercises, help readers set goals and then formulate plans and develop skills to achieve those goals.

Part III, "The Job Search: Organizing Your Search," looks at how to find job leads and examines the details of résumé writing, interviewing, and marketing skills. You will have an immediate opportunity to apply new skills when working through the exercises. Even people who do not plan to seek new employment immediately will benefit greatly from the information in Part III.

This edition of *The Career Adventure* takes a fresh look at the adventure of career planning from a Canadian perspective. It includes resources and information relevant to people living in all regions of Canada, with consideration given to the Canadian labour market, diverse cultures, and post-secondary education and training opportunities. The information is just as relevant to young adults beginning to embark on their careers as it is to those who are making mid-career changes.

Useful and stimulating exercises are grouped at the end of each chapter with suggestions for group discussions. These exercises and discussions give you the opportunity to more fully integrate and synthesize the information presented in the text. They also encourage you to grow through interaction with peers, instructors, administrators, and the community. Internet resources and suggested readings are offered throughout the book to help you expand your information base and give you alternative sources for further investigation and learning.

The world around us plays a dramatic and constantly changing role in our career adventures. However, it is the adventurer who guides the journey and determines the outcome. Recognizing what information is needed, knowing how and where it can be found, and understanding what can be done with it are the keys to achieving any and every goal. *The Career Adventure* was written to help you acquire the skill and confidence to see the goal and achieve it!

# Acknowledgments

This book could not have become a reality without the generous support and encouragement of the following people. I would like to thank them for their efforts.

Dr. Lamarr Reese, Terry Maiwurm, and Leonard Banks supported my growth and development as a career counsellor. They were exceptional resources in the development of particular ideas for the book and in helping me to better understand co-operative education and its value to students. Brenda Krueger and M. L. Smith shared with me their ideas about personality development and co-operative education. I would also like to extend my appreciation to Tony Allen, who was invaluable in helping me more fully understand the significance of diversity in career issues. A big thank you to Bruce Anderson for guidance on electronic transmission of résumés. My thanks also go to Jon Sergeant, the Bureau of Labour Statistics, for assistance with labour trends data.

Karen Witt, Ann Hall, and Dodie Munn allowed me to enjoy the special relationship that comes from shepherding students through career decision making in the Adult Re-Entry classes. The staff members of the Career Planning and Placement Center, the Experience-Based Education Department, and the Learning Resources Center of Sinclair Community College aided me in locating materials and helped me to understand more fully the challenges that students encounter when making career decisions in a college setting. Their help was invaluable.

My thanks to Dr. Priscilla Mutter, who taught me about letting go and finding balance. My special thanks to Del Vaughan for the opportunity he gave me to work with students under his leadership—a peak experience as a career professional. I would also like to extend my gratitude to Dr. Jean Cook for her active promotion and support of my goals and dreams and her continuing belief in my ability to make them a reality.

I am very grateful to the following reviewers, who read this material in various stages of its development and offered ideas as to how it might be improved: Mikel J. Johnson, Emporia State University; Carole J. Wentzel, Orange County Community College; Jan L. Brakefield, University of Alabama; Pat Joachim Kitzman, Central College; Eve Madigan, Los Angeles Trade Technical College; Dave Sonenberg, Southeast Community College; Pablo Cardona, Milwaukee Area Technical College; Katy Kemeny, Lansing Community College; Cliff Nelson, Hinds Community College; and Maria Mitchell, Reading Area

Community College. Students will find the book more readable and more helpful as a result of their efforts.

I would also like to thank Sande Johnson, Cecilia Johnson, Pam Bennett, JoEllen Gohr, and Gay Pauley for their guidance and support as editors and production coordinators of this book.

Finally, I would like to thank my parents, Claude and Marcia Kelnhofer, for instilling in me a strong work ethic and a basic respect for all types of work. Their influence led me to a deeper understanding of the meaning of work and career in our growth and development as human beings.                          SMJ


I, too, have many people who have supported and encouraged me on my career adventure. I wish to express my gratitude to the following people without whom this book would not have become a reality.

First, thank you to Carmen Batsford and Dave Ward of Pearson Education Canada. Carmen suggested that I should begin writing and encouraged me to do so, and Dave took interest in this project and encouraged me to write this book, offering support and encouragement along the way. Also, thank you to Jon Maxfield for his guidance, feedback, and professionalism, Linda Cahill, for her excellent work copy editing the manuscript, and the many other staff at Pearson who produced this book. Thank you, also, to the reviewers who provided thoughtful and insightful suggestions and feedback.

Thank you to my colleagues at Kwantlen, including Susanne Dadson and Ron Flaterud who supported and mentored me into my roles as counsellor, instructor, and writer; Susan Morris and Renu Seru who shared their ideas and course materials that inspired such a textbook; Dennis Dahl for his stimulating discussions on research, writing, and career development; and our Dean, Derek Nanson, for his ongoing support, understanding, and flexibility that allowed me to undertake this project. I also want to thank the many Kwantlen students who have trusted me to guide them in their growth and learning and who, in turn, have helped guide me in mine.

And finally, thank you to my family. A very big thanks to my mother for caring for my daughter when I work, and to both my parents, Jose and Rosalina Moniz, who through living example have provided me with the values of honesty, caring, respect, love of learning, and desire to strive for excellence. Thank you to my husband, Joey, who has been at my side since I was 18 and who has encouraged, supported, and shared life with me. And last, but always most, my daughter, Julia, who has always understood why mama has to work, even though she doesn't always like it. Thank you for sitting beside me drawing me pictures on so many days, so that I could just get the rest of the chapter finished.                                                          SM-L

# About the Authors

## Susan M. Johnston

With approximately 20 years of experience in career development and counselling, Susan M. Johnston has had the opportunity to work closely with hundreds of students and clients who have chosen to take on the challenge of career planning. As an instructor in career planning and a private practice career advisor, she has guided individuals through the process of self-assessment, career exploration, and decision making to achieve their career goals. Prior to her classroom and private practice experience, she held positions at Sinclair Community College in the area of Cooperative Education and with the Career Planning and Placement Center. In addition to her teaching and counselling services, she is currently providing career planning consulting services to secondary schools seeking to update and implement career development programs.

Susan graduated *summa cum laude* from Wright State University with a B.A. in Communications and holds an M.S.Ed. in Counselling from the University of Dayton. In past positions, she has been on assignment with the State Department in India for the U.S. Information Agency, and prior to her experience as an educator, she was a contract negotiator for the U.S. Air Force. She is an active member of the American Counseling Association, the National Career Development Association, and the Ohio Counseling Association. She also has written a number of articles and presented workshops in the areas of career planning and balancing roles.

Susan is married to Jack W. Johnston, a man who is regularly mistaken for Paul McCartney. Unfortunately, when she was growing up, Susan's favourite Beatle was Ringo; fortunately, as Jack has aged, he has begun to look more like Ringo. He is the CEO of DAPSCO, a business services corporation.

Susan is a pacifist whose oldest son, Charles, is a U.S. Marine of whom she is insufferably proud. He is also a student at the Ohio State University. Susan's middle son, Mitch, is a varsity soccer player and co-captain of his high-school soccer team. She and Mitch took swing dance lessons recently and were a hit at the Mother–Son Dance. Her youngest son, Russ, is a total football monster as the offensive guard for his championship team.

## Sandra Moniz-Lecce

Sandra Moniz-Lecce has a Bachelor of Arts degree in psychology from Simon Fraser University and a Master of Arts degree in counselling psychology from the University of British Columbia. Since 1996, she has held a faculty position at Kwantlen University College, where she teaches Career and Academic Success courses and provides counselling for students. Both personally and through her work as a counsellor and instructor, Sandra has gained insight and experience in career exploration and decision making.

Sandra's husband, Joey, has been her partner at her side throughout her own career adventure. He has supported her through her education and career changes. At the centre of their life is their 6-year-old daughter, Julia, who since birth has reaffirmed what is truly important in life.

# Introduction

Welcome to the exciting, chaotic, perhaps even scary process of career decision making! We are all involved in our own real-life career adventure. We are constantly challenged to understand more deeply who we are and what we are looking for in our lives and our careers. This process of defining a career is an adventure—a discovery of who you are and what you will do with your life. Understanding yourself and the meaning of your life is an important aspect of growth and self-worth in our culture. One of the ways in which you express yourself is through your career.

## The Difference between a Career, an Occupation, and a Job

The terms "career," "occupation," and "job" are commonly used interchangeably to mean the same thing. However, their meanings are very different. It is necessary for you to be clear on the differences between them because how you define these terms may impact the process you establish for yourself in career decision making.

The term "career" is defined as one's progress through roles in life. Career development is a process which begins in early childhood and continues throughout life. A career is the accumulation of all of your life's work, including work that is paid or unpaid, at home, in the community, or at school. This is the overall work history of your life and not to be confused with the term "occupation."

An "occupation" is a profession, trade, or field of work where one is trained and/or employed. For example, one's occupation may be a librarian, baker, tile setter, artist, or writer.

A "job" is work that one does within a particular occupation. A person may have various jobs throughout his or her life, moving from one company to another or from one position to another within the same occupation, or have jobs in entirely different occupations. For example, a person might have worked in customer service at the Bay and at Canadian Tire. In this case, he or she has had two jobs working within the same occupation. However, if a person works in customer service at the Bay and then as a firefighter for the local fire department, he or she would have had two jobs in two different occupations. The accumulation of all of one's roles, whether paid or unpaid, would be considered a career.

It is important to understand the differences between these terms. Sometimes people feel overwhelmed with career decision making because they believe that they are making the ominous decision of "their career." They believe that they must decide on the "career" they will have for the rest of their lives, when really, what they are doing is making a decision in their career. They are really in the midst of the process defined as their life career, and what they are doing is deciding on a job or an occupation in that career. Making a decision on a job or even on an occupation is usually not as threatening because most people will make these decisions and change jobs and occupations numerous times throughout their lives and careers.

The world of work in Canada has changed dramatically over the years. No longer is it realistic to assume that you will be working in the same occupation for one company, with promotions along the way, until retirement. Nowadays, the career process is much less linear and much more flexible and reflective of the cycles of change that occur in nature, society, and individuals. As times change, as people change, career paths also must change to fulfill new needs.

Career decision making is about making changes and decisions throughout your career and at any point in your career. It requires making decisions about jobs and occupations and the path your life work will take. A career is a primary path for personal growth, a way to define, discover, and expand at the same time. It is a source of economic support, emotional strength, and a means for self-discovery. Making career choices involves finding arenas that will meet your needs and offer you opportunities for genuine growth and fulfillment.

## The Importance of a Career

In Canadian culture, work has very significant meaning. For most people, it is more than a pastime or a means of providing income for basic necessities. Rather, it plays a significant role in defining who they are and how they live their life. This is evident even in the language that we use in meeting people and introducing ourselves. Inevitably, the first question people ask when meeting someone new is "What do you do?" This is an important question for people trying to get to know one another. Also interesting is that rather than answering with something like "My job is to ...," or "I work doing ...," people will almost always answer, "I *am* a ..." The "am" denotes that a person's occupation is a descriptor of who they are. For this reason, careers are important to people.

Career development is directly related to one's personal identity formation and self-esteem. Psychologists have long recognized that people have a need to work and contribute to society. Fulfilling this need is a key component of personal identity formation and finding meaning and satisfaction with life. When someone's work successfully fulfills the needs they have in their career, they usually feel more satisfied, meaningful, and better about themselves. This feeling can also affect pleasure in other aspects of life. However, the reality is that people do not always obtain pleasure and satisfaction in their work. As people and society change, needs also change, which often means people must make changes in their careers in order to seek fulfillment.

This book offers a model for career development. It will guide you through the process of career decision making and deciding on a satisfying occupation.

## How This Book Is Organized

There are three basic steps required in this process. They are Self-Awareness, Occupational Research, and Job Search.

The first step, **Self-Awareness**, is addressed in Chapters 1, 2, and 3. These first three chapters will focus on furthering your learning about yourself. They will help you to look at your needs, motivations, values, skills, interests, abilities, and personality. This is the starting point in your career development. It is important to realize that this aspect of the process will require some introspection and can only be done by you. No one can tell you about yourself—you know yourself better than anyone else does.

Once you have expanded your awareness of yourself, the next step in the process is to increase your awareness of the world of work. The second part of the book will focus on **Occupational Research**. In Chapters 4, 5, 6, and 7 you will learn about different occupations, the labour market, and job trends, and about decision making and goal setting. This step of the process will require you to consider what you know about yourself and about the labour market in order to begin to make decisions and set goals. You will start to narrow in on occupations that will meet your needs and those of the changing labour market. While it is important to do something we love, it is equally important to be sure that there will be need for that work now and in the future.

The last part of the process is **The Job Search**. Chapters 8, 9, 10 and 11 will provide information on preparing yourself for available opportunities in a chosen occupation. This part of the book will address developing job leads, networking, résumés, making contact, and interviewing. Having knowledge and skills in a particular field is only one component of career success. In addition, you need to showcase your abilities so that you will have a competitive edge in the job search.

Finding your career is a lifelong process. Increased self-awareness, knowledge of the labour market, and refined job search skills allow you to grow, learn, gain insights, and make satisfying decisions throughout your career.

## Beginning the Adventure

Learning about yourself and the work world, researching options, and making decisions—all of these steps are challenging and may create anxiety for you. It may feel at times as if you are about to leap off a cliff into the unknown. Make up your mind that you are ready to jump into your career adventure. As you do, your strength and confidence will increase because you know:

◆ *You will be doing everything possible to ensure success.* You will do the homework and the research, and you will feel secure with the information that you gain. You are a bright person who is capable of making the right choices. You are ready and well prepared to do this.

◆ *Even if your worst fears become reality and you are not satisfied with your choice, you can always change your mind.* You will be prepared to handle obstacles that come along. Besides, you have plenty of time to "wiggle your way" toward your ultimate goal. Your effort now will put you ahead of the game later. This is a lifelong process.

And remember ... this is an adventure! The freedom to examine who you are and the world in which you live and then to move toward a personal goal is a precious privilege—one that countless people around the world would risk everything to have. Cherish the freedom and excitement that this discovery process offers you. Whether you are 18 or 50, the career choices you make are the reflections of who you are. Yes, the process may be chaotic and confusing at times. But it is the adventure of your lifetime. Go after it and enjoy the freedom and excitement of your career development!

# Part I

# Self-Awareness

## Learning about Yourself

The only place to start the career adventure is with *you*. Knowing as much as possible about yourself is critical to the decisions you will make in the future. This is your chance to discover and appreciate the things that make you a unique individual.

The adventure begins by examining different areas of your life and experiences. The goal is to make any aspects that are vague or unclear become more real and concrete. These components of who you are will gain meaning as you learn to relate them to your everyday life and translate them into possible career choices. Self-assessment reveals who you are more clearly. Then you can connect with an occupation that brings you meaning and fulfillment.

## Part I will include
## Objectives

**Chapter 1:** Creating Your Dream
**Chapter 2:** Discovering Yourself: Motivations, Life Stages, and Values
**Chapter 3:** Continuing Your Self-Discovery: Skills, Personality, and Interests

- ◆ To reflect on who you are and who you would like to be.
- ◆ To understand what motivates you.
- ◆ To gain awareness of your interests, values, personality, skills, and abilities.
- ◆ To learn about life stages and growth in adult life.

# Chapter 1
# Creating Your Dream

*Twenty years from now you will be more disappointed by the things that you didn't do than by the ones you did do. So throw off the bowlines. Sail away from the safe harbour. Catch the trade winds in your sails. Explore. Dream. Discover.*

MARK TWAIN

To start, let's dream a bit ...

Dreams, fantasies, hopes, or whatever you wish to call them, are essential elements in career decision making. You may have met people who say, "I've wanted to be a nurse (teacher, doctor, writer, and so on) ever since I was a child and here I am, and I love every minute of it." Sometimes it's that simple. Some lucky people have a dream or a vision of what they want to become. They pursue it and make it happen. However, for most people it may not be that easy.

Dreams, fantasies, and hopes are worth considering because they can provide us with information about our ideals, what we want, and what is important to us. One way to begin is to think back about the dreams you had as a child. What did you think your life would be like? What did you see yourself doing as an adult? What did you dream about?

Jot down the answers to these questions. How does it feel to think back to a time when anything seemed possible—a time before other responsibilities and obstacles may have eclipsed your dreams and made them unrealistic?

Do those dreams still appeal to you? Do they hold the same promise and excitement that they did when you were younger? Are they still possible as career choices? Or have you lost interest in the occupation that at one time seemed like the right one? Have you changed? Has the career you dreamt of changed?

## Who You Are and Who You Would Like to Be

A few years ago, Jack sought career counselling because he was struggling to decide between attending college or university or finding a job. Jack had many interests and could not zero in on one specific occupation. Finally, a counsellor asked him just to imagine what he would do if he could do anything at all. He kind of snorted and said, "That's easy. I'd like to be a hockey player for the Vancouver Canucks." His natural response revealed that he enjoyed athletics and competition. Now he had to identify some options that might utilize those strengths in the unglamorous world of everyday life. "Well," the counsellor ventured, "if you couldn't do that, then what else do you think you might like?" He said, "I could play basketball for the Toronto Raptors."

Jack's dreams were admirable but probably unrealistic. He was focused on an idealized vision of himself, which made it hard for him to translate that vision into real-life terms.

Dreams allow us to see possibilities that may exist within us. They give us insights into ourselves and what we want. Although it is enjoyable to imagine ourselves as superheroes, using our unique gifts to bring ourselves and others fulfillment, it is perhaps more important to identify realistic goals that encompass at least a piece of the dream. Some of your interests and needs may be satisfied by the occupation that you enter; however, others may be fulfilled outside of work in your personal life, hobbies, and in your leisure or recreational activities. For example, if you can't be Wayne Gretzky and play on a professional sports team, perhaps you can coach or perform in another athletic setting and still find satisfaction. You might work toward a position as a manager or a trainer, or perhaps you might find that playing on a recreational team would satisfy some aspects of your dream.

Figure 1.1 shows that, with luck, you can look forward to a career that may extend to the age of 70 or more, allowing you many, many years to get in touch with your true self. Inherent in that process is time to make choices, rethink those choices, and possibly change them to achieve more satisfying outcomes. This is all part of living and learning. The trick is to keep your eye on the dream (even if it changes) while learning and working with it so that it reflects your evolving identity. As you gain life experience, you will continue to develop a sense

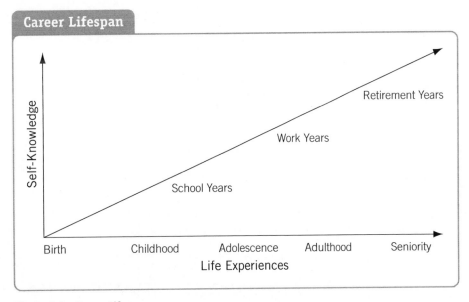

**Figure 1.1**  Career Lifespan

of yourself and to understand your needs, interests, and goals and consider these as you seek a new direction in your career.

At every point in the process, it is important to stay in tune with your needs, interests, and goals. While it is necessary to consider the effects of decisions on people in our lives, it is easy to let our insight become clouded by what others want. That is, many people who look for new occupations spend a great deal of time putting other people's needs first. Some people struggle to discern what they want and how they feel, because they are unaccustomed to putting their own feelings first. This may mean that they enter into occupations that please others but not themselves.

It may be difficult to put aside the needs of those you love. However, at least in the initial phase of the career decision making process, it is necessary that you allow yourself to be as free as possible to consider every option and every dream. Throughout the book, you will have ample opportunity to identify obstacles and to develop strategies for overcoming them. For now, your primary task is to look honestly at your needs and hopes and to translate those into goals that will help you achieve self-expression and fulfillment.

## TAKE A CLOSER LOOK
### 1.1 Occupation List

When people think of occupations, they often think of the obvious ones—doctor, lawyer, teacher, etc.—when in fact, there are thousands of different occupations. This exercise will help you expand your awareness of occupations that you may never have thought of before.

Brainstorm and create a list of as many occupations as you can think of. Can you list 100? 1000? 10 000?

_____

_____

_____

_____

_____

_____

_____

_____

_____

Share your list with someone. Can they add any more to your list?

Highlight the occupations that spark your interest or that you might want to learn more about.

### TAKE A CLOSER LOOK
### 1.2 Visualization

Look at the list of occupations that sparked your interest from Exercise 1.1. Visualize yourself in these occupations. Which occupations seem to be the best fit for you and which ones don't? Circle the ones you think would suit you best.

### TAKE A CLOSER LOOK
### 1.3 Dream

Open your mind and dream. Visualize your life in one of the occupations from Exercise 1.2. What would your work-life look like? How would you create meaning for yourself from this work?

### TAKE A CLOSER LOOK
### 1.4 Career Lifespan

Go back and look at the diagram in Figure 1.1. Drawing a similar diagram, create your own career lifespan. Plot a point signifying the beginning of your life and one for where you are now. Then connect the two points with a line. On this line, record significant times, experiences, and events in your life so far. Then extend the length of the line to signify your future. Consider the dreams you visualize for your future and record the events and experiences you would like to have for the rest of your life. Record both your short-term and long-term goals.

# Chapter 2

# Discovering Yourself

## Motivations, Life Stages, and Values

*Once I had abandoned the search for everyone else's truth, I quickly
discovered that the job of defining my own truth was far more complex
than I had anticipated.*

INGRID BENGIS

Discovering who you are is a lifelong process. At this point in your life you are likely in the midst of this process of learning about your true self—not the person your parents want you to be, not the person your spouse and close friends think you should be, not the person your kids expect you to be, but the person you are. Self-discovery is a complicated process with no simple formula. However, it is the first and most important step in determining your career goals.

The model of self-awareness presented here begins a process that in many ways will be self-propelling. Once you begin, you may find that you need little prompting to continue. In this chapter you learn more about your motivations, life stages, and values. The next chapter continues this process of self-discovery by helping you to explore your abilities and skills, personality, and interests.

People who are younger may struggle a bit with some areas of self-awareness that they have not yet encountered, and people with broad life experiences may be a bit overwhelmed as they sort through the various aspects of life. Change always involves some discomfort and anxiety. This is only the starting points from which you will continue your self-exploration. So be patient and remember that this is a lifelong process.

## Motivation

Motivation is the force that moves you to form goals and strive to achieve them. You may have heard high achievers referred to as having "a fire in the belly," an image that pictures someone who is consumed from within by a passion to reach a goal. Motivation is the "fire" or fuel that drives you forward.

# Calvin and Hobbes

by **Bill Watterson**

**Panel 1:** IF YOU STICK YOUR TONGUE OUT FOR A LONG TIME, IT DRIES UP! TRY IT!

**Panel 2:** WHY WOULD ANYONE WANT HIS TONGUE TO DRY UP?!

**Panel 3:** BECAUSE THEN IT FEELS REALLY WEIRD WHEN YOU TOUCH IT. / I'LL TAKE YOUR WORD FOR IT.

**Panel 4:** SOME PEOPLE JUST AREN'T OPEN TO REVELATORY EXPERIENCES.

Clearly, not all people are motivated by the same things or by the same amount of drive. Some people struggle just to get up in the morning, while others drive themselves to the brink. Much of what motivates us originates in our psychology and culture.

Abraham Maslow, a noted psychologist, developed a model that describes how needs influence motivations. Maslow's "Hierarchy of Needs" has been used for the past 30 years to explain what moves people and gives their actions meaning. The model is shown in Figure 2.1.

Maslow suggested that human nature requires us to have our needs met in a pattern resembling a "climb" up a pyramid to a peak. To advance to the higher levels of need, you must first satisfy the needs at the base.

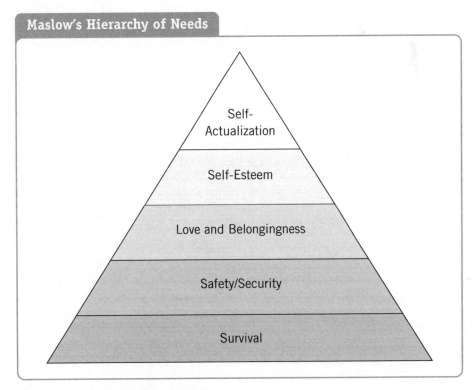

**Maslow's Hierarchy of Needs**

- Self-Actualization
- Self-Esteem
- Love and Belongingness
- Safety/Security
- Survival

**Figure 2.1**   Maslow's Hierarchy of Needs

Think of it this way: You are one of the first inhabitants of a scarcely populated region of Earth.* As a primitive human, you depend on a few basic skills and tools, passed on to you through your particular tribe. These skills and tools represent the accumulated knowledge of your group. Through a series of misadventures, you become separated from your tribe and are forced to survive on your own until you can get back to the safety of the group.

Every day of this separation is a challenge to find enough food to eat and to keep your body healthy while living in the harsh environment. You find a cave, cozy and dry, and you manage to find plants and a few edible bugs for nourishment. You have food, clothing, and shelter—you have met the needs of Maslow's most basic level, Survival.

You hear a noise outside the cave. Fortunately, you know how to make a fire, and the one at the mouth of your cave will keep unwelcome predators away. Your club is nearby and you feel quite secure. You have now reached the second level, Safety, or Security.

Still, you miss your home. You can't help recalling your family. You would gladly return to the warmth of the home you knew with them. You may be warm and safe in your own cave, but you are alone, missing the benefits of Maslow's level three, Love and Belongingness. Then, you hear someone calling to you in the rudimentary language of your tribe. You listen and then respond. Soon you are reunited with your friends and family, who valued you enough to send out a search party. A happy reunion follows, and you are able to fully satisfy your need for love and belongingness.

Your return to the group is an occasion for great celebration. It seems that while you were gone, the tribe really missed you and your valued skills. They are delighted to hear the exciting tales of your harrowing adventure. You are a significant participant in the group and have assumed an important role in your community. This level, Self-Esteem, represents your need to value your own importance and ability and your need for the tribe to value you as well. According to Maslow, esteem needs are basic to your growth as a healthy human being.

Advancing to the highest level, Self-Actualization, requires being sensitive to the inner voice, which speaks within each of us. Self-actualization is the process of becoming everything that you are capable of and experiencing a sense of fulfillment and satisfaction with your choices in life. Only a small percentage of people ever reach and sustain this level. According to Maslow, in order to reach self-actualization, you must first proceed through the other levels. After all, it would be very difficult to experience contentment with your life choices if you had to focus primarily on seeking food to satisfy your hunger, or shelter to keep you safe.

It is common to be grappling with decisions and opportunities on different levels, especially when those decisions relate to your career. Many people simultaneously struggle with the challenges of preparing themselves for second careers and also supporting their families by remaining in jobs they've long since outgrown. They may be forced to cope with the frustrations of a job that is going nowhere, yet their efforts toward change elevate them to a higher level on Maslow's hierarchy, enhancing their self-esteem and expanding their vision for the future.

* Thanks to Felix Marshall for the inspiration of the cave man scenario.

2

Discovering Yourself   CHAPTER 2   **9**

# Life Stages

Prior to the advent of psychology as an acknowledged field of study, philosophers believed that there were only two life stages, childhood and adulthood. Even after theorists began to question this assumption, they still believed that adolescence was just a brief detour in the growth of humans and that growth essentially stopped when we physically reached adulthood. Now, on the basis of Erik Erikson's work and that of other psychologists, we realize that physical maturation is hardly the end of our growth as human beings. In fact, we continue to change and adapt throughout our lives.

There is still much to learn about each life stage, and psychological research is continually adding to our knowledge of adult growth. Figure 2.2 illustrates Erikson's model of the life stages and the experiences associated with each of them.

Much research still needs to be done concerning life stage development and how it translates to everyday living. We do know that each stage identified by Erikson presents different opportunities for growth through the events associated with that life stage. While some events may be linked to particular life stages, people can also experience events typically associated with one life stage during another part of their life. They may re-encounter experiences they thought they

## Life Stage Development

| Birth to Age 12<br>Childhood | Cognitive and social development; period of value development; modelling according to gender. |
| Age 13 to 18<br>Adolescence | Beginning of identity formation; period of intense questioning and testing of real versus ideal. |
| Age 18 to 22<br>Independent<br>Adulthood | Continuation of identity formation; attempts to establish independent life and perhaps an intimate relationship. |
| Age 23 to 28<br>Adult<br>Identity | Establishment of external place in society, i.e., decisions concerning career, relationships, personal experiences. |
| Age 29 to 32<br>Questioning | Attempts to integrate life choices; possible questioning of prior decisions with subsequent changes. |
| Age 33 to 35<br>Settling | Seeking stability; acceptance of adult decisions with goal of "rational" growth. |
| Age 36 to 45<br>Life Meaning | Reassessment; realization of mortality may initiate "midlife crisis." |
| Age 46 to 60<br>Resolution/Renewal | Based on midlife transition, may hold renewed vitality and challenge or loss of vigour and resignation. |
| Age 60 to 85<br>Retirement | Depending on health, possible "bonus" career to be realized on own terms; sense of satisfaction with life choices or despair over unsatisfying outcomes. |

**Figure 2.2**   Life Stage Development

had already dealt with conclusively. For example, in your early 20s, you may have chosen and entered into an occupation and assumed that this would become your occupation for life. Then, suddenly, in your 40s, you become restless in this occupation, or perhaps economic or technological issues force you out. You begin to reassess your life and your career, and consider making changes. Although this is one of the growth experiences associated with the Adult Identity stage typically resolved in early adulthood, you may face it again in later life. The resolution of this stage depends on a range of issues and how well you are able to work through and resolve conflicts, transitions, and change. Understanding the process of life stage development makes one fact dramatically clear: We all go through periods of growth and change. The inevitability of our growth makes finding an occupation that offers satisfaction and meaning a compelling goal.

Throughout our lives we are faced with decisions as we attempt to reach our goals. Yet, seldom do our decisions yield clear-cut outcomes, satisfaction guaranteed. The truly important issues are frequently ones that we visit more than once. In our increasingly open and flexible culture, we have many opportunities to revisit past choices and to make new decisions. This is true even in the area of career decision making. It is becoming more and more common for people to change occupations throughout their lifetimes. That is, no longer do people begin working in their 20s and retire from that same occupation in their 60s. Instead, nowadays it is common for people to change jobs numerous times, and to change occupations anywhere from three to five times throughout their lives. Therefore, it would appear that career decision making is truly a lifelong process.

A well-chosen career path can bring a lifetime of growth and fulfillment. It can provide an outlet for using your unique talents, developing yourself through challenge and competition, learning to steady yourself through the trials of adult life, and reaping the rewards of doing a job to the best of your ability.

# Values

Values are the things that we consider important or desirable. They represent needs that ideally become more clear and firm as we mature and learn more about who we are. As these values "crystallize" they shape our behaviour and help us set goals. Values are shaped by our families, friends, culture, traditions, religious beliefs, schools, textbooks, media, and the whole range of our life experiences. As we go through life, we encounter a variety of people and events, and view them through the perspective of our values and their meaning to us.

While we may have only a small number of internalized values influencing us, they compete with each other to shape our actions through a complex structure of interrelationships. Let's say, for instance, that you value altruism, a concern for the well-being of others. You also value independence and autonomy. Your inclination toward altruism might encourage you toward a career of volunteer work in your community. Unfortunately, volunteer work alone would not provide you with the money you would need to live independently and accommodate your value of independence and autonomy. The decision becomes even more complex if you have a need for prosperity. Only when values are prioritized can their competing influences be organized in a coherent pattern, a pattern that facilitates self-understanding and decision making.

Research seems to indicate that while our attitudes and interests may change as a result of life experiences, our values remain relatively stable. We change and are influenced by life experiences, but our basis for understanding and evaluating our world seems to be fairly consistent over time.

Think of your own life. While you may not continue to prize the same things you did in high school, your life is still a reflection of the core values you were exposed to when growing up. You've probably moved beyond the youthful idealism of your teenage years to a more mature view of the world and your place in it. Experiences gained through school, work, relationships, parenting, or any number of roles in the community can influence your perspective and give you a broader view of life without changing your values.

The following example might better illustrate the nature of values. Jeanne values self-reliance, and as a result, owning her own home is important to her. Therefore, she begins to look for a house and soon finds one that is suitable. She buys it and, now that she owns her own home, she no longer continues looking for a home. Instead, she devotes her energy to maintaining and enhancing her new home. Jeanne's basic value of owning a home as a way of being self-reliant has not changed but, as a result of her new experiences and growth, her actions have. Although at some point she may outgrow the house and look for another, her values remain, and she adjusts to meet the changing needs they reflect.

The same process may be influencing your present search for a new occupation. Perhaps your decision to look seriously at your career direction is a result of maturity and growth while still reflecting your deeper, unchanged values. Sometimes you may feel strongly about certain values in the abstract, but find yourself struggling with how those values are manifest in reality. For example, you may value equality in the workplace and "equal job opportunities for all," as a way of equalizing and providing opportunities for groups of people who have been closed out in the past—until just such a program results in a job rejection or demotion. In that case, it is a real test either to hold on to your original value or to question your belief.

Other situations may also bring values into direct conflict. For example, while you may look the part of the perfect corporate employee, your ability to relate with your "friends on the block" when you leave the office may make you feel as though you are living a double life. Do you keep your life divided, juggling your views to fit the situation you are in, or do you find ways to harmonize your life? More threatening would be the situation in which one or the other side of your life demands your total commitment. While it is unlikely that would ever happen, your value for loyalty to friends and community may come into conflict with your value to succeed financially. Being able to resolve the tensions between those values will influence the direction of your life and career.

Our values ripple through every aspect of our lives to a greater or lesser extent. When we talk about jobs and the satisfaction we feel with our career choices, we can focus on a smaller, more manageable number of characteristics. We can begin to assess how our values affect our job/career priorities. Knowing clearly what your values are will enhance your ability to choose a gratifying career.

# Katarina's Story

Katarina was facing her first career-planning class with a mixture of anticipation and skepticism. For a while now, she'd been thinking and talking about what occupation she might consider, and it made her queasy to consider a whole course devoted to the subject. The fact that she was no closer to a decision than she had been five years ago made her all the more apprehensive. After all the options and programs and possibilities she had considered, how could one class make a difference?

When she reached the classroom the first day, the instructor hadn't arrived yet. Katarina took a seat near the front and looked over the textbook for the class. It looked like it would be fun to do the self-assessment exercises. She was surprised there wasn't more information about what careers were "hot." Within minutes the instructor for the class arrived and began to take attendance. Katarina glanced around the room at her new classmates. The classroom was filled with people like her, some 18 or 19 years old, just getting started. Others looked older and she assumed they might be re-entering the workforce or making changes in their career directions. Katarina sat up and listened intently as the instructor explained what would happen during the course. She remained unsure about whether the assignments would make any difference in her search for an occupation.

The first assignment was to "capture," or identify, a career dream and to share it with the class. Katarina struggled to pinpoint a career dream that she could tell the class. Every time she thought of an occupation that sounded interesting or fun, she came up with all the reasons why it just wouldn't work for her. When it was Katarina's turn to share her career dream at the next class, she knew she had to say something, so she flatly said she had always wanted to be a nurse. She was disappointed with herself, though, and after class she approached the instructor and explained her problem. The instructor said that sometimes when people are in situations in which they haven't had the chance to try out different types of roles or jobs, they may find it hard to choose. But just thinking about possibilities and considering them doesn't mean one is bound to them. It's just the first step in the process of satisfying hopes and needs. The instructor suggested that she try to get in touch with her feelings about herself and her hopes. That's all the career dream represents … not a hard reality.

Katarina left the class feeling better. She was ready to work on the assignments for next week, the work values assessment, and a life-stage development exercise. As she worked through the exercises, she reminded herself several times not to get stuck on making a final decision yet. She focused on being patient and letting her needs and interests surface slowly through the self-assessment process. She found out that her life stage involved establishing an independent life and continuing to form her identity. Her work values were focused on helping and influencing others and finding a way to be creative.

That seemed to strike a chord. She had always enjoyed art and had often been complimented on her work. As she considered the different possibilities in the exercises, she came upon the idea of teaching art, an idea she had never seriously considered before. Katarina began to believe that there might be an occupation for her after all.

## TAKE A CLOSER LOOK
### 2.1 Maslow's Pyramid

Take a look at the model of Maslow's Hierarchy of Needs and fill in the space with one- or two-word descriptions of ways in which you perceive your needs might be met at each level.

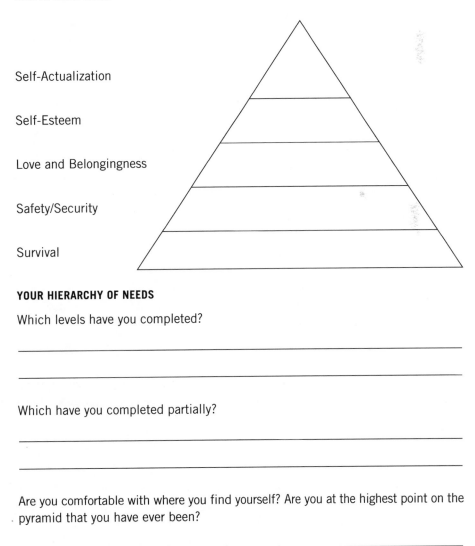

Self-Actualization

Self-Esteem

Love and Belongingness

Safety/Security

Survival

**YOUR HIERARCHY OF NEEDS**

Which levels have you completed?

_____

_____

Which have you completed partially?

_____

_____

Are you comfortable with where you find yourself? Are you at the highest point on the pyramid that you have ever been?

_____

_____

Are you looking forward to advancing to the next level? Why or why not?

_____

_____

Are you "stuck" in your present level? Why or why not?

_____

_____

Can you get "unstuck"? Do you want to?

_____

_____

Think about what is motivating you right now to examine your life and where you are going. At which level do your motivations place you?

_____

_____

Summarize what you have learned from the discussion of Maslow's hierarchy and how it relates to you and your motivations.

_____

_____

*Discuss these questions with your group or with the class.*

_____

### TAKE A CLOSER LOOK
### 2.2 Your Current Life Stage

Age ____20____    Life Stage _Independent Adulthood_

Review Figure 2.2. Find your life stage based on your age. Read the brief description corresponding to your age. Does the description reflect the way you see your current life stage?

_____

_____

If not, can you think of what circumstances in your life may have influenced your situation?

_____

_____

What do you hope to accomplish during this life stage?

_____

_____

*Discuss your reactions with your group or with the class.*

## 2.3 Distinguishing Your Values

Look at the list of values that follows. These values describe a variety of attributes associated with various work settings. Using the following scale, rate the degree of importance of each in choosing an occupation for yourself.

1—NOT IMPORTANT AT ALL     3—REASONABLY IMPORTANT

2—SOMEWHAT IMPORTANT     4—VERY IMPORTANT

____1____ *Help society:* Do something to contribute to a better world

____3____ *Help others:* Be involved in helping others in a direct way

____2____ *Work with others:* Close working relationships with a group

____1____ *Competition:* Pit my abilities against others with win/lose outcomes

____3____ *Work under pressure:* Face situations with time constraints or where the quality of my work is judged critically

____4____ *Power and authority:* Control work activities of others

____1____ *Influence people:* Be in a position to change attitudes or opinions of others

____3____ *Work alone:* Conduct work by myself, without contact with others

____2____ *Knowledge:* Pursue knowledge, learning, and understanding

____1____ *Personal growth:* Engage in work that offers me the opportunity to grow as a person

____1____ *Creativity:* Engage in creative work, e.g., art, graphic design, photography, program planning, interior design, writing, composing, performing, and so on

____4____ *Variety:* Have responsibilities that offer variety in content or setting

____4____ *Stability and security:* Have a work situation that is predictable, with probability that I can keep my job

____4____ *Recognition:* Be recognized for the quality of my work

____2____ *Excitement:* Experience a high degree of excitement at work

____2____ *Profit gain:* Have a strong possibility of earning large amounts of money

____2____ *Location:* Work in a place near my home, with a short drive or bus ride

____2____ *Fun:* Work in a setting where I am free to be playful, humorous, exuberant

____1____ *Autonomy:* Have work responsibilities that allow me freedom to determine how and when the work is accomplished

____2____ *Status:* Have a position that carries respect within the community

____2____ *Advancement:* Have the opportunity to work hard and see rapid career advancement

_____ *Productive:* Produce tangibles, things I can see and touch

_____ *Aesthetic:* Create things that are beautiful and contribute to making the world more attractive

_____ *Achievement:* Experience a feeling of accomplishment for a job well done

_____ *Environment:* Work in a pleasant, clean, comfortable setting

_____ *Supervision:* Work as part of a team that is managed with fairness and appreciation

Now list the values you rated with a 4: very important.

_____

_____

Note the values you rated with a 3: reasonably important.

_____

_____

Do you see a pattern emerging? Can you see groupings that point to similar values in certain areas?

_____

_____

Take a look at the values you ranked with a 4. Ask yourself, "Is this important to me because *I* want it or because it will please others or win their respect and acceptance?"

_____

_____

Keep in mind that even if your values do not change, your priorities might as some needs are satisfied and others emerge. As you grow and change, continue to reassess and prioritize your values.

_____

_____

*Discuss some of the new insights you may have discovered through this exercise with your group or the class.*

**TAKE A CLOSER LOOK**

**2.4 Pulling It All Together**

What dreams did you start with?

_____

_____

Where are you on Maslow's hierarchy?

_____

_____

What life stage are you in right now and what issues related to that stage are you currently considering?

_____

_____

_____

What do you want to accomplish in this life stage?

_____

_____

_____

What three work values did you respond to most strongly?

_____

_____

_____

How has identifying some of the factors that are important to you affected your understanding of yourself and your career decisions?

_____

_____

_____

## A Look Back

As a result of the first stage of your career adventure, you should have a good sense of the issues surrounding your motivations, the life stage you are in, the pressures associated with it, and information about your values concerning work and career. These areas of self-assessment all have a direct bearing on your career choice and will be considered again in later chapters.

For now, it is important to realize that the unique combination of innate gifts and individual experiences with which you have been blessed are resources you will use to select an occupation and to find within yourself the courage and enthusiasm to make that choice a reality.

## Other Sources and Suggested Reading

*Live the Life You Love in Ten Easy Step-By-Step Lessons* by Barbara Sher
This book encourages creative approaches to getting in touch with your identity and finding the means for expressing yourself in your life and career.

*Major in Success: Make College Easier, Fire Up Your Dreams, and Get a Very Cool Job* by Patrick Combs
This book offers a good look at the whole process in a hip, fun format.

*What Color Is Your Parachute? A Practical Manual for Job-Hunters and Career-Changers 2004* by Richard Nelson Bolles
This is an update of the classic manual for job hunters and those changing occupations. It addresses the entire process of career decision making in a light, easy reading style, including some exercises and activities.

## Web Sites and Internet Resources

**www.jobboom.com/conseils/top100A.html**
Developed by Human Resources Development Canada, this is a very useful site that lists and describes the top 100 Internet sites for learning and employment, each categorized under relevant topics.

**www.kwantlen.ca/library/Internet/job.html**
Kwantlen University College's library has a very good site with links to many other Canadian sites. The librarians have evaluated a number of sites and listed some of the best. The sites are categorized according to different aspects of employment and career development.

**www.cdm.uwaterloo.ca/index.asp**
The University of Waterloo's Career Services presents a comprehensive home page that includes a look at the steps involved in career decision making.

# Chapter 3
# Continuing Your Self-Discovery

## Skills, Personality, and Interests

*Your vision will become clear only when you look into your heart. Who looks outside, dreams. Who looks inside, awakens.*

CARL C. JUNG

In the previous chapter, you began the process of self-assessment. This chapter gives you an opportunity to expand your knowledge of yourself by looking at your skills and abilities, personality, and interests.

These three areas are valuable sources of information for developing your career decisions and will enrich your insight into your needs and how they can be met through your career.

## Skills and Abilities

The term "skills" is somewhat synonymous to "abilities" but has a more technical connotation. Generally, skills are those capabilities that can be acquired and developed through exposure to and repetition of a task or learning process that may take place in a classroom or a lab, through training or study, or in a workplace. On the other hand, abilities are those talents or powers that are typically innate gifts and may be enhanced and developed to their maximum potential through study, training, or practice.

"Abilities" refers to those qualities that are an intrinsic part of you and the way that you relate to the world. An ability may be something as fundamental as understanding mathematics easily, or it may be as intangible as facing a crisis calmly. Both of these are qualities that enable you to bring special talent to a particular situation.

What are your unique talents and gifts? Your ability to identify and tap into both your inner capabilities and your skills will not only give you added confidence, but will also make you more marketable in the work world. Identifying and categorizing career skills and abilities and matching them to specific occupations will provide you with information for making career choices and for marketing yourself to employers.

Human Resources and Skills Development Canada (HRSDC) has a number of publications that explain how skills are related to career markets. The *National Occupational Classification* (NOC) (which will be discussed in more detail in Chapter 4) lists approximately 30 000 occupations and their required skills and abilities. The NOC is an excellent resource that may be useful to you in evaluating your skills and abilities and exploring how they may be relevant to further career development. *The Dictionary of Occupational Titles* is also a useful resource for information about different occupations.

The skills and abilities listed in Figure 3.1 are grouped according to three categories: data, people, and things. As you survey the abilities and skills categorized, you may immediately see areas in which you consistently possess high-level skills. You may have become aware of these abilities through school, athletic events, hobbies, leisure activities, or other situations apart from paid employment. Your task is to focus on what you have learned in the past and what your talents are now. You will identify settings for applying those talents in a later section.

## Calvin and Hobbes                                          by Bill Watterson

## Transferable Skills

Understanding your abilities and skills is vital to discovering who you are and what you have to offer, but this knowledge may not always determine your specific career path. Sometimes we may find the things at which we are best have not yet found a market in the world of work. Nevertheless, among your innate talents may lie the seed of your future occupation.

Most of your skills, whether rudimentary or highly developed, are transferable. Transferable skills are those that can be used in a variety of occupations and work settings. If you have a particular ability that gives you a great deal of satisfaction, it may be the key to an occupation in which you can apply that ability in one form or another.

Transferable skills are different from job-specific skills, or work content skills. Work content skills are skills directly related to a unique job description, such as operating a bulldozer, editing videotapes, or conducting lab tests. Identifying your transferable skills can help you develop alternative career options. These skills are an especially valuable asset for career changers who have many talents but are seeking new ways and new settings in which to use them. Your transferable skills are often those you have used successfully during activities that you enjoyed. Using these skills gave you a strong sense of satisfaction.

The Government of Canada recently conducted a national research study to examine the skills that are transferable from one work setting to another. Human

## Skills and Abilities Inventory*

### DATA

*Synthesizing:* Putting ideas and facts together in new ways to explain how things work; developing new ideas and theories.

*Coordinating:* Organizing things; planning projects; deciding in which order things must be done; checking to be sure the steps are done on time and correctly.

*Analyzing:* Studying information to find out what it means; deciding how to solve a problem.

*Compiling:* Collecting, arranging, or combining facts about data, people, or things and reporting the results.

*Computing:* Using arithmetic; reporting the results of computations and applying the data from those results.

*Copying:* Writing, listing, or entering numbers or letters exactly as seen.

*Comparing:* Deciding if data, people, or things are alike or different. Using rules to decide degree of difference.

### PEOPLE

*Mentoring:* Helping people deal with problems; giving legal, scientific, clinical, spiritual, or other professional advice.

*Negotiating:* Talking over ideas, information, and opinions with others in order to reach positive solutions.

*Instructing:* Teaching people (or animals) by explaining, showing, or watching them practise; giving advice on a topic in which you have expertise.

*Supervising:* Directing workers by giving orders and explaining duties; making sure they do the work on time; acting as a team leader.

*Entertaining:* Amusing others; saying or doing things that people find interesting; working on stage, radio, or TV.

*Persuading:* Winning others over to purchase a product or service, or agree on a point of view.

*Speaking/Signalling:* Talking or making motions so people can understand and receiving information in return; giving verbal directions clearly and concisely so that listeners understand.

*Serving:* Helping people or animals; carrying out others' wants or wishes.

*Taking Instruction/Helping:* Doing as you are told; following orders without deciding whether they are right or wrong.

### THINGS

*Setting Up:* Changing parts on machines; fixing mechanical objects if they break down; knowing how to operate several different machines.

*Precision Working:* Being responsible for making things that fit exact rules or standards; deciding which tools or materials to use to meet the specifications.

*Operating/Controlling:* Starting, stopping, and watching machines or equipment to be sure they are operating correctly; watching gauges, dials, and other devices, and changing valves or controls as needed.

*Driving/Operating:* Steering or guiding machines or tools; estimating distance, speed, and direction.

*Manipulating:* Moving, guiding, placing, or working things using your body or tools; selecting tools, objects, or materials.

*Tending:* Starting, stopping, and watching machines work; watching timers or gauges; making changes based on rules.

*Feeding/Offbearing:* Filling up or emptying machines that are run automatically or by other workers.

*Handling:* Moving or carrying things.

*Adapted from Marilyn Maze and Donald Mayall, *The Enhanced Guide for Occupational Exploration,* First Edition. Copyright © 1991 by Jist Works, Inc., Indianapolis. Reprinted with permission.

**Figure 3.1**    Skills and Abilities Inventory

Resources and Skills Development Canada has interviewed over 4000 people across Canada working in more than 200 different occupations. This study, called the *Essential Skills Research Project* (ESRP), resulted in a list of nine skills deemed to be "essential skills" used in nearly every occupation at one level or another. These skills are considered to be necessary for learning, work, and life.

The nine essential skills[1] are:

*Reading Text*: Reading material that is in the form of sentences or paragraphs; generally involves reading notes, letters, memos, manuals, specifications, regulations, books, reports, or journals.

*Document Use*: Tasks that involve a variety of information displays in which words, numbers, icons, and other visual characteristics (e.g., line, colour, shape) are given meaning by their spatial arrangement. For example, graphs, lists, tables, blueprints, schematics, drawings, signs, and labels are documents used in the world of work.

*Numeracy*: Use of numbers and thinking in quantitative terms.

*Writing*: Writing texts and writing in documents (for example, filling in forms); non-paper-based writing (for example, typing on a computer).

*Oral Communication*: The use of speech to give and exchange thoughts and information.

*Working with Others*: Working with others to carry out tasks; working co-operatively with others; self-discipline to meet work targets while working alone.

*Continuous Learning*: Participate in an ongoing process of acquiring skills and knowledge.

*Thinking Skills*: Five different types of cognitive functions that are all interconnected.

*Computer Use*: Indicates the variety and complexity of computer use within the occupational group.

In addition to Canada, other countries in the world, including the United States, Australia, and Great Britain, have also agreed that these skills are necessary in virtually all occupations and in daily living. HRSDC expanded on these and has developed skill profiles for various occupations. These can be accessed through the National Occupation Classification guides (NOC). (See Web Sites and Internet Resources at the end of the chapter.)

## Employability Skills

The Conference Board of Canada has also formulated a list of what it considers to be necessary skills, abilities, attitudes, and behaviours for the workplace. These are called Employability Skills 2000+ (see Figure 3.2). The skills are divided into three categories: fundamental skills, personal management skills, and teamwork skills. The Conference Board of Canada regards this list to be applicable whether one is self-employed or working for others, in almost any occupation.

---

[1] Adapted from Human Resources and Skills Development Canada. *Essential Skills and Workplace Literacy Initiative.* Reproduced with the permission of the Minister of Public Works and Government Services Canada, 2004. Accessed September 29, 2004 at **www15.hrdc-drhc.gc.ca/English/general/understanding_ES-e.asp**.

## Employability Skills 2000+

*The skills you need to enter, stay in, and progress in the world of work—whether you work on your own or as a part of a team.*

These skills can also be applied and used beyond the workplace in a range of daily activities.

| Fundamental Skills | Personal Management Skills | Teamwork Skills |
|---|---|---|
| The skills needed as a base for further development | The personal skills, attitudes, and behaviours that drive one's potential for growth | The skills and attributes needed to contribute productively |

**Fundamental Skills**

*You will be better prepared to progress in the world of work when you can"*

**Communicate**
- read and understand information presented in a variety of forms (e.g., words, graphs, charts, diagrams)
- write and speak so others pay attention and understand
- listen and ask questions to understand and appreciate the points of view of others
- share information using a range of information and communications technologies (e.g., voice, e-mail, computers)
- use relevant scientific, technological, and mathematical knowledge and skills to explain or clarify ideas

**Manage Information**
- locate, gather, and organize information using appropriate technology and information systems
- access, analyze, and apply knowledge and skills from various disciplines (e.g., the arts, languages, science, technology, mathematics, social sciences, and the humanities)

**Use Numbers**
- decide what needs to be measured or calculated
- observe and record data using appropriate methods, tools, and technology
- make estimates and verify calculations

**Think & Solve Problems**
- assess situations and identify problems
- seek different points of view and evaluate them based on facts
- recognize the human, interpersonal, technical, scientific, and mathematical dimensions of a problem
- identify the root cause of a problem
- be creative and innovative in exploring possible solutions
- readily use science, technology, and mathematics as ways to think, gain and share knowledge, solve problems, and make decisions
- evaluate solutions to make recommendations or decisions
- implement solutions
- check to see if a solution works, and act on opportunities for improvement

**Personal Management Skills**

*You will be able to offer yourself greater possibilities for achievement when you can:*

**Demonstrate Positive Attitudes & Behaviours**
- feel good about yourself and be confident
- deal with people, problems, and situations with honesty, integrity, and personal ethics
- recognize your own and other people's good efforts
- take care of your personal health
- show interest, initiative, and effort

**Be Responsible**
- set goals and priorities balancing work and personal life
- plan and manage time, money, and other resources to achieve goals
- assess, weigh, and manage risk
- be accountable for your actions and the actions of your group
- be socially responsible and contribute to your community

**Be Adaptable**
- work independently or as part of a team
- carry out multiple tasks or projects
- be innovative and resourceful: identify and suggest alternative ways to achieve goals and get the job done
- be open and respond constructively to change
- learn from your mistakes and accept feedback
- cope with uncertainty

**Learn Continuously**
- be willing to continuously learn and grow
- assess personal strengths and areas for development
- set your own learning goals
- identify and assess learning sources and opportunities
- plan for and achieve your learning goals

**Work Safely**
- be aware of personal and group health and safety practices and procedures, and act in accordance with these

**Teamwork Skills**

*You will be better prepared to add value to the outcomes of a task, project, or team when you can:*

**Work with Others**
- understand and work within the dynamics of a group
- ensure that a team's purpose and objectives are clear
- be flexible: respect, be open to and supportive of the thoughts, opinions, and contributions of others in a group
- recognize and respect people's diversity, individual differences, and perspectives
- accept and provide feedback in a constructive and considerate manner
- contribute to a team by sharing information and expertise
- lead or support when appropriate, motivating a group for high performance
- understand the role of conflict in a group to reach solutions
- manage and resolve conflict when appropriate

**Participate in Projects & Tasks**
- plan, design, or carry out a project or task from start to finish with well-defined objectives and outcomes
- develop a plan, seek feedback, test, revise, and implement
- work to agreed quality standards and specifications
- select and use appropriate tools and technology for a task or project
- adapt to changing requirements and information
- continuously monitor the success of a project or task and identify ways to improve

Source: *Employability Skills 2000+* Brochure 2000 E/F. 2000. Ottawa: The Conference Board of Canada. Reproduced with permission.

**Figure 3.2**    Employability Skills 2000+

In addition to being called employability skills, essential skills, or transferable skills, these skills are sometimes also referred to as "soft" skills. However, having them can give you a firm advantage.

Becoming aware of your strengths and weaknesses in each of these skills areas can benefit you in many ways. First, you will realize that you already have some of the skills that are required for many fields of work. This can help you gain confidence to pursue your goals. Second, realizing these strengths will be an advantage in marketing yourself to potential employers. You can assure employers that you possess these employability skills, deemed essential by most employers. And third, becoming aware of these essential transferable skills can provide you with information regarding skill areas to focus on for further personal development.

## Emotional Intelligence

As you examine your skills and abilities now, it is not the time to start tallying your limitations and numbering the obstacles. Researchers suggest that success and well-being are derived from a host of qualities unrelated to intelligence and physical capability. For instance, in 1995, Daniel Goleman authored the book *Emotional Intelligence: Why It Can Matter More Than IQ*. In this book he discusses the concept of "emotional intelligence," distinguishing it as something different from cognitive intelligence. Goleman and other theorists believe that emotional intelligence is as important, if not more important, than cognitive intelligence for succeeding in the real world.

Unlike cognitive intelligence, emotional intelligence is less influenced by genetics. Also, while cognitive intelligence tends to remain fairly constant throughout adulthood, emotional intelligence continues to develop as one gets older and, most importantly, can be learned and refined. Goleman identifies a number of qualities that allow people to excel in life. These "emotional intelligence" qualities include:

♦ *self-awareness*: the ability to recognize your own feelings as they take place and respond in a thoughtful, disciplined manner;

♦ *altruism*: a concern for the well-being of others;

♦ *personal motivation*: the drive to persist and achieve;

♦ *empathy*: the ability to understand and feel what others are feeling and communicate empathy appropriately;

♦ *the ability to love and be loved*: experiencing growth through intimacy and sharing.

These qualities can be learned and nurtured by quality relationships and good choices. They are cultivated through opportunities that naturally occur as part of life, opportunities to practise and refine these skills. Goleman believes that emotional intelligence is the root of effective leadership and managerial success. Others suggest that it is also effective in managing stress and improving health, well-being, and performance.

The very fact that you have chosen to examine the issues related to careers and your own growth shows your emotional intelligence is guiding your progress. This process will continue to nurture your development as a successful adult with a flourishing career and a full, rewarding life.

### The Workplace of the Future

In 2002, at a conference on new employment challenges, the Honourable Claudette Bradshaw, Canadian Minister of Labour, stated that fewer than 50% of workers in Canada today hold what we would have called a "regular job" 20 years ago. She was referring to the fact that people are increasingly employed by contract or non-traditional work. More and more, the lines between traditional work and the rest of life are fading as fewer people are working 9 to 5 for one specific company until retirement, and more people are becoming self-employed, setting up home-based businesses, teleworking, telecommuting, providing work on a contract basis, and/or working for various employers at any given time. This is a trend that is predicted to continue into the future. The Minister further commented that "all of us need to adjust to these new employment relationships, going far beyond the traditional definition of employment."

Globalization, advances in technology, and changes in demographics are all having an impact on the rapidly changing face of the workplace of the future. In order to keep up with these changes, people need to take initiative; they need to be flexible, adaptable, able to change, creative, focused, willing to take risks, independent, and team players. Overall, you need to have the skills and abilities that can take you from one work experience to another and be self-reliant and responsible for your own life and career development. Work will likely always be a part of people's lives. As the world and its people change, the structure of work also will change, and you necessarily must change with it.

# Personality

The examination of one's personality is a particularly interesting area of self-assessment. Your personality is composed of all your individual qualities. Your attitudes, behaviours, activities, and emotional reactions come together in your personality. Your personality reflects the way you view and respond to the world and the way you show the world who you are.

Ask any parent who has more than one child—they will repeat what psychologists believe: Everyone has a distinct personality. Even identical twins, who share the same genetic makeup, take in and respond to their world differently. This uniqueness among individuals is a subject of endless fascination and study. Geneticists are beginning to trace some attitudes and behaviours to specific genes, a process that may reduce personality assessment to something resembling statistical analysis. For now, however, we rely on the work of psychologists to help us view how personality influences our lives.

However, personality is just one of many variables in career decision making. People with very different personalities may be drawn to the same occupation, and people of a similar personality type may find themselves at opposite ends of the occupation spectrum. There are quiet, introspective salespeople and outgoing, gregarious librarians. Personality is only one dimension that influences career choice.

Have you ever been involved in a conversation in which someone says, "Oh, she's a typical teacher (banker, engineer, politician)"? Sometimes people make assumptions about someone's personality on the basis of their profession and vice versa. Some professions call to mind extreme, stereotypical traits. In the following section, remember that personality is only one factor to consider in your career choice. Keep all possibilities open.

## Jung's Psychological Types

An early pioneer in the area of personality development was Carl G. Jung, a Swiss psychiatrist and contemporary of Sigmund Freud. Jung developed a theory of psychological types in conjunction with an overall theory of personality development to explain the normal differences between people's behaviour. Jung's typology led to the creation of a highly useful model for understanding personality.

Jung's theory maintains that people's personalities are influenced by inborn tendencies, early experiences, environment, and family. Jung believed that people's personalities are a direct result of how people use their minds to gather information, make decisions, and relate to the world. According to Jungian theory, there are four pairs of personality preferences, each pair describing opposite types. Jungian typology maintains that people will have a preference for one type over the other in each of the following dimensions:

Extroversion (E) or Introversion (I)

Intuitive (N) or Sensing (S)

Thinking (T) or Feeling (F)

Judging (J) or Perceiving (P)

Jung maintained that some preferences will be more dominant than others. You will generally rely on those dominant preferences and use them almost automatically. However, when situations demand, you can choose to use those preferences that come less naturally. For example, although a person might be described as introverted, he or she may act more extroverted when at a party or performing on stage. It might take more energy for the naturally introverted person to be extroverted, but it is possible. That is, all preferences may be available for you to use, but some may be more easily accessible and come more naturally, like using your right or left hand, for example. You might be able to use both hands when you need to, but one might be more dominant, stronger, and more competent, and it might take more concentration and effort to use the other hand. The same is true for the opposites of each dimension. While you may have each opposite at your disposal, one may come more naturally than its opposite, which may require more effort and concentration. Neither is wrong or right, just different but equally valuable.

## Myers-Briggs Type Indicator®

Several researchers have built upon Jung's theory and have developed assessment instruments to help people understand the characteristics of their personality. One of the most popular personality instruments used today is the Myers-Briggs Type Indicator® (MBTI). It was developed by a mother-and-daughter team Isabel Myers and Katharine Cook Briggs, and it is considered to be a reliable tool for helping people understand different personality types.

The MBTI provides scores for personality preferences on four scales based on Jung's typology. The Extroversion (E)/Introversion (I) scale measures your source of energy in relating to the world. The Sensing (S)/Intuition (N) is your perceiving preference measuring what you pay attention to when you gather information. The Thinking (T)/Feeling (F) is your deciding preference or how you make decisions. And finally, the Judging (J)/Perceiving (P) scale measures how you prefer to deal with life. These preferences will be examined in more detail.

### Extroversion (E)/Introversion (I)

The dimension of Extroversion (E)/Introversion (I) refers to the mode through which a person relates to the world. It describes how a person gets and expends energy. If your preference is for Extroversion (E), your orientation is directed toward the outer world of people, things, and actions. While an introverted person gets energy by being alone, an extroverted person gets energy by being with others. Extroversion is usually displayed through outgoing behaviour.

If your preference is for Introversion (I), you are oriented toward and energized primarily by your inner world of thoughts, ideas, emotions, and impressions. You might exhibit traits associated with quiet, reflective, or deliberate behaviour.

Extroversion and introversion influence how each of the other preferences operates in our personality.

### Intuitive (N)/Sensing (S)

Intuitive (N)/Sensing (S) relates to the way a person takes in information. It describes what you pay attention to when you take in information. Sensing (S) types tend to pay attention to information taken in using their five senses. They tend to be more comfortable with specifics and prefer tangible results and literal interpretations. If you are matter-of-fact and rely on tangible experience, then you probably prefer Sensing (S).

Intuitive (N) types pay attention to information using their "sixth sense." They tend to focus on what might be or what could be rather than what is. If your dominant way of gathering information allows you to handle several different things at once, see the "big picture," and work easily with generalities and possibilities, but you find it difficult to manage details, your typology would likely be labelled Intuitive (N).

### Thinking (T)/Feeling (F)

Thinking (T)/Feeling (F) function relates to how one prefers to make decisions. People who have a preference toward the Thinking (T) type tend to make decisions based on facts and data and to rely on thinking to decide in a logical and objective way. They are able to remain calm in a crisis, prefer level-headed objectivity, and are noted for their logical viewpoints.

People who have a preference toward the Feeling (F) are persons who are highly sensitive to feelings, their own and others'. They rely on feeling to decide and consider the impact of feelings on the decision. They are rewarded by interacting with others and value getting along well with people.

### Judging (J)/Perceiving (P)

The last category was originally termed "rational" and "irrational" by Jung. As with the other terms above, the current terms, "judging" and "perceiving," are not meant to be interpreted literally. Jung's original "rational" component, now dubbed Judging, referred to a reflective, linear response that leads to a particular judgment with little tolerance for ambiguity. The "irrational" component was related to the Perceiving function and referred to an ability to perceive intangibles and to function well despite disorganization and ambiguity.

The Judging (J)/Perceiving (P) dimension describes which function (intuitive/sensing or thinking/feeling) a person prefers to use to live day to day. People who prefer the Judging (J) type like to live a planned and organized life and do not like unexpected changes. They like to make decisions efficiently and confidently and prefer to use a deciding (thinking/feeling) process in dealing with the outer world.

Perceiving types prefer to live in a flexible and spontaneous way. They like to keep things open and to allow for new information. They are highly adaptive and do not like feeling tied down with routines and schedules. They prefer to use a perceptive process (intuitive/sensing) in dealing with the outer world.

### The 16 Personality Types

The different combinations available by using these four dimensions (E/I, N/S, T/F, J/P) provide 16 different "personality types" (see Figure 3.3). Using the MBTI to identify your preference on each of these dimensions, you can get some idea of your personality "type." For example, if you prefer introversion, intuitive, thinking, and judging, your type would be INTJ.

**The 16 Personality Types**

| ISTJ | ISFJ | INFJ | INTJ |
|------|------|------|------|
| ISTP | ISFP | INFP | INTP |
| ESTP | ESFP | ENFP | ENTP |
| ESTJ | ESFJ | ENFJ | ENTJ |

**Figure 3.3**   The 16 Personality Types

The MBTI has been well researched and its corresponding four-letter codes correlate well to specific occupations. It seems that people of a particular type are often drawn to similar occupations. For example, ISTJs often enter into occupations such as business managers, bankers, or police officers, while their direct opposite ENFPs are attracted to counselling, music, or entertaining. If you wish to take the MBTI, it is only available from someone who is certified to administer that instrument. The person administering the MBTI should be able to assist you in exploring further how the code can be interpreted as it relates to your career selection.

It is important to remember, however, that such instruments are not intended to be 100% accurate, or to be predictors of behaviour any more than a crystal ball would be. They are only tools in the overall process of growth and self-examination. Nevertheless, used with discretion, they can enhance your insight of who you are and help in your self-assessment.

There are various adaptations of the MBTI, and other instruments purporting to measure personality, available on the Internet. However, it must be noted that these have not been as thoroughly scrutinized, and may not be as reliable as the MBTI, which must be administered by a qualified person.

Another well-known instrument that has also been developed based on Jung's typology is the Keirsey Temperament Sorter. The Keirsey Temperament

Sorter can be found in the book *Please Understand Me* by David Keirsey and Marilyn Bates and through the Internet Web site (see Web Sites and Internet Resources at the end of the chapter). Keirsey and Bates have devised extended profiles for each of the 16 four-letter types derived from Jung's theories. The profiles in *Please Understand Me* are summarized in Figure 3.4 and offer a way of gaining insight into your unique view of the world. The Web site also offers descriptions for each personality type.

It is always a good idea to discuss the results of this or any other instrument with a qualified career counsellor who can provide you with information regarding access and interpretation of these assessments. Try Exercise 3.4 at the end of the chapter. If you take the MBTI or the Keirsey Temperament Sorter, share the results with your group or the class and your feelings about learning your personality type. Do the results match what you predicted or were you surprised?

## Your Four-Letter Personality Type

**ENFJ**  ENFJs are the charismatic leaders who prize co-operation and value their interpersonal relationships over everything. Tolerant, empathetic, and highly intuitive, they are drawn to careers in counselling, teaching, ministry, the media, and performing.

**INFJ**  An exceptional sense of intuition contributes to the complexity of INFJs. Their need to give of themselves makes them exceptional therapists and ministers. Caring, creative, and visionary, they also find satisfaction in writing and teaching.

**ENFP**  Intense, emotional, and authentic are several words that describe ENFPs. Their enthusiastic approach to any task can be a powerful influence on others. They love being creative but become restless when bogged down with routine details. Careers in sales, politics, advertising, and writing are suitable outlets for their talents.

**INFP**  INFPs are the dedicated idealists, capable of deep commitment to a cause or a person. Sensitive and understanding, they prefer harmony and can handle complicated situations but may bridle if forced into a stifling routine. Architecture, psychiatry, college teaching, or missionary work would appeal to INFPs.

**ENTJ**  The ENTJs of the world are the leaders who take charge, provide structure, and drive a group forward. They are impatient with things that don't contribute to achieving the goal, whether they are structures that impede progress, illogical approaches, or people's feelings. Dedicated to their goals, ENTJs usually choose management and leadership positions in a variety of fields.

**INTJ**  Confident and decisive, INTJs are the creative pragmatists who are continually looking for new and better ways to accomplish something. Highly intuitive, they can become lost in the challenge of developing an innovative approach to a problem. Scientific research and engineering are fields that offer an outlet for their abilities.

**ENTP**  The sensitive and intuitive ENTPs are the problem solvers who can bring others along by using charm and enthusiasm. They enjoy improvising and innovating but only if the solutions work in the real world. This style can be awkward because ENTPs are not known for their attention to advance preparation. Nonconformists at times, they can be excellent teachers because they are always looking for new ways to get their points across.

*continued*

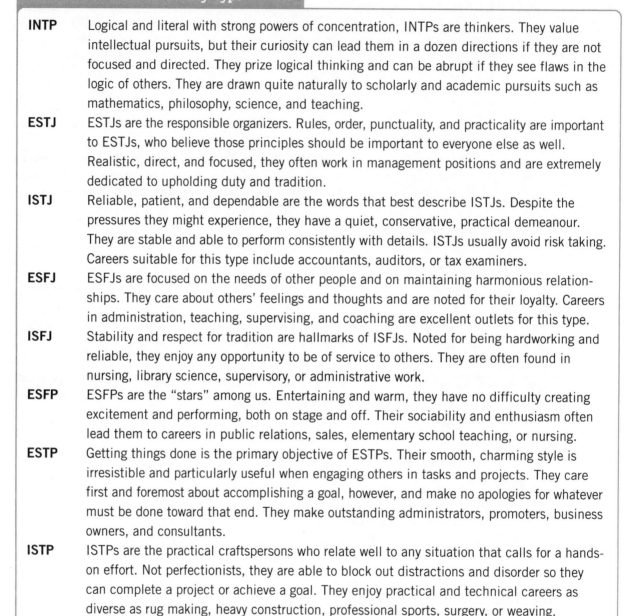

**Your Four-Letter Personality Type** continued

**INTP**    Logical and literal with strong powers of concentration, INTPs are thinkers. They value intellectual pursuits, but their curiosity can lead them in a dozen directions if they are not focused and directed. They prize logical thinking and can be abrupt if they see flaws in the logic of others. They are drawn quite naturally to scholarly and academic pursuits such as mathematics, philosophy, science, and teaching.

**ESTJ**    ESTJs are the responsible organizers. Rules, order, punctuality, and practicality are important to ESTJs, who believe those principles should be important to everyone else as well. Realistic, direct, and focused, they often work in management positions and are extremely dedicated to upholding duty and tradition.

**ISTJ**    Reliable, patient, and dependable are the words that best describe ISTJs. Despite the pressures they might experience, they have a quiet, conservative, practical demeanour. They are stable and able to perform consistently with details. ISTJs usually avoid risk taking. Careers suitable for this type include accountants, auditors, or tax examiners.

**ESFJ**    ESFJs are focused on the needs of other people and on maintaining harmonious relationships. They care about others' feelings and thoughts and are noted for their loyalty. Careers in administration, teaching, supervising, and coaching are excellent outlets for this type.

**ISFJ**    Stability and respect for tradition are hallmarks of ISFJs. Noted for being hardworking and reliable, they enjoy any opportunity to be of service to others. They are often found in nursing, library science, supervisory, or administrative work.

**ESFP**    ESFPs are the "stars" among us. Entertaining and warm, they have no difficulty creating excitement and performing, both on stage and off. Their sociability and enthusiasm often lead them to careers in public relations, sales, elementary school teaching, or nursing.

**ESTP**    Getting things done is the primary objective of ESTPs. Their smooth, charming style is irresistible and particularly useful when engaging others in tasks and projects. They care first and foremost about accomplishing a goal, however, and make no apologies for whatever must be done toward that end. They make outstanding administrators, promoters, business owners, and consultants.

**ISTP**    ISTPs are the practical craftspersons who relate well to any situation that calls for a hands-on effort. Not perfectionists, they are able to block out distractions and disorder so they can complete a project or achieve a goal. They enjoy practical and technical careers as diverse as rug making, heavy construction, professional sports, surgery, or weaving.

**ISFP**    The dreamers among us are probably ISFPs. Capable of intense feeling and highly tuned to physical sensation, they seek out opportunities for tangible experiences. The outdoors is a primary setting for their career interests as is the art studio, with its potter's wheel and brightly coloured paints.

**Figure 3.4**    Your Four-Letter Personality Type

## A Cautionary Note

Please note several important issues when considering the categories or types just described:

◆ Everyone is gifted with each of the traits mentioned to a greater or lesser degree. The mix is unique to each person. For example, no one is always extroverted or consistently introverted. We adapt and incorporate behaviours that may lie on different ends of the continuum. The categories simply allow us to identify better the areas in which we feel most comfortable, and they, in turn, influence our responses and actions.

◆ There is no right or wrong attitude or function, no good or bad trait or response. Each of us enjoys our own special "recipe" of attitudes and functions that combine to form how we meet the world and how the world meets us. There is no right or wrong way to be you. In fact, Jung's definition of true maturity involved the ability to learn who you are and accept the gifts and richness of your attributes, rather than try to figure out how you can change yourself to be something you are not.

◆ The codes described here are helpful tools in understanding a person's overall orientation but do not fully represent all the complexities that make up an individual's personality. No human being can be reduced to or explained by a set of letters. Nonetheless, we continue to use any means available to understand better what it means to be human.

◆ Finally, the career possibilities suggested here are necessarily a limited list of occupations. Don't be discouraged if a career option you may be considering isn't listed or conflicts with your personality type. The options suggested are designed to help you focus your career decision making; they are not life sentences to limit and control you. Trust your inner voice and follow its wisdom.

## How Personalities Complement One Another

Part of Jung's definition of maturity included accepting yourself for the special person you are. Jung also suggested that it is important to our growth to accept other people and their different ways of being.

David Keirsey and Marilyn Bates, the developers of the Keirsey Temperament Sorter, have studied personality and its influence on relationships in depth. Keirsey and Bates's model breaks down personality types from the original four-letter codes to two-letter codes that are associated with particular temperaments. Figure 3.5 shows the two-letter temperament codes and the corresponding four-letter codes.

Each of the two-letter codes in this model is associated with specific temperament traits, as noted in Figure 3.6. These traits describe the behaviours and attitudes associated with the people with whom we might work, be friends, or choose as mates. In Figure 3.6, see if you can pick out yourself, either from your code or the description. Then pick out those of your friends and acquaintances.

Now that you have an idea of Keirsey's temperament codes, try Exercise 3.6 at the end of the chapter to see how you react to the personality differences you encounter.

## Two-Letter Temperament Codes

| NT | SP | SJ | NF |
|------|------|------|------|
| INTP | ISTP | ISFJ | INFJ |
| ENTP | ESTP | ESFJ | ENFJ |
| INTJ | ISFP | ISTJ | INFP |
| ENTJ | ESFP | ESTJ | ENFP |

**Figure 3.5**   Two-Letter Temperament Codes

## Keirsey's Temperament Types and Traits

| | | |
|---|---|---|
| **NTs:** | About 12% of the population<br>Want to understand ideas<br>Never satisfied with results | Competent<br>Self-critical<br>Driven, seek knowledge |
| **SPs:** | About 38% of the population<br>Impulsive, enjoy a crisis<br>Add "electricity" in any setting | Artists and performers<br>Highly changeable<br>Dislike deadlines |
| **SJs:** | 38% of the population<br>Responsible and aware of duty<br>Drawn to education, churches,<br>   hospitals as job settings | Prefer orderly setting<br>Rule/law-oriented |
| **NFs:** | 12% of the population<br>Very articulate and influential<br>Strive for self-actualization | Seek meaning in life<br>Often drawn to writing<br>Spiritual |

**Figure 3.6**   Keirsey's Temperament Types and Traits

# Interests

Regardless of your age, you probably know what kinds of activities and subjects draw you in and cause you to be excited and passionate. Or perhaps, if you are a bit more subdued in your responses, you might refer to certain things that make you feel comfortable and at ease with yourself. These activities, or entities, are commonly known as your interests.

Interests can be powerful predictors of suitability for a type of work. You may find occupations that match your values, fit your motivations, and correspond well with your life stage, but if your interests lie in other areas, you may be dissatisfied with your choices. Typically, if you are strongly attracted to a certain occupational field, you may decide to pursue it despite a host of potential obstacles. Just take a trip to Hollywood and you will find hundreds, even thousands, of people whose interest in the entertainment industry outweighs other considerations. They will endure daily rejection, substandard living conditions, and years of uncertainty in hopes of being one of the chosen few who becomes a star.

John L. Holland is one theorist who has explored the issue of interests and their relation to career choice. Holland's theory suggests that there are six basic personality types and that most people fit into either one of the personality types or a combination of the types. In his model, a person's personality type is largely determined by his or her interests.

Holland's theory maintains that vocational choice is often a reflection of one's personality type. People seek situations in which they can use their skills and express themselves in positive ways. Frequently, people of similar interests are drawn to the same vocation. If you can identify your personality type by interests, then you can match your type with occupational choices that would complement your personality type. Tracing these "links" will open up a series of occupational possibilities that you can explore.

If you have had a variety of life experiences, you may find the process of identifying your interests and preferences much simpler than someone who is younger or has not had different opportunities. Your knowledge about yourself and the world of work will be reflected in your interests and preferences. Young people with less exposure to a broad range of experiences may find this a bit challenging. Identifying your interests is an important step to self-understanding. The following six personality types identified by Holland may help you identify your interests.

## Holland's Personality Types

### Realistic

People in this category usually prefer physical tasks, athletics, and outdoor activities. They enjoy working with their hands and using tools, utensils, and machines.

### Investigative

Investigative-type people are usually quiet, inquisitive, or analytical, and may be observant and enjoy academic and scientific pursuits.

### Enterprising

People of this type usually enjoy persuading or influencing others. They may seek leadership or management situations and are comfortable organizing to achieve group goals. They prefer working with people in a leadership role.

### Artistic

People of the artistic type usually prefer situations in which they can be creative and artistic. They may be flamboyant and imaginative, enjoying settings that are free of structure. Some are visionary and independent.

### Conventional

Conventional type people usually prefer structure and order. They are comfortable with details of any variety—facts, numbers, any kind of data—and they find satisfaction in bringing situations to closure.

### Social

People in this category usually gravitate to other people, regardless of the setting. They may have strong verbal and written communication skills and a special attraction to the helping professions.

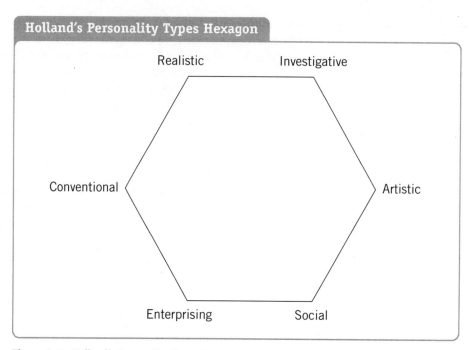

**Figure 3.7**    Holland's Personality Types Hexagon

Figure 3.7 illustrates Holland's six types arranged in a hexagon shape. The types nearest to each other are more closely related than those that are opposite each other on the hexagon. Most people's personality types will usually be identified by one dominant type and influenced to a lesser extent by one or two others. Once you identify the types where most of your interests lie, you can start matching your interests with those of people working in particular occupations. Exercise 3.7 at the end of the chapter will help you examine some of your interests and identify related occupations.

In addition to Exercise 3.7, a number of vocational interest inventories are available to assist you in identifying your interests and how they may relate to certain occupations. Holland's Self-Directed Search: A Guide to Educational and Vocational Planning (SDS), the Career Assessment Inventory (CAI), and the Strong Interest Inventory (SII) are among the most widely recognized instruments. Each of these assessments is based on Holland's personality codes and offers a more comprehensive list of related career options. Holland's Self-Directed Search also includes measurement instruments for assessing leisure and educational interests. These instruments are usually available through career counsellors, who will assist you in interpreting the results. Your responses can be used as a basis for developing possible career options.

Along with pencil-and-paper instruments, there are also interactive computerized guidance systems available. These programs provide self-assessment and career-exploration exercises. Career Cruising™ and Choices are two examples of online career guidance systems used by counsellors to help people research their interests, values, and experiences. These assessments automatically cross-reference your findings with related occupations.

It might be useful for you to complete an interest inventory in order to assess your interests and how they might relate to occupational choices. After you've had a chance to complete one of the assessments, share the results with your group and discuss how you feel about the results. Do they match what you might have chosen for yourself? Or were you surprised?

Keep in mind that your interests are subject to change. Your priorities may shift as you grow, and this may affect the influence of your values. Your interests may also shift and adapt. The results of any assessment you take now are merely a "snapshot" at this point in your career decision-making process.

## Li's Story

Li was starting her first college term in a few weeks but felt totally lost. She had determined her class schedule on the basis of the answer to one critical question: "What program will make it easiest for me to get a job when I graduate?" Li had looked over the college calendar, wondering what all the department codes and class numbers meant. She had thought about talking with an advisor but was afraid she would look foolish if she didn't know what she wanted to do.

As the first day of classes approached, Li realized that she was getting closer and closer to taking a path about which she felt increasingly uncomfortable. Her schedule was packed with math and science classes required for the engineering technology program. She dreaded the classes and was having a hard time seeing herself working in that field. Something didn't fit.

Li finally admitted to herself that she needed help in finding out what would be a better fit for her. She made an appointment with a career counsellor. The counsellor, Ron, spent some time talking with Li about why she had decided on engineering technology in the first place. Li felt embarrassed when she told him that she had chosen it because she was good with numbers and knew that she would be able to get a job in the field. Ron wasn't surprised and suggested that while many students make decisions with even less consideration than that, it might be helpful if Li took some self-assessment instruments, such as the MBTI and the Strong Interest Inventory, before she made any major decisions. The greatest task for her would be to think more about what she enjoyed doing. She might eventually decide that engineering technology was indeed a good choice but if not, she would have a good idea of other options.

After completing the assessment instruments, Li wrote down all the activities and skills that interested her and matched her values. She had always enjoyed working with numbers but not the upper-level math that was required for engineering. She was an orderly person who felt good when everything fit together nicely. She was definitely interested in developing a marketable skill that would lead to job security. When she met with Ron to discuss the results of her assessments, she was thinking about accounting as a possibility. The interest instrument and the personality indicator confirmed that accounting was one option that might be a good fit for Li.

There was a great deal that Li still had to find out, both about the field she was considering and about herself. However, she felt more confident knowing there was a process that would help her sort out what she wanted and how to achieve her goals.

Look at the skills and abilities in Figure 3.1. Do you see any areas that you recognize in which you excel or possess a high level of capability?

_____

_____

How do you know you have these skills? Describe the setting in which you were able to demonstrate your ability.

_____

_____

Describe a specific incident associated with your demonstrated capability in which others recognized your skills.

_____

_____

What were the outcomes—tangible or intangible—of your having used that ability?

_____

_____

Describe your feelings while you were performing this skill and afterward.

_____

_____

Are you aware of any skills and abilities you possess that are not listed?

_____

_____

Do you recognize any categories of skills under which these "unlisted" skills would fit?

_____

_____

_Discuss your reactions with your group or the class._

**TAKE A CLOSER LOOK**

**3.2 Your Transferable Skills**

Of all the skills you enjoy using, choosing ones that are transferable can help you envision yourself in different work settings and can suggest career choices to explore further. You will identify your transferable skills by focusing on achievements or peak experiences that gave you a sense of satisfaction and fulfillment.

In the following space, list five achievements that you think were peak experiences, ones that allowed you to use your skills with good results. Note the details of your achievement, delineating the specifics of the event or task so that your notes resemble a job description. For example, rather than "Responded to a customer complaint," you might write "Greeted the customer, listened attentively to the complaint, asked questions to determine the exact nature of the problem, discussed possible remedies, contacted the relevant department, gathered information, resolved customer problem." After describing the event or events, list the skills that were necessary to achieve the results. For the above-mentioned episode, you might write down skills such as listening, remaining calm, negotiating, interpreting information, enlisting co-operation, and investigating and organizing resources. If necessary, review the skills listed in this chapter to help you identify those skills most critical to each of your specific achievements. The most important factor is that anything counts, whether you used a skill at work, school, home, or as part of a hobby. Your skills can be a valuable part of your career plan, so include everything that comes to mind!

**ACHIEVEMENT EVENT #1**

_____

_____

Facts Pertaining to Event

_____

_____

Skills Used to Achieve Results

_____

_____

**ACHIEVEMENT EVENT #2**

_____

_____

Facts Pertaining to Event

_____

_____

Skills Used to Achieve Results

_____

_____

**ACHIEVEMENT EVENT #3**

_____

_____

Facts Pertaining to Event

_____

_____

Skills Used to Achieve Results

_____

_____

**ACHIEVEMENT EVENT #4**

_____

_____

Facts Pertaining to Event

_____

_____

Skills Used to Achieve Results

_____

_____

**ACHIEVEMENT EVENT #5**

_____

_____

Facts Pertaining to Event

_____

_____

Skills Used to Achieve Results

_____

_____

*Do you see a pattern of skills emerging? Discuss your reactions with your group or with the class.*

_____

## TAKE A CLOSER LOOK
### 3.3 On-the-Job Know-How

Review the information from Employability Skills 2000+ in Figure 3.2. Now recall your achievements, prior work experiences, and current educational situation, going through each skill to see how you rate. On the chart below, rank your level of skill by circling the number that you think best reflects your level, 1 representing little or no skill and 10 representing maximum achievable skill. Try to be as candid and honest as possible. This is part of finding out what you need to do to find your place in the world of work. It will help you know what you need to do to be competitive. Remember, *where* you acquired the skills is irrelevant here, just consider your level of development in each of these skills.

**Fundamental Skills**

| | | | | | | | | | | |
|---|---|---|---|---|---|---|---|---|---|---|
| Communicate | 1 | 2 | 3 | 4 | 5 | 6 | 7 | 8 | 9 | 10 |
| Manage Information | 1 | 2 | 3 | 4 | 5 | 6 | 7 | 8 | 9 | 10 |
| Use Numbers | 1 | 2 | 3 | 4 | 5 | 6 | 7 | 8 | 9 | 10 |
| Think & Solve Problems | 1 | 2 | 3 | 4 | 5 | 6 | 7 | 8 | 9 | 10 |

**Personal Management Skills**

| | | | | | | | | | | |
|---|---|---|---|---|---|---|---|---|---|---|
| Demonstrate Positive Attitudes & Behaviours | 1 | 2 | 3 | 4 | 5 | 6 | 7 | 8 | 9 | 10 |
| Be Responsible | 1 | 2 | 3 | 4 | 5 | 6 | 7 | 8 | 9 | 10 |
| Be Adaptable | 1 | 2 | 3 | 4 | 5 | 6 | 7 | 8 | 9 | 10 |
| Learn Continuously | 1 | 2 | 3 | 4 | 5 | 6 | 7 | 8 | 9 | 10 |
| Work Safely | 1 | 2 | 3 | 4 | 5 | 6 | 7 | 8 | 9 | 10 |

**Teamwork Skills**

| | | | | | | | | | | |
|---|---|---|---|---|---|---|---|---|---|---|
| Work with Others | 1 | 2 | 3 | 4 | 5 | 6 | 7 | 8 | 9 | 10 |
| Participate in Projects & Tasks | 1 | 2 | 3 | 4 | 5 | 6 | 7 | 8 | 9 | 10 |

How do you rate? Do you see areas in which you might improve your skill level?

_____

How can you improve your skills in the areas where you see weaknesses?

_____

_____

*Discuss your responses with your group or with the class.*

_____

Let's examine each of Jung's eight categories separately to see which might describe you and your preferences. Place a check next to the phrases under each category that most accurately describe your style or preference. Mark down your "gut" reaction. Try not to read too much into each statement.

**EXTROVERSION**

❏ Prefer fast pace
❏ Enjoy variety

❏ Enjoy interacting with people
❏ High energy
❏ Open, self-disclosing
❏ Will talk with anyone about anything

_____ Total
_____ Category preference (E or I)

**INTROVERSION**

❏ Prefer planned activities
❏ Do one thing at a time until each task is completed
❏ Work in a setting with a low activity level
❏ Like to get away by yourself
❏ Enjoy working on things "in your head"
❏ Prefer to weigh all factors before deciding

_____ Total

**INTUITIVE**

❏ Prefer the "big picture"
❏ Enjoy many things at once
❏ Seek new challenges

❏ Give weight to intangible factors
❏ Impatient with literal interpretations
❏ Eager to learn

_____ Total
_____ Category preference (N or S)

**SENSING**

❏ More comfortable with specifics
❏ Prefer working with details
❏ Uncomfortable with unfamiliar challenges
❏ Strict adherence to accuracy
❏ Resistant to "gut-level" responses
❏ Prefer literal interpretations

_____ Total

**FEELING**

❏ Sensitive
❏ Value others' feelings
❏ Enjoy interacting with people
❏ Work at relationships
❏ Subjective
❏ Capable of feeling deeply

_____ Total
_____ Category preference (F or T)

**THINKING**

❏ Orderly
❏ Enjoy working with numbers
❏ Not easily influenced by others' feelings
❏ Focused
❏ Calm under stress
❏ Objective

_____ Total

**JUDGING**

❏ Prefer step-by-step planning
❏ Thoughtful
❏ Motivated to reach closure
❏ Decisive
❏ Organized, linear
❏ Unrelenting in pursuit of goal

_____ Total
_____ Category preference (J or P)

**PERCEIVING**

❏ Comfortable with open-ended situations
❏ Tolerant
❏ Sensitive to intangibles
❏ Able to function despite disorganization
❏ Hesitant to exclude options
❏ Aware of full implications of issues

_____ Total

Note the letter from each category that shows your personality preference and indicate each preference below.

Your code _____   _____   _____   _____

          E or I     N or S     F or T     J or P

*Based on your responses to the checklist, you will come up with one of the four-letter personality codes listed in Figure 3.3.*

## TAKE A CLOSER LOOK

### 3.5 A Glimpse in the Mirror

Now that you have learned a bit about your possible personality type and some of its characteristics, reflect briefly on how you see yourself.

From the previous exercise on personality type, what did you find your psychological type might be?

**YOUR FOUR-LETTER PERSONALITY CODE**

On these lines, note some key words from the text that are associated with your personality type.

_____     _____

_____     _____

_____     _____

Do these key words represent traits that you feel are true of you?

_____

_____

Look at the other descriptions, especially for those personality types that have letters in common with your own. Do any of the key words describing other personality types remind you of yourself? Note those key words here.

_____     _____

_____     _____

_____     _____

Learning more about some of the characteristics associated with personality types has probably given you a better sense of some occupational fields that might appeal to you and bring you satisfaction. List some of your ideas here.

_____

_____

*Discuss the results of this exercise with your group or with the class.*

### 3.6 Love–Hate between Types[2]

If you have taken the MBTI or the Keirsey Temperament Sorter, then you know your four- and two-letter codes. If not, try to determine which group you might be most comfortable in from the brief descriptions offered earlier.

Now divide up your class or group by two-letter types, with NFs and SPs in one group and SJs and NTs in the other. Once you are divided into groups, discuss the following question in your group. Have one member keep track of your responses.

What traits do you most dislike in the people in the other group?

_____

_____

_____

Have one person in your group read your responses aloud to the main group.

Now consider this question: What traits do you most like in the people in the other group?

_____

_____

_____

Again, share your impressions with the main group.

Surprised? Yes, for all the "strangeness" represented by the other personalities we encounter, we have to admit that they do have a lot to offer as well. Every group needs its creative, impulsive energy source along with dedicated, orderly producers. The beauty of the mix is in the balance it offers.

*Discuss your feelings about your type and the opposites as you view them now with your group or with the class.*

### 3.7 Assessing Your Interests

Take a look at the following interest areas and the related occupational titles. Based on your preferences, write out the possible occupational choices that are related to your interests.

| INTEREST AREAS | RELATED OCCUPATIONS |
|---|---|
| *Artistic*<br>Creative activities<br>Endeavours requiring imagination and innovation | Art, Music, Dance, Fine Arts, Theatre, Design, Commercial Art, Advertising, Writing, Sketching, Composing, Acting |

---

[2] This exercise is adapted from the work done by Dr. Bruce Taylor, Janet Kalven, and Dr. Larry S. Rosen, based on Keirsey and Bates's *Please Understand Me.*

*Social*

| | |
|---|---|
| Helping activities | Education, Counselling, Human |
| Activities that offer outlets for idealistic action | Services Work, Political Science, Health Care, Law Enforcement |
| Teaching, leading groups | |

*Conventional*

| | |
|---|---|
| Methodical activities | Accounting, Business Management, |
| Activities requiring efficiency and systematic skills | Computer Systems, Clerical and Administrative Services |
| Following defined procedures and routines | |

*Enterprising*

| | |
|---|---|
| Managerial activities | Management, Business and Hospital |
| Endeavours requiring high energy and self-confidence | Administration, Purchasing, Human |
| Planning projects, selling, promoting, and supervising | Resources, Public Administration, Retailing |

*Realistic*

| | |
|---|---|
| Tangible activities | Architecture, Automotives, |
| Activities requiring operation and use of tools | Engineering, |
| Working outdoors, tinkering with machines, sports | Drafting and Design, Quality Control Engineering, Graphics Production |

*Investigative*

| | |
|---|---|
| Problem-solving activities involving independent, intellectual tasks using natural curiosity and scientific methods to solve problems | Sciences, Medicine, Research, Laboratory Procedure and Analysis, Computer Programming and Systems Analysis |

My interests are in: _____

Possible occupational areas: _____

## TAKE A CLOSER LOOK
### 3.8 Pulling It All Together

"Li's Story" is about her coming to a new understanding of herself. After reading her story, you can probably see more clearly how looking at the different aspects of who you are can help you discover possible career directions. While the process can certainly include a more intuitive approach, it may help to set forth specifically the key factors that have been explored in this chapter, namely:

What skills did you identify as most important to you and your growth?

_____

_____

What transferable skills did you identify?

_____

_____

How did you rate in employability skills?

_____

_____

What were your four-letter and two-letter personality types?

_____

_____

What are some of the traits and characteristics associated with your personality type?

_____

_____

On the basis of your responses to the interest exercise, what was your interest area?

_____

_____

What are the occupational areas related to your interests?

_____

_____

If you were able to complete a personality or interest instrument, what occupational choices did you discover?

_____

_____

Did your process of self-assessment confirm the possibilities that you had considered or did it suggest that you had not considered before?

_____

_____

List some occupations that you are interested in exploring and learning more about.

_____

_____

_____

_____

## A Look Back

Your career adventure is taking you further along the path of insight into what an occupation might offer you. In this chapter, you examined your abilities, skills, personality, and interests. You explored those skills and abilities that are most rewarding to you and identified those that might be important in the workplace of the future. You developed a better understanding of your personality type and some of its characteristics. You also began to assess your interests and those activities and settings that appeal to you. Additionally, you probably have a clearer understanding of how those aspects of your personality relate to possible career choices.

If you are feeling frustrated and somewhat confused at this point, don't worry. Those feelings may be a sign that some of the assumptions you have held are in flux. You may be facing the reality of the work world for the first time—a significant step in itself. Over time, your feelings will resolve themselves as you adjust to what lies ahead. Keep a positive attitude and you may find things will fall into place very soon. On the other hand, if you're feeling sure of yourself because you got just the results you had expected, be prepared. You never know what you may encounter as you continue your career adventure. That's what makes this process exciting. Keep an open mind.

Part I focused on increasing your self-awareness. In Chapter 1, you reflected on who you are and your dreams for yourself. In Chapter 2, you examined your values and motivations, and in Chapter 3, your skills and abilities, personality, and interests. The purpose of these three chapters was to help you begin to understand these important aspects of yourself and how they relate to your career decision making.

At this point you may be feeling somewhat confused and may be trying to make sense of all this information. Your task now is to synthesize what you have learned about yourself and to begin to generate a list of occupations that may fit well with the important aspects of yourself that you have identified. One of the best ways to do this is to summarize the results of your self-assessment and look for convergence among the factors involved. Each circle in Figure 3.8 represents an aspect you have considered in these first three chapters. The point in the centre is where they all converge. This is where you should concentrate your occupational search. Use this diagram to help you identify the aspects you need to consider when searching for an occupation. Then identify occupations that might best fit these aspects.

In Part II, we will turn our focus from the inner self to the external world of work. You will continue refining your list of occupations that you may be interested in learning more about. You will also learn about the labour market and job trends.

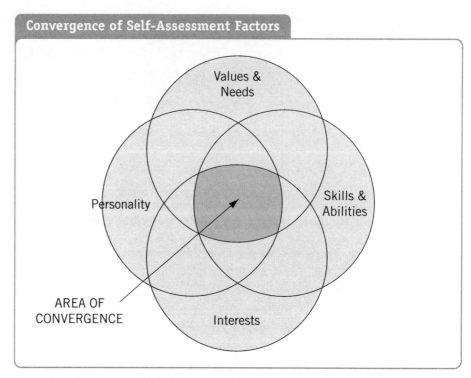

Figure 3.8 Convergence of Self-Assessment Factors

 ## Other Sources and Suggested Reading

Career Cruising™
This computerized assessment is interesting and easy to use. It is available online with subscription at **www.careercruising.com** and on CD-ROM. Many colleges, universities, and career resource centres maintain subscriptions.

Choices
This career assessment tool is produced by Bridges Transitions Inc. It is available on CD-ROM and online at **www.bridges.com/canada/index.htm**. The online version is available with subscription by colleges, universities, and career resource agencies. It delivers self-directed career and education-planning tools.

*Do What You Are: Discover the Perfect Career for You Through the Secrets of Personality Type* by Paul D. Tieger and Barbara Barron-Tieger
This book examines personality types and possible career choices that complement each other.

*Making Vocational Choices: A Theory of Careers* by John L. Holland
The Holland system of personality types and their relationship to career choice is explained in depth in this useful book.

*Personality Types: Jung's Model of Typology* by Daryl Sharp
A basic guide to Jung's theory of psychological types.

*Please Understand Me* by David Keirsey and Marilyn Bates
This book takes a closer look at personality types and their influence in the various aspects of life. The concepts are based on the personality theories of Carl Jung.

*Type Talk and Type Talk at Work* by Otto Kroeger, with Janet M. Thuesen
   Both of these books explore and expand on the Keirsey Temperament
   Sorter model and offer interesting insights on the impact of personality
   in contemporary work settings.

# Web Sites and Internet Resources

**www.keirsey.com**
This site offers the Keirsey Temperament Sorter from which to derive Jung's
four-letter code.

**www.mdani.demon.co.uk**
An in-depth examination of Jungian psychology, including an online
personality test.

**www15.hrdc-drhc.gc.ca**
Human Resources and Skills Development Canada's Web site, full of very
useful, relevant, up-to-date information.

**www.conferenceboard.ca/education/learning-tools/employability-skills.htm**
This is the Web site of the Conference Board of Canada with access to
information on Employability Skills 2000+.

**www.jobfutures.ca**
This site is developed and maintained by the Government of Canada. It
provides useful information about 226 occupational groups and describes
the work experiences of recent graduates from 155 programs of study.

**www23.hrdc-drhc.gc.ca**
The NOC 2001 Web site contains the classification structure and descriptions
of 520 occupational unit groups and includes over 30 000 occupational titles.

**www.jobsetc.ca**
This is a Government of Canada site that has quizzes to help you identify
your interests and working style.

**www.yorkregion-vcrc.com**
York Region's Virtual Community Resource Centre. This Web site offers practical
information regarding career planning, changing careers, and the transition
from school to work. There are various links available to self-assessment inventories, business profiles, labour market information, and occupation profiles.

**http://careerbookmarks.tpl.toronto.on.ca**
This Toronto Public Library page contains a number of links to useful
assessment sites.

**www.hrsdc.gc.ca/en/hip/hrp/career_awareness/quizzes/quizzes1.shtml**
HRSDC provides some links that can direct you to career quizzes and
information.

**www.cdm.uwaterloo.ca/step1.asp**
The University of Waterloo's Career Services offers an online guide to lead
you step by step in your career decision-making process.

# Part II

# Occupational Research

## Learning about the World of Work

Being free to deeply examine who you are can be exciting and enlightening. Now it is time to explore aspects of the outside world and their influence on your career decision. By this time you may be considering a number of career possibilities that you identified through the self-awareness process in Part I of this book. You are ready for Part II, your next step in the career adventure.

A key factor in your career decision will be knowledge of the current labour market. As you make your career decisions, it is important to consider a broad range of information and issues. Some issues relate to the basics of the position in which you have an interest—duties, salary, setting, and availability of openings. Other information crucial to this process relates to the general job market—the impact of technology on our way of doing work, trends in managing workers, and the influence of global competition.

As you continue to gather information, the primary goal of this text is to help you focus on the place in the career spectrum where your unique personality, interests, skills, and abilities can best be used and your individual needs can best be met.

## Part II will include

## Objectives

**Chapter 4:** Exploring the World of Work: Researching Occupations, the Labour Market, and Future Job Trends

**Chapter 5:** Networking: Establishing Contacts and Support

**Chapter 6:** Trying an Occupation: Gaining Experience, Education, and Training

**Chapter 7:** Decision Making and Goal Setting: Putting It All Together

- ◆ To be aware of resources for acquiring information on different occupations.
- ◆ To develop contacts in your field of interest.
- ◆ To use information interviewing to network and research occupations.
- ◆ To gain hands-on knowledge and experience of the field you are considering.
- ◆ To put together all information acquired about self and occupations and to use this information to make career decisions.
- ◆ To establish short-term and long-term goals.

# Chapter 4
# Exploring the World of Work

## Researching Occupations, the Labour Market, and Future Job Trends

*I skate where the puck is going to be, not where it is.*

WAYNE GRETZKY

At this point in the career adventure, you have the opportunity to explore the world of work. This part of your search is extremely important. As you plunge into the process of deciding on an occupation and preparing for it, you will benefit from understanding the labour market. Without this knowledge, manoeuvring in the job market might be similar to jumping off a high-diving board without knowing how to swim. You might survive, but you would definitely be in over your head.

This phase of the career decision-making process will yield much valuable information and perhaps a few surprises. The information-gathering process is an ongoing part of career planning throughout your life. You will continually use the skills that you develop as you investigate the job market, accept a position, change fields, and continue to grow in your career.

When you make a career move, your expectations for success are naturally raised. This is especially true if you have invested in years of planning, training, or a post-secondary education. You envision a higher-paying, high-level job that matches your academic skills. That's okay, as long as your expectations are grounded in reality. In other words, consider the example of an electronics student who might be thinking about opening a shop offering VCR repair service. Her first step is to find out if there is a market for this type of work. She might find that because VCRs are sold so inexpensively now and most people are updating to DVDs, there is very little demand for people to repair VCRs. It is possible that the potential income in this occupation will be low, and this type of work may eventually be phased out. Therefore, she may or may not still wish to pursue this goal. It is worthwhile for her to consider the labour market and job trends before she makes her decision and sets her goals. Some people will pursue their dream occupation, regardless of where it may lead. Being committed to a career goal is fine, but anticipating what lies ahead on your path is essential.

In this chapter and those that follow, you will learn how to conduct research on occupations you may be considering. This will give you information you need to make decisions and prepare for your chosen occupation. There are a variety of tools and resources designed to assist you in the process.

In this chapter, we explore how to research occupations and learn about them, the labour market, and future job trends by using information technology, government resources and publications, and career resources centres as a means for collecting information.

# Using the Internet to Research Occupations

It is now possible to use the Internet to research organizations, job leads, and other career-related information. If you have a computer, modem, Internet software, and an Internet service provider, then a typical search will yield literally hundreds of thousands of references. It is an incomparable source of information, but can offer too much of a good thing. With just the touch of a button, you can be buried under Web sources that may hold valuable information or may be a maze of useless data and advertising. A few simple steps will make the time you spend on the Internet more productive.

1. *Use two or three search terms, clarifying with markers.*

    ◆ Use *and* or a *plus sign* (+) to narrow your search (trades AND women + training);

    ◆ Use *or* or a *slash* (/) to broaden your search (college OR university, college/university);

    ◆ Use *not* or a *minus* (−) *sign* to indicate a word that should not appear (lions NOT CFL, lions−CFL);

    ◆ Use *near* when the words should be close to each other (cost NEAR accounting);

    ◆ To limit a search to an exact phrase, put it in quotation marks; typing Career Information System without quotation marks yields over 5 million returns on **google.ca**. "Career Information System" yields 1790.

2. *Use guidelines provided at the search engine sites to facilitate your search.* Each search engine has tips on the best way to gather data. Take a few minutes to familiarize yourself with the recommended shortcuts.

3. *Use sources that you can rely on.* Some search engines offer directories, or online guides, that are evaluated by experts. These vertical portals, or "vertals," save time by linking you when possible directly to the most useful sites. Some library Web sites also have direct links to Web sites that have been evaluated by librarians.

4. *Evaluate Internet resources before relying on the data found there.* Keep the following in mind when reviewing information found on the Internet.

    ◆ Who is the author? Is the author the originator of the data? What are his or her credentials, background, education, experience?

    ◆ What organization supports the site? What is the relationship between the author and the site sponsor? Does the site sponsor monitor the information or is the author biased in favour of the sponsor?

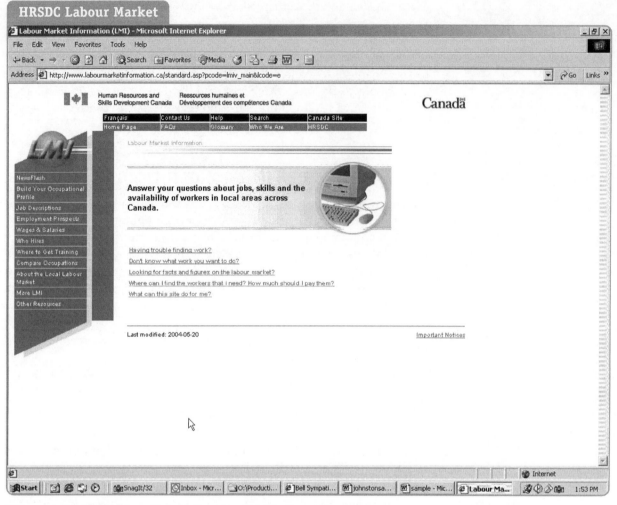

**Figure 4.1** The HRSDC Labour Market Information Web Site Home Page

Source: Human Resources and Skills Development Canada. 2004. HRSDC Labour Market Information Web Site Home Page. Reproduced with the permission of the Minister of Public Works and Government Services Canada, 2004. Accessed September 29, 2004 at **www.labourmarketinformation.ca/standard.asp?pcode=lmiv_main&lcode=e.**

◆ Is the information current?

◆ What is the purpose of the data? To inform? To persuade? To explain?

◆ For which audience is the information intended?

◆ How does the information offered compare to other sites and non-Internet sources?

Figures 4.1, 4.2, and 4.3 offer examples of Web sites that you might wish to visit as you search the Internet. All of them are Human Resources and Skills Development Canada (HRSDC) Web sites. Figure 4.1 is a Web site dedicated to labour market information. Figures 4.2 and 4.3 are from the *Job Futures* Web site. These will be discussed in more detail later in the chapter.

Most libraries now offer Internet access to their patrons. The Internet provides you with a valuable resource for information to conduct your career exploration, particularly if you use the above suggestions when you search. There are many useful Web sites for you to use in your occupation research.

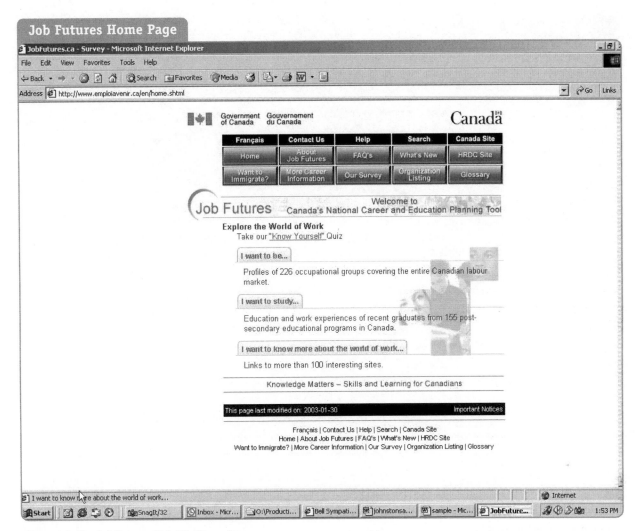

**Figure 4.2** The Job Futures Web Site Home Page

Source: Human Resources and Skills Development Canada. 2004. Job Futures Web Site Home Page. Reproduced with the permission of the Minister of Public Works and Government Services Canada, 2004. Accessed September 29, 2004 at **www.emploiavenir.ca/en/home.shtml.**

## Online Career Guidance Systems

In the last chapter, you explored your skills, interests, and personality in an attempt to find an occupation that might suit you. In addition to the information available in print form, there are also a number of computerized systems, some available online as well as in CD-ROM format, that are valuable resources in making career decisions. These resources offer tools both for self-assessment and for information regarding occupations, job markets, and educational institutions. While a session with a computer may never take the place of face-to-face counselling with a professional, many people can still benefit from using these resources.

The computerized guidance systems that are currently available offer a variety of programs and modules from which to choose. Two of the most popular programs available with Canadian editions are Career Cruising™ and Choices.

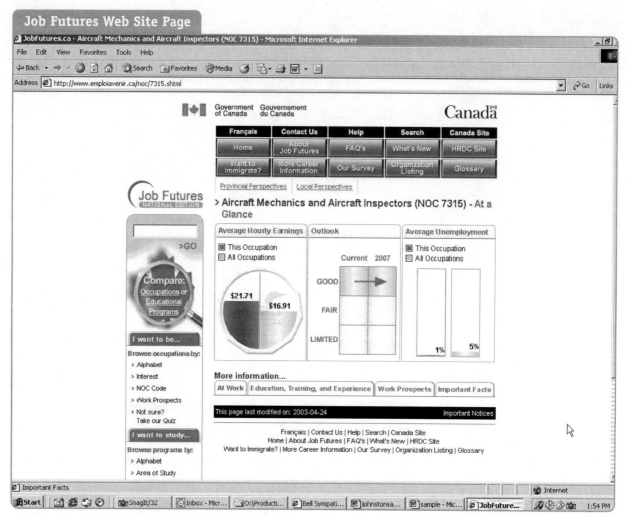

**Figure 4.3** Sample Web Page from the Job Futures Web Site

Source: Human Resources and Skills Development Canada. 2004. Job Futures Web Site Page. Reproduced with the permission of the Minister of Public Works and Government Services Canada, 2004. Accessed September 29, 2004 at **www.emploiavenir.ca/noc/7315.shtml**.

## Career Cruising™

This computerized career information system is available online at **www.careercruising.com** and on CD-ROM. However, one must have a licence to use it. Many colleges, universities, career resource centres, libraries, and career counsellors subscribe to this program and have it available for use. Career Cruising™ matches students' self-assessment responses with occupations and then provides a complete database of information about occupations. It offers a user-friendly program that includes in-depth occupational information, interviews with people working in the occupations, and a database of colleges and universities that provide the necessary training for the occupations.

Most valuable is the depth and amount of information about careers and the world of work that is available at the touch of a button. People can learn more about specific jobs, salaries, duties, outlook, and what professionals like and dislike about their jobs. An added benefit lies in each system's ability to store student information and responses, allowing the student to return to the program for long-term use.

## Choices

Choices is published by Bridges, a Canadian company based in Kelowna, BC. Bridges offers the Choices program in CD-ROM and online at **www.bridges.com/canada/index.htm**, with elementary, high-school, post-secondary, and agency and HR versions. It uses personality theory to assist users to identify occupations that might suit them and provides information about occupations, job banks, educational institutions, and job-searching skills. It is intended to be a self-directed career and educational planning tool.

As with any tool that you use to make a career decision, computers can make the process more manageable. But, just as you have found with interest inventories and personality exercises, they do not provide a magic answer that will lead you directly to the occupation of your dreams. As a resource, they allow you access to a wealth of information and may assist you in gaining insight, but they will never completely replace the hard work necessary to make a career choice.

Ask your instructor or counsellor whether any of the programs mentioned previously are available for your use. If so, schedule an appointment to use the system. Discuss your experience with the computer-assisted career guidance system with your group or with the class.

# Government Resources and Publications

"Don't forget, Charlie, I want to see your high school diploma *tomorrow* or I'm gettin' me another Frialator man!"

There are two very useful resources published by the Government of Canada for anyone interested in occupational research, the labour market, and/or future job trends. These are the *National Occupational Classification* (NOC) and *Job Futures*. The NOC lists and classifies approximately 30 000 occupations in the Canadian labour market. *Job Futures* provides information on the Canadian labour market as a whole, and there are also specific publications of *Job Futures* for individual provinces and territories that supply local labour market information. These resources will provide you with a base of knowledge from which to broaden your occupational research.

## The National Occupational Classification (NOC)

The NOC is the definitive document for cataloguing occupations in Canada, listing over 30 000 occupational titles. It provides a standardized definition of positions and duties, grouping positions according to occupational clusters and skills. The occupations described in the NOC are organized by numerical codes that match a job's skills and functions. Figure 4.4 shows a sample page from the NOC that is now also available online (see Web Sites and Internet Resources at the end of this chapter).

**Sample NOC Online Page**

@ 2213 Meteorological Technicians

Back | Forward | Stop | Refresh | Home | AutoFill | Print | Mail

Address: @ http://www23.hrdc-drhc.gc.ca/2001/e/groups/2213.shtml

@ Live Home Page | @ Apple | @ iTools | @ Apple Support | @ Apple Store | @ Microsoft MacTopia | @ MSN | @ Office for Macinto

Human Resources Development Canada | Développement des ressources humaines Canada

Canada

| Français | Contact Us | Help | Search | Canada Site |
| Home | Order Our Products | FAQ | Related Links | HRP Directorate |

NATIONAL OCCUPATIONAL CLASSIFICATION

Occupational Descriptions

Index of Titles

Matrix

Training Tutorial

Career Handbook

Search 2001

NOC 1992

2001

**Quick Search**

[ GO ]

Find an occupational description by entering its four-digit NOC code.

2213    Meteorological Technicians

Meteorological technicians observe weather and atmospheric conditions, record and interpret meteorological data, transmit and report on recorded information, and provide meteorological information and advice to the general public, the transportation industry and the media. They are employed by the Atmospheric Environment Service of Environment Canada and by the armed forces, private consulting companies, resource and utility companies and by provincial governments.

Example Titles

aerological technician
avalanche controller
climate data processor
climate service specialist
climate service technician
ice service specialist
meteorological inspector
meteorological technician
officer-in-charge, weather station
operations technician, weather station
surface weather observer
weather service specialist

>>View all titles

Main duties

Meteorological technicians perform some or all of the following duties:

- Observe, record and transmit atmospheric and weather information including air pressure, temperature, humidity, wind, precipitation, cloud and ultraviolet conditions
- Observe, chart and report on ice conditions in navigable waters
- Provide weather information to various users such as pilots, farmers, shipping industries and news media
- Inspect and service various weather service installations and maintain equipment and instruments
- Analyze and interpret weather data
- Maintain climatological databases and participate in the production of weather maps and charts
- Observe snow conditions and participate in programs to control avalanches in mountainous terrain.

Employment requirements

- Completion of secondary school is required.
- Completion of a meteorological technician program provided by the Atmospheric Environment Service is required.
- Initial training may be up to one year, with subsequent specialized training available.

Classified elsewhere

- *Meteorologists* (2114)

Classification Structure - 2

Last Modified: 2004/10/27                    ▲                    Important Notices

**Figure 4.4** A Sample NOC Online Page

Source: Human Resources and Skills Development Canada. 2001. National Occupational Classification, Example of an NOC online page—2213 Meteorological Technicians. Reproduced with the permission of the Minister of Public Works and Government Services Canada, 2004. Accessed September 24, 2004 at **www23.hrdc-drhc.gc.ca/2001/e/groups/2213.shtml**.

A typical listing for an occupation in the NOC includes the position's four-digit occupational code, the occupational title, the industry designation in which the job is categorized, any alternative or related titles, a brief description of the tasks associated with the position, and employment requirements including education and training.

The occupational titles in the NOC are divided into 10 categories:

**Category No.**

0    Management Occupations

1    Business, Finance, and Administration Occupations

2    Natural and Applied Sciences and Related Occupations

3    Health Occupations

4    Occupations in Social Science, Education, Government Service, and Religion

5    Occupations in Art, Culture, Recreation, and Sport

6    Sales and Service Occupations

7    Trades, Transport, and Equipment Operators and Related Occupations

8    Occupations Unique to Primary Industry

9    Occupations Unique to Processing, Manufacturing, and Utilities

Each of these 10 categories is then further subdivided into major groups, for a total of 26 major groups, and each major group is subdivided even further. Each subdivision becomes more and more specific, from field of work or industry to specific occupational titles. Each occupational title has a four-digit code, with each digit of that code signifying a particular aspect. For example, the first digit of the code denotes the number, from the 10 categories, to which the occupation belongs. The second digit specifies the skill level, education, or training required; "1" indicates the requirement of a university degree and "4" indicates on-the-job training.

The NOC has a separate index that alphabetically lists all 30 000 occupational titles and their accompanying four-digit codes. There are at least two ways to look up information in the NOC. First, if you already know the title of the position you are interested in, you can go directly to the index, look up the code for that title, and then locate the information by looking up the code in the NOC. On the other hand, if you are not sure of the title of an occupation but are interested in working in a certain field, you can go directly to that section in the NOC and browse through the titles within that category.

The NOC is a useful tool for understanding the jobs found throughout Canada's labour market and for career decision making. Exercise 4.1 at the end of this chapter is designed to familiarize you with the NOC so that you can take advantage of this extensive resource. Exercise 4.2 is designed to help you expand your exploration.

## Job Futures

As your career search expands, other occupation-related information becomes more important, such as opportunities for growth and availability of jobs. Most people want to know "In which field will I be sure to get a job?" or "Which job pays the most?" These are important questions, but only two factors for you to consider in your career choice. There are other factors, for example, the future outlook of the occupation, the day-to-day work requirements, and the education or training required.

Some of the most readily available and comprehensive resources on job prospects and the Canadian labour market are published by the Department of Human Resources and Skills Development Canada (HRSDC). Because of the constant changes influencing the workforce, HRSDC has developed tools to help Canadians keep pace with these changes and succeed in their careers. One of these tools is *Job Futures*.

*Job Futures* provides useful information about 226 occupational groups and describes the work experiences of recent graduates from 155 programs of study. It provides information about occupations and their prospects for the future. It also describes the demographics of people currently employed in various occupations and the likelihood for openings and growth in the occupation. In addition, it indicates how students have fared once they have completed their program of study, whether they have become employed in their field, how much they are earning, and whether they are satisfied with their chosen occupation.

*Job Futures* is available at your local college, university, or public library. It is available both in print form and online at **www.jobfutures.ca**. More and more career-related information is now available online because it can be easily accessed, updated, and revised to stay current. The current issue of *Job Futures* offers projections on employment for the next few years. It categorizes all occupations it lists in terms of their prospects for growth in Canada. Occupations are categorized as having either good, fair, or limited work prospects. Relevant data on skills, training, requirements, worker characteristics, and labour market information can be as close as the library or your computer.

As mentioned earlier, Figure 4.2 displays the home page for *Job Futures* online, and a sample page from *Job Futures* is shown in Figure 4.3. *Job Futures* uses the same four-digit codes as the NOC; therefore, cross-references to NOC are available. The *Job Futures* Web site also provides links to community HRSDC offices that offer information relevant to local communities.

HRSDC also publishes *Job Futures* specific to the different regions of Canada. These, too, are available in print and online, and cover topics similar to the national version of *Job Futures*, with information that is more specific and relevant to particular Canadian regions. Some of the regional versions are called *Work Futures* while others are called *Job Futures*. See the resources at the end of this chapter for the publication for your local region.

## Labour Market Information

In addition to the NOC and *Job Futures*, there are a number of other government resources available in print form and online that contain a wealth of useful information on occupations. More specifically, these resources provide information on national, regional, and local labour markets. For instance, HRSDC maintains a Web site devoted to labour market information. This site is available at **http://lmi-imt.hrdc-drhc.gc.ca**. Here, you can search local labour markets; descriptions of occupations, wages, and salaries; employment prospects; who's hiring; and where to get training. HRSDC offices can also be a resource for labour market information and other career-related programs and services.

Aside from government-funded resources and publications, there are also books published by economists and futurists that examine the labour market. Two good sources of labour market information are *Making Career Sense of Labour Market Information* published by the Canadian Career Development Foundation, available in print and online, and *Canada's Best Careers Guide* by Frank Feather. Both these resources provide an overview of how work in Canada is changing, and they examine occupations of the future.

Another valuable resource for current career information is your local university or college career centre. On some campuses, it may be called career services or perhaps career counselling. Whatever its name, it is one of the best places to find many of the resources mentioned in this chapter as well as to obtain career counselling. Many college and university campuses offer career counselling and workshops or seminars for students and/or community members. Also, as a bonus, many career centres have libraries that store up-to-date information about local and regional companies, their products, and the local economy.

Because Canada is such a large country, with unique characteristics from one region to the next, the labour market information changes from one region to another. Solid research on labour market information or job prospects can be complicated and requires the accumulation of information on regional and global economies, demographics, trends, and much more. As you review *Job Futures* and other sources of labour market information, you may be tempted to view the data presented as the final authority on job availability. Although the information is helpful within the context of national or regional trends, the specifics about the job outlook in your community may differ. These publications are very useful but are only a start in your investigation. You will acquire a broader perspective on an occupational field and learn detailed facts about the work as you explore further and continue with your occupational research.

There are some questions you should keep in mind as you pursue research about the occupations that interest you. Getting answers to these questions will provide you with valuable information about the occupation and its future possibilities. As you research, try to gather information on the following questions:

1. *What is the future outlook for the occupation?*

   Gather information regarding future opportunities in this occupation. Are job opportunities likely to increase or decrease? Is there much competition for jobs in this field? Consider whether this work is likely to change in the future and, if so, how? Find out how the occupation has changed over the years and consider how it might change in the future.

2. *What does the work involve?*

   Try to get a picture of what the day-to-day work involves. Find out about the tasks, activities and responsibilities, the hours and working conditions, and where the work is performed. Could you picture yourself doing this work every day?

3. *What is the best way to prepare for this occupation?*

   Research what required skills, education, and training are necessary to enter into the line of work. Are there specific programs that employers prefer? What skills and training will be required to enter into the occupation in the future? This is particularly important if the occupation is one that will require many years of education and preparation. Anticipate what will be required in the future in order to do the work.

Making direct contact with people employed in the field you are interested in can be one of the most useful ways of gathering answers to these questions and continuing your occupational research. People working in the field can be one of the best sources of information about the occupation and its future work prospects. Networking and information interviewing are two valuable ways of acquiring information from people directly involved. These will be discussed in the next chapter.

One thing seems certain: The world of work has changed dramatically over the last century. Industrial-age jobs are now being replaced by knowledge-based jobs. This change has been labelled the "new economy," which is driven by technology and information, and differentiated from the "old economy," which was based on resources. Jobs in the goods-producing sector have diminished while jobs in the service sector have increased. This is a result of changes in productivity due to technology as well as changing demographics and population needs. Population growth, age, health, education, immigration, lifestyle, and economy are among some of the factors that influence the changing labour market.

## Future Trends

In the last section, we discussed the complexity of the labour market and how to acquire information about it. To have a solid understanding of an occupational field, take the time to look at more than just the information related to a specific position. It is important to be informed on the job and the occupation as a whole, as well as the labour market in which it exists. Be aware of both the national and local trends and economic and cultural trends that affect our society.

Futurists such as Frank Feather contend that Canada, and the rest of the world, changes constantly. In his book, *Canada's Best Career Guide*, Feather maintains that in order to understand what the future of Canada will be, we must understand the trends that influence the future. As major institutions struggle to meet the challenges that change presents, individuals have to stretch their emotional, psychological, and physical resources to meet the new demands. Now more than ever, your understanding of how trends in our society and culture will

## Calvin and Hobbes        by Bill Watterson

affect your career is essential to your success and satisfaction in that field. Knowing what to expect places your decision in a context that will enable you to choose wisely and prepare yourself for what lies ahead.

Researchers have identified a number of trends that will have a lasting impact on the world of work. The following is a compilation of a few noteworthy themes that are currently being played out in our workforce:

◆ *The workforce will reflect the increasing diversity of our society.* The increase in the average age of our population will be a factor in the changing composition of the workforce. As baby boomers reach retirement age, the impact will be realized in those occupations that have the highest concentration of aging workers.

◆ *Workers will attempt to reintegrate home and work life.* Companies and workers will find new ways to make work and home life compatible, reversing a 100-year trend. On-site child care, job sharing, and working from home are examples of innovations that are already benefiting some corporations by helping to create increased worker loyalty and greater profitability. Corporations will need to be innovative in an attempt to create "a great place to work" through additional services like counselling on health, legal, and financial matters as well as more personal and community service time.

◆ *A greater number of jobs will be created in many small businesses rather than from the large business sector.* New business start-ups will continue to offer the greatest opportunity for employment. Large businesses will continue to trim employees and contract for work in an effort to remain competitive and show profits. New business relationships will assure economic survival by adding capabilities through new strategic alliances without adding cost or growth to the organization. The so-called "old economy" corporations, made from bricks and mortar, will survive and thrive depending on how well they can integrate new dot-com features into their culture. Competition will come from unexpected places, as travel agents found when they realized that their greatest threat wasn't from the travel agency across the street but from the personal computer that their former clients could now use to book their own trips.

◆ *Competition from foreign countries will contribute to the continued growth of a global economy.* Opportunities for growth in foreign markets will push the economy to open further while we struggle to keep up with scientific and technical competition from abroad. Corporate alliances across disciplines and national borders will rival political alliances, creating new power bases, new leadership roles. Globalization and technology are inextricably linked and will continue to change the way we interact. E-commerce, online education, and telecommuting—even intercontinental telecommuting—will become increasingly common. Information technologies will reshape the way work and resources are distributed.

◆ *Increasingly, the nature of work will demand a knowledge-based workforce.* Jobs requiring little skill and training are disappearing. Technology and the global economy have increased the need for further training after high school and made it a prerequisite to employment even in entry-level positions. Manufacturing will continue to shift jobs to foreign competitors until computer technology takes over the production setting. When this takes place, some manufacturing jobs could be reclaimed if our workforce is prepared with the required higher-level skills. College and university graduates from some disciplines, specifically health, engineering, education, and information technology, will be in high demand while others will find themselves facing diminished opportunities and underemployment.

♦   *Further change will take place in the relationship between employees and employers.* Human resources planning will play a major role in establishing the way workers interact with their employers. The traditional career path of upward mobility through one organization to retirement is already a thing of the past. "Outsourcing," or contracting, portfolio or freelance and temporary employees who work on an as-needed basis has become a way for corporations to reduce overhead and save money. People will become self-employed contractors, contracting to various companies throughout their careers. In all organizations, "human capital," the organization's investment in its employees and their ability to innovate and respond quickly to market forces, will determine which organizations will survive. Employees will take responsibility for their careers, recognizing that performance and skill development are what count. Employers who are willing to respond by sharing profits and encouraging employee participation in the organization's success will create the synergy necessary to keep pace with the marketplace.

As you can see, our world will be undergoing dramatic change as we transition from the old industrial economy into the "new economy." You will be part of that change. Being informed on these and other issues will provide you with an invaluable base from which to make decisions.

As you pursue your career, you may find that the rapid rate of change is continually shifting the shape of your occupation. You may find that you continually need further training or upgrading to stay current in your field. There seem to be a number of factors that have a strong influence on the employment success that people achieve. Your success may be determined in large part by:

♦   *The occupational field you pursue*—Some fields of work will continue to enjoy growth and job availability.

♦   *The employability skills you develop*—Your ability to demonstrate the employability skills that are deemed valuable to employers will make you a preferred candidate for employment.

♦   *The level of education and training you acquire*—Most job openings today require some form of education and training beyond high school. The "new economy" places a high value on continuous learning, and it is expected that most new jobs created in the future will require some form of post-secondary education or training.

♦   *The level of actual work experience you've had*—Any opportunities to become involved in hands-on work experience is an asset. Paid and unpaid experiences provide skills that can transfer to work environments. Begin to build your credibility for later employment. This includes co-op positions, internships, and volunteer and part-time jobs.

All these are variables that you can control. Even more important, knowing what you want, knowing what to expect, making your choice, and working hard have a greater impact than any external forces.

Next is an example of how one student used the resources discussed in this chapter to make his decision.

## Mitch's Story

Mitch was struggling to find a place for himself in the world of work. Mitch's father had worked his entire life as a carpenter in the construction trade. Mitch had always been around skilled tradespeople and had wielded a hammer since he was five years old. He loved the work environment and the sense of satisfaction he received from working with his hands but was uncomfortable with the instability of the construction business. He had seen his father suffer through periods of instability and wanted a more secure occupation. His family supported his decision to continue his education as a way to broaden his experience and allow him more autonomy in his career.

Unfortunately, he wasn't sure what occupation could give him the same satisfaction as carpentry and also provide opportunity for growth. Mitch looked up "construction" in the NOC. Under that main heading he found areas that sounded interesting to him, such as engineering, safety officer, telecommunications, and equipment mechanic. As he scanned the various categories, he found several that offered opportunities for growth combined with the hands-on skills with which he was familiar. Architecture and civil engineering were possibilities that would require a bachelor's degree or more, while programs in drafting and surveying were available at the two-year college level.

Mitch's research on the Internet led him to the *Job Futures* Web site, and the information there indicated that the job outlook for civil engineers and construction managers was expected to be good for the next few years whereas the prospects in drafting were expected to be just fair.

Mitch realized through further research that both occupations were highly dependent on economic changes and would be among the first affected in a recession. Mitch was prepared for this because of his knowledge about the construction field. He believed that he could compete for employment in the predicted economic environment. His family's support and his prior success in meeting his employer's requirements were good indicators of his future success. Long-term trends further contributed to his belief that population growth in his province would require skilled tradespeople for many years to come.

His initial research behind him, Mitch now set out to find how accurate his understanding was regarding the occupations he found interesting. His next step was to begin talking with people who actually worked in these fields. Mitch knew that the road ahead might offer obstacles, but he was beginning to feel that he would be realistically prepared for whatever happened.

## 4.1 Finding Your Way around the NOC

At first glance, the NOC can seem imposing. After your initial experience using it, you will feel at home. Most public, college, and university libraries have the NOC in their reference section. It is also available online.

To begin, page through the print volume and get a feel for how it is set up. As you can see, the jobs appear in occupational groups; thus, many of the job descriptions in a group may be very similar.

Read the following job titles. Using the alphabetical index listing for the NOC, find the corresponding NOC four-digit code.

| | |
|---|---|
| Correctional officer | _____ |
| Costumer | _____ |
| Athletic coach | _____ |
| Preschool teacher | _____ |
| Nurse | _____ |
| Director of motion pictures | _____ |
| Curator | _____ |
| Educational psychologist | _____ |
| Car repairer | _____ |
| Electronic engineer | _____ |

You may find more than one subheading that designates the specific circumstances in which each job is performed. Using the four-digit code, look up a few of the descriptions. Note the differences between jobs with similar titles and the categories into which jobs are classified.

In the following spaces, list on the left the occupations that you identified in your self-assessment from Chapters 2 and 3 as ones you would like to explore further—especially those from the interest and personality exercises that you completed. Then find the corresponding NOC code in the alphabetical index. Next, locate the definition in the main text and jot down a few of the key points mentioned there. As you review the definition, note the job titles and descriptions related to the one you are looking up. Do those sound interesting as well?

Occupation to Explore _____ NOC Code _____

Key points _____

Occupation to Explore _____ NOC Code _____

Key points _____

Occupation to Explore _____ NOC Code _____

Key points _____

If you have access to the Internet, now try the NOC online at **www23.hrdc-drhc.gc.ca**. Here you can view the most recent version of the NOC. Click on its picture and you will go to the home page where you can view the index of titles, the occupational descriptions, and the matrix.

You can search by alphabetical listing, key words, four-digit codes, or skill type and level. Try searching using each of these methods.

Below, list some occupations that seem interesting to you.

| OCCUPATIONS | DETAILS | RELATED OCCUPATIONS |
|---|---|---|
| _____ | _____ | _____ |
| _____ | _____ | _____ |
| _____ | _____ | _____ |
| _____ | _____ | _____ |

Did the information you found in the NOC help you get a better idea of what occupational data are available? Were your expectations confirmed or were you surprised by some information? If you have had a job, look it up in the NOC. Does the description match what you recall doing?

*Discuss the results with your group or with the class.*

## TAKE A CLOSER LOOK
### 4.2 A Family of Jobs

Start by surveying the National Occupational Classification Matrix poster included with the NOC or the NOC Major and Minor Group Structure at the front of the NOC binder. This shows all the categories of occupations listed in the guide. Review the summary and note how the interest areas and different fields are grouped, how they are related, and how they differ.

Now turn to the NOC alphabetical index. Look up the job titles that you identified in your self-assessment exercises. Note the four-digit code associated with one of those titles, and jot the number down in the space below.

**JOB TITLE** _____     **FOUR-DIGIT CODE** _____

Using the first digit of the four-digit code, look up the interest area in the main text. Review the occupations listed there. Using the next digit of the four-digit code, find the skill level related to the job you are researching. Look closely at the information on interests, skills, and settings associated with this work group. Write down this information below.

**KIND OF WORK**

_____

_____

Skills and abilities needed

_____

_____

_____

How do you know you would like or could learn this kind of work?

_____

_____

_____

Preparation necessary

_____

_____

_____

Other information

_____

_____

_____

Are you aware of any related jobs or occupations that you may not have considered before?

_____

Do the skill requirements of the positions you have researched indicate that you will need to acquire new skills or further training in order to perform the job duties?

_____

The exercise you have just completed has helped you to look beyond what might have seemed like your only choice. It is important to keep a positive, open focus on what you are trying to achieve. Your goal is to pursue a full, rewarding career, not to fall into a trap from which you must later free yourself. Try to stay positive and flexible. It will help broaden your notion of what will work for you.

_Discuss your findings with the group or class._

## TAKE A CLOSER LOOK
### 4.3 Putting Predictions in Perspective

Choose one of the job titles you identified in the NOC exercises above, and use _Job Futures_ in print form or online to find information that addresses projections for this occupation. Answer the questions on the basis of the information you gather.

How specific is the information related to this occupation? Does it mention actual job titles or a broad category of jobs?

_____

_____

How does the information about the job compare to that found in the NOC?

_____

_____

Does the information cover projections nationally, provincially, or locally?

_____

_____

Are the projections specific (statistical, percentage of increase) or general (expected to grow, expected to decline)?

_____

_____

Is this information helpful? Explain.

_____

_____

What else should you consider when researching a particular job's outlook for future growth?

_____

_____

Where can you get additional information?

_____

_____

As you gather data about possible occupations, try to suspend your inclination to throw out any possibility that might present a challenge. Be sure that you have exhausted every possibility before you dismiss any options. Have faith in yourself and your ability to achieve your goal.

_Discuss with your class or group the information you have uncovered._

**4.4 Pulling It All Together**

Now that you've taken a look at specific occupations, you have a base from which to make choices about your career. Use this as a way to consolidate your information.

What occupations did you find from the NOC and Internet search that seem to offer you what you are seeking?

_____

_____

_____

What does *Job Futures* indicate about the field/job in which you are interested?

_____

_____

_____

What future trends do you recognize from your research, observations, media, etc. that may be relevant or significant in terms of your occupational choice?

_____

_____

_____

*Discuss the results of your exploration up to now with the class or with your group.*

## A Look Back

At this point in your career adventure, you have acquired a great deal of knowledge about the different types of occupations that appeal to you and could meet your needs. You are familiar with resources available online and those in print available in the library that offer specific information about the duties, settings, skills, salaries, and outlook for various occupations. You are also familiar with online career guidance systems that can provide you with a perspective on related jobs and skill areas. Computers with access to the Internet may be available to you as a source to further your career search, and your college career centre has valuable resources from which you can learn more about the national and local labour markets. Finally, you have begun to broaden your exploration to include learning about overall economic and social trends and their effect on present and future job markets. With all of this new knowledge, you are creating a sound basis for making an informed career decision.

## Other Sources and Suggested Reading

The resources discussed in this chapter are the best place to develop a perspective on your chosen occupational field. In addition, your university, college, or public library has numerous publications available from which you can obtain even more information.

The resources cited are a few of those we have found most useful for students exploring their career choices.

*Canada's Best Career Guide* by Frank Feather
> This book discusses future trends and the Canadian labour market. It includes lists of the best and worst career prospects for the future.

*Encyclopedia of Careers and Vocational Guidance*, 11th Edition, published by Ferguson Publishing Company (U.S. publication)
> This is a four-volume encyclopedia describing approximately 540 occupations within 14 different industries. Occupations are listed alphabetically and include information and educational and training requirements.

*Job Futures Canada* published by Human Resources and Skills Development Canada (HRSDC)
> Available in print form and online, it describes various occupations and their prospects for employment in the future.

*Making Career Sense of Labour Market Information* published by the Canadian Career Development Foundation
> Available in print and online, it discusses information on the labour market and its relevance to career decision making.

## Web Sites and Internet Resources

Some of the most valuable information on the Internet is provided by Human Resources and Skills Development Canada.

**www.jobfutures.ca/en/home.shtm**
This is the Web address for the national edition of *Job Futures*. For information on *Job Futures* related to a specific province or territory, go to **www.emploiavenir.ca/en/provincial.shtml.** From there, you can link to Web sites for each province or territory. You can also go directly to these sites by the following addresses:

Alberta, Northwest Territories, and Nunavut:
**www.hrsdc.gc.ca/en/gateways/where_you_live/regions/ab-nwt-nu.shtml**

British Columbia:
**www.workfutures.bc.ca**

Manitoba:
**www.hrsdc.gc.ca/en/gateways/where_you_live/regions/mb.shtml**

New Brunswick:
**www.hrsdc.gc.ca/en/gateways/where_you_live/regions/nb.shtml**

Newfoundland and Labrador:
**www.hrsdc.gc.ca/en/gateways/where_you_live/regions/nl.shtml**

Northwest Territories:
**www.jobfutures.stats.gov.nt.ca**

Nova Scotia:
**www.hrsdc.gc.ca/en/gateways/where_you_live/regions/ns.shtml**

Ontario:
**www.ontariojobfutures.net**

Prince Edward Island:
**www.pei.jobfutures.org/en/frames/home.html**

Quebec:
**www150.hrdc-drhc.gc.ca/emploi-avenir**

Saskatchewan:
**www.saskjobfutures.ca**

Yukon:
**www.workfutures.yk.ca**
**www23.hrdc-drhc.gc.ca**

The *National Occupational Classification* (NOC) is available online and provides information on over 30 000 occupational titles.

**http://lmi-imt.hrdc-drhc.gc.ca**
This is the HRSDC Web site devoted to labour market information.

**www.jobprofiles.org**
Provides profiles and descriptions of a number of different occupations. Each was prepared by a person working in the occupation.

**www.umanitoba.ca/counselling/careers.html**
The University of Manitoba's Student Counselling and Career Centre provides a Web site with information on almost 200 occupational options, including links to other sites relevant to each occupation.

**www.bls.gov/oco**
This U.S. Web site, the United States Federal Occupation Information, Occupational Outlook Handbook, offers similar information to the NOC in Canada.

# Chapter 5
# Networking

## Establishing Contacts and Support

*It's not always what you know, but who you know.*

AUTHOR UNKNOWN

It wasn't long ago that the definition of "network" was limited to a type of hardware we associate with electronic components. For the past 20 years, however, we have expanded the meaning of the word to include a system of relationships that can have a dramatic effect on you and your career. Indeed, networking is a necessary part of establishing and maintaining a rewarding, meaningful career.

A network is a group of work and social acquaintances knowing who you are and what you do or hope to do. It can include people from the most informal of settings, such as the woman who sits next to you at the ballpark, or formal business associates, such as the president of the company where you once worked. Both of these people are members of a club and may not even know it. It's the "Friends of You" (FOY) Club. Obviously, the word "friends" in this case is used to refer to anyone who might be in a position to assist you in your career.

Whether the members of the FOY Club are familiar to you on a close or more distant basis is of little importance. What is important is:

◆ *Your network is unique to you.* No one else has the exact same combination of relatives, acquaintances, and associates. Your FOY Club is a distinctive asset that is unique and valuable.

◆ *Your network can be expanded to meet your career needs.* It would be easy to limit your club membership to only those people whom you have met up to now. There are dozens of others—friends of "friends of you," if you will, who could play a role in your career growth. All you have to do is meet them ... a task that can seem intimidating, but is in fact, easy. We will discuss how to do this in this chapter.

◆ *Your network will help you understand the local career market much better than any resource you can examine in a library.* Talking to people who are actually working in the field in which you are interested will provide you with a balanced insight into the job as well as an understanding of job availability, good places to work, and future trends in the field.

◆ *Your network will help you to begin establishing yourself in your chosen field.* If you don't already know anyone who is working in a particular occupation that you are exploring, now is the time to meet them. The people you meet now may be there later, when you are ready to enter the field, waiting to give you a welcome boost.

◆ *Your network can be a means of visualizing yourself in your new profession.* As you meet with people at their places of work and talk with them, you will begin to imagine yourself actually performing the job. You will also begin to learn the language of a new line of work. This initial phase of visualization in a profession will be a sustaining vision as you move toward your goal.

The process of invigorating your network so you can put it to work begins by organizing the members of your current network, your FOY Club.

## Identifying Your Existing Network

Your existing network is likely more extensive than you might think. It is not uncommon for people to find that a family member or neighbour or previous classmate is working in a field in which they are interested. You might be surprised by the number of people you can name as part of your FOY Club. Use Exercise 5.1 at the end of this chapter to help you identify the range of your network. Begin by listing any friends and acquaintances who could tell you more about their careers.

Granted, you may already know that many of the people on your list are working in jobs that hold no interest to you. Nevertheless, you might find someone in your circle of contacts who is working in the field you are investigating or who knows someone working in the field. If not, don't be concerned. You are about to enlarge the circle.

## Expanding Your Network

The best first step is to contact people with whom you are comfortable and familiar. After you have gathered leads and information from them, take the leap— reach out beyond the familiarity of your existing network to the larger community.

To expand your network, start by identifying resources that you believe will yield names relevant to your field of interest. Keep a record of names, telephone numbers, and business addresses of people who work in a field you might be interested in. Even if you don't know anyone in the occupation you're interested in, you may know someone who knows someone in that line of work.

If you find that your present circle of contacts is limited, don't despair. There are other avenues by which to continue your exploration. One of the most effective methods of expanding your network is to become acquainted with the members of the professional organization associated with your field of interest. These groups usually meet monthly to discuss topics relevant to the profession and to network among themselves. Students are often able to arrange membership at a reduced fee. These meetings can provide a gold mine of information about the professions and available jobs. If you have zeroed in on a particular field that has a local professional organization, get in touch with the person in charge of new members and inquire about attending meetings or obtaining referrals. Most organizations are happy to work with someone who may later join the group.

Along with formal professional organizations, informal networking groups are a valuable resource for referrals and information. These groups are often more accessible than professional associations. You might find listings in your local newspaper under "group meetings." If not, keep your ear to the ground when contacting new people and find out what you can about how they network. This is another route toward finding a group that will offer encouragement and support.

If you have already worked in a particular occupation and are now undertaking a career change, then your professional network may already be quite extensive. Everyone with whom you have worked in prior positions is a member of your FOY Club. Even if they work in occupations that don't interest you, they are another source of contacts and information. More significantly, if you were a valued member of your former associates' work group, you can ask them for advice, information, and recommendations. You need only to enlist them into your group.

Volunteering and involvement in community groups and organizations is another way to build your network. If possible, become involved in community work that is related to the field you are interested in pursuing. Not only is this an excellent way to begin networking with those working in the field, it is also a good way to learn first-hand about the occupation. Even if it is not possible to become involved in volunteer or community work directly related to the occupation you are interested in, getting to know people in your community can help you create leads to "people who know people" in the field.

Another way to find leads is through your local post-secondary schools. Many colleges and universities have lists of alumni who are available to assist students in their career investigations. Check with the career services or alumni offices at your local post-secondary institution to see if they offer this service. Alumni are an excellent resource for job market information and are usually glad to help, so feel free to approach them for a brief phone or in-person interview, even if you feel a little uncomfortable. Once you've done it, you'll find it gets easier and easier.

If by chance your local college or university does not offer this service, it's time to head back to the library in search of directories for local companies and organizations. Public libraries and college and university libraries have resources such as *The Canadian Key Business Directory* by Dun & Bradstreet of Canada, *The Career Directory* by R. W. Yerema and K. Chow, *The National Business & Communications Directory* by Newline Publishing, and the *Canada Student Employment Guide* by the Student Employment Network. These directories offer an array of information about local and national organizations. You will find information on the type of business these companies do, their addresses, phone numbers, perhaps a brief historical synopsis, or even the names of the organization's executives. The primary value of checking these directories is to locate specific organizations that might employ people in your field of interest. You might also find names of possible network partners in the directories of professional organizations, chamber of commerce publications, or in local newspaper articles highlighting companies.

Of course, for many occupations, you need go only as far as the Yellow Pages to find the names of many people who are working in a particular field. The

Better Business Bureau also publishes a directory of its membership. There are numerous businesses and professionals listed in these types of directories.

Internet contacts can assist you with information about professions and jobs through contact with listserv groups, "bulletin boards," and online chat. While these contacts can yield a great deal of information, remember that the information is only as good as its source. It may be difficult to determine the validity of the contact you've made. More significantly, something that holds true about an occupation in eastern Canada, for example, may mean little if you live in the Northwest Territories. Also, getting data from the Internet is an easy way to do research, but it may do nothing to help you meet people who could be helpful down the road. There is one other point of caution about trying to meet network contacts through the Internet. It has its own pitfalls, such as being taken advantage of by unscrupulous individuals. Using the Web is no substitute for meeting people face to face.

The key factor in expanding your network is making contact with the actual persons who are performing the work that interests you. You might be directed to the receptionist, customer service, or the human resources office. Try to get the name of the person who is doing the work you are interested in and ask for him or her specifically by name. Once you actually talk with the person who can help you, you are much more likely to arrange a meeting. This meeting is called an information interview.

# Information Interviewing

Information interviewing, the process of meeting face to face with a professional in the field you are researching, is one of the most valuable methods for gathering data about an occupational field. This type of career research was popularized during the 1970s by Richard Nelson Bolles in his book *What Color Is Your Parachute?* and has become an integral part of any career or job search.

When contemplating information networking, the first question most people ask is "Whom will I interview?" As mentioned earlier, the easiest place to start is with your existing network, those contacts and acquaintances already in the FOY Club. They are your networking partners right now. With very little effort, you can enlist their help in your career exploration.

Once you have decided whom you will interview, it is useful to begin a data sheet. This data sheet can help you keep track of the information you collect about the occupation you are researching and about the business or organization you are contacting. It is important that you do some research on your own before the information interview so that you already know something about the occupation before the interview. Begin collecting information for your data sheet before the interview, and then record the information as you acquire it before, during, and after the information interview. Keep the data sheets on file in your computer, file cabinet, or even on index cards. This information may be useful again when you are ready to work in the field. Someday, you might want to interview for a job with one of these companies, or even begin your own business, and you will already have some valuable information at hand.

Figure 5.1 is an example of what a data sheet might look like.

## Occupation Information Data Sheet

Information interview with: _____    Date/time: _____

Title: _____    Regarding occupation: _____

Company: _____    Address: _____

Phone no.: _____

Major responsibilities of occupation: _____

Day-to-day work: _____

Skills and education required: _____

Best way to prepare/train for occupation: _____

Working conditions: _____

Positive aspects: _____

Negative aspects: _____

Salary range: _____

Advancement in the field: _____

Other related jobs: _____

Projected employment outlook for the future: _____

Similar work in other areas of Canada, in other countries: _____

Useful advice: _____

Other information: _____

**Figure 5.1** Occupation Information Data Sheet

## Arranging the Information Interview

You have now reached the part of networking that typically causes the most anxiety: arranging appointments for information interviews. These may be your first business phone conversations, or this process may bring back memories of other business conversations, or it may be that the idea of calling someone with a request makes you hesitate.

If you experience anxiety or hesitation, try to relax and take one step at a time. Remember, you are conducting research and this is part of your assignment. Feel confident in asking for information and insight—the people you speak to undoubtedly have been helped by others before them ... and you will likely have the opportunity to do the same for someone else someday. Besides, people love to talk about themselves, and you're going to give them the chance to do just that.

To start, try the following role-play exercise with someone to get a feel for how it works.

**Operator:** Good morning, Acme Engineering.

**You:** Good morning. May I please speak to Ms. Charlotte Ramsey?

**Operator:** One moment, please.

**Ms. Ramsey:** Engineering, Charlotte Ramsey.

**You:** Hello, Ms. Ramsey. My name is Pat Black and I am a student at the University of Saskatchewan here in Saskatoon. I am conducting research into occupations related to engineering. I'm not looking for a job, just some information. I am wondering if you would have 15 or 20 minutes to chat with me at your convenience about your job and about engineering in general.

**Ms. Ramsey:** I'm quite busy. I'm not really sure I can help you.

**You:** I'm sure that any information you can share will be very valuable to me, and I promise I won't take more time than you can spare. Perhaps I could come out and chat with you next week some time? Say Tuesday perhaps?

**Ms. Ramsey:** Well, all right. Next Tuesday at 10:30 a.m. would be good. I can talk to you for a short time then.

**You:** Thank you, Ms. Ramsey. I look forward to meeting you.

How did the dialogue feel? Maybe a little stiff the first time, but you'll become more comfortable with it as you practise and use it. Exercise 5.3 at the end of the chapter will help you establish your own script.

Once you complete Exercise 5.3 and practise a bit, you will be ready to make calls. Choose a time and a place where you will not be disturbed. As a courtesy to the person you are contacting, avoid making calls on Monday morning, a particularly busy time for most people. When you are making the actual calls, suggest a date for the interview that is completely open for you so that your contact does not have to rearrange his or her schedule to accommodate your needs. Once you have a date and time set, write it down on your data sheet for that company.

A word on voice mail: You may find that your call will be answered by a machine or an electronic messaging system (voice mail). If you are uncomfortable with the idea of leaving your name and number on voice mail, you may wish to keep trying until you reach the person. You may become quite frustrated since some people use messages as a way of screening calls. If this happens, leave a brief message stating your name, why you're calling, and when you will try to reach the person again. If you are still unsuccessful in contacting the person directly, you may then want to leave a number where you can be reached. Don't wait for them to call you, though. In the long run, it may be more productive for you to try reaching someone else who is more accessible.

## Preparing for the Information Interview

You have successfully arranged a meeting! It is time to do your homework and prepare yourself for the interview. The most important fact to remember is that this meeting is not a job interview. Meeting with contacts to inquire about their field is part of your ongoing career exploration, not a campaign to obtain a job. It is very important that you remember this throughout the interview process as most people will not look favourably on a request for an information interview that then shadily turns into a job interview.

Think of the information interview as simply an opportunity to acquire information about an occupation in order to decide whether it may be right for you and, if so, how you may best prepare for it. It is for gathering information, nothing more. Focusing on this will free you and your network partner from the pressures associated with job seeking.

Preparing yourself for an information interview requires you to focus on two aspects: your appearance and the questions you will ask. The simplest aspect of any network meeting is making sure that you dress appropriately. If you can, find out how people at the company dress. Respect your interviewee and take the time to conform to the dress code of his or her environment. Appropriate dress for an office setting usually consists of a tie, jacket, and dress trousers for men, and a blouse, jacket, and skirt, a suit, or a simple dress for women. However, this type of dress may not be appropriate for interviewing someone who works as a tradesperson. In this case, anticipate how the person might dress and dress accordingly. Slacks, a collared shirt, and casual shoes usually work well for men or women. Make sure that your clothes are neat and clean, your hair is combed, and your nails trimmed.

Promptness is essential. Ensure that you are on time by planning and trying the route to the meeting a day before (remember to factor in rush hour traffic). On the day of the meeting, arrive at least five minutes early as a way of demonstrating your dependability and to give yourself time to relax before the appointment.

The second aspect of your preparation should focus on the questions you wish to ask your new contact. You may have only 15 to 20 minutes, so it is best to ask clear, concise questions. You should not be wasting the interviewee's time with simple, basic questions that you can answer easily for yourself through some quick research. Save the interview for the more complex questions. For example, rather than asking a question such as, "Are there any other businesses in this line of work?" which can be answered by a quick look in the Yellow Pages directory, ask a question such as, "Do you anticipate there being a need for more businesses such as this one in the future?"

The following are some examples to help you get started preparing your own list of questions. Consider what you would need to know in order to make an informed decision about whether to pursue this occupation and how to go about preparing for it. For example, consider questions such as:

- What are the specific duties associated with your position?

- What is a typical day like in this work?

- How did you obtain your present job?

- Can you give me any suggestions as to how I might best prepare myself to enter this field?

◆ Where do you see this field going within the next five to ten years?

◆ Do you see there being increased opportunities in this field?

◆ What do you like most about your job?

◆ What do you like least about your job?

◆ Whom else would you recommend I speak with who knows about this field?

## Conducting the Information Interview

An information interview is different than a job interview in one primary way: You are in charge. That means that it is up to you to be prepared, to take initiative, and to direct the interview. Begin by introducing yourself and shaking the person's hand. Confirm the amount of time allotted to the interview and reiterate why you have requested the information interview. Then begin with your first prepared question.

You will be responsible for keeping track of time, steering the course of the questions and discussion, and ensuring that you get the information that you need. The information interview should be conducted professionally, yet be casual and friendly. Try to view it as an opportunity to build rapport and get to know the person and the work he or she does, rather than as an interrogation of question after question.

However, any interview with a professional in the occupational field you are exploring should include questions about that person's specific duties. After you have interviewed several contacts, you will see how people with the same job titles may perform very different jobs. Also, asking how the person got into his or her position will give you an idea of how career paths evolve.

The other questions you might ask focus on the type of preparation needed to enter the field and what might happen in the field in the future. If your allotted interview time is quite short, you might be limited to just these questions. You may find, however, that the person is willing to expand the interview beyond the time limit. Most people are quite generous with their time when they are discussing something they enjoy.

Plan enough questions for the time you have allotted for the interview, but be flexible enough that you can improvise, too, as the conversation progresses. Take advantage of any opportunity to pursue a topic that interests you even if it deviates from your prepared set of questions. You can always get back to those or leave them for another interview with someone else.

Also, be prepared to discuss your interest in the occupation. Review in your mind how you came to choose this path—this will encourage a meaningful exchange. If you are in the middle of a career change and are comfortable sharing your experiences with your network partner, you will have an excellent opportunity to connect on a professional level. Your background and maturity can be a plus, but avoid talking negatively about a former employer or company. The world of work is much smaller than we might think.

Keep track of time and, once the agreed-upon time is coming to an end, let the interviewee know by saying something like, "I am aware that our time is almost up." This will show that you respect the person's time and do not want to take advantage of it. If the interviewee indicates that a few more minutes would be all right, continue with one or two more questions; otherwise, wrap up the interview. You might wrap up by asking if there is anyone else he or she would recommend you speak to about the field. This will provide you with another contact for an information interview and the opportunity to expand your network. End the interview by shaking hands and thanking the interviewee for the information and time spent.

If you were to draw a picture of your network after meeting a few contacts, you might find that it looks like a road map. In some respects it is a road map that intersects with you. As you interview more and more people, you may hear the same names repeated as "the people to know" in your field. If you have already met them, then pat yourself on the back. You have made valuable contacts and, if you were well prepared, you probably made a good impression. If you haven't made contact with one of these key people, you may want to do so. Such a meeting could prove valuable later on.

## Following Up

After your information interview, follow up with a thank-you letter or note within a day or two. This brings your first encounter with that person to a favourable closure. This closure does not necessarily mean that you will have no further contact, however. Remember, your interviewees become members of the FOY Club, and you might be in contact with them again at some future point.

If, as a result of your information interviews, you decide to make a commitment to enter that occupation, you may want to include that in your thank-you note. Figure 5.2 is an example of a short note that might be sent to your interviewee. If it is appropriate, mention that you hope to be able to call on this person in the future for advice and insight. As your study of the field continues, you may wish to write to those contacts you have made through the networking process to update them on your search and progress. These individuals may be key players in the realization of your professional goals.

# Finding Mentors and Sponsors

Having a contact helps you to understand an occupation or how a local labour market has developed, but your contact may provide even greater benefits. Occasionally, you may encounter an individual who is willing to do more than just give information. This person may play the role of mentor or sponsor, which can have a significant impact on your career. However, finding someone to provide that support can be tricky.

The roles of mentor and sponsor have become a more visible reality during the last quarter century. Mentors and sponsors have long been around in an informal context, usually assisting young men through the transitions of their careers. When women began to enter the world of work, often they found that they were excluded from the relationships and informal settings where mentoring commonly occurs. Therefore, women began actively to seek out individuals who could support them in their professional lives.

Some of the contacts became mentors, people who were experienced in their field, who could offer insight, encouragement, and a steadying influence on

**Thank-you Note**

85 Green Street
Saskatoon, Saskatchewan
S2K 1Y1

March 23, 2005

Ms. Charlotte Ramsey
Acme Engineering, Inc.
376 Industrial Parkway
Saskatoon, SK
S7K 2R5

Dear Ms. Ramsey:

Thank you for the opportunity to meet with you last Tuesday to share your insights on industrial engineering. Our discussion was most helpful and has confirmed my interest in pursuing industrial engineering as my profession.

I will be continuing my studies toward my degree at the University of Saskatchewan in the fall. Your informed perspective has been of great value to me. Thank you for your time and consideration and for the information you shared.

Sincerely,


Pat Black

**Figure 5.2** Thank-you Note

young people trying to succeed. Others became sponsors, individuals who were willing to actively promote a newcomer for opportunities within their organizations.

These alliances are certainly advantageous, but they are not without risk. Unscrupulous individuals have exploited some young workers, and some professionals have been victimized by young people pushing for a career boost. People on both sides of the relationship have experienced betrayal, scandal, and ethical blunders. This does not have to be the case, though. The advantages of having a mentor usually far outweigh the disadvantages.

The best opportunities to develop positive mentoring relationships usually occur in actual work settings, where you can get to know someone well. In turn, that person will have the chance to see you at work and to establish a feeling of mutual respect and trust. Sometimes new workers, people who partake in a training practicum, co-op work experience, or volunteer setting, encounter a co-worker who will take the time to advise and encourage them. The person who extends a helping hand might then become a source of continuing support.

Occasionally, prior to work experience, a person from your network may suggest that you keep in touch with them as you continue your academic work. If you are comfortable with the suggestion, this person may become a mentor or even a sponsor. If you are unsure, discuss the situation in detail with your instructor, counsellor, parents, or your partner. Make sure that all contacts with your potential mentor/sponsor take place in a professional setting and involve issues related to your career and training. If you become uncomfortable with any aspect of the relationship, you are not obligated to continue. Simply end the association.

You may be wondering how mentors and sponsors benefit from these relationships. Many professionals enjoy the experience of nurturing fresh talent. In addition, the more successful they are in developing a corps of gifted new workers within their organization or within their field, the more their reputation in the company and the field is enhanced. If they are successful in establishing you as a hot new addition to their company, they have just added another loyal member to their own Friends of You Club. Keep that in mind. Networking never ends.

## Job Shadowing

A different type of information interview is known as job shadowing. This process involves an extended interview in which you accompany a professional as he or she carries out the duties of a typical day's work. While this set-up is not as commonly utilized as an information interview, it is becoming recognized as a valuable career education tool. The most visible sign of this trend is "Take Your Child to Work Day," when working men and women arrange for their children to observe them at their work settings. This effort is intended to raise the consciousness of our young people about career possibilities and has led to the general acknowledgment that all young people need to know more about the career marketplace.

You can learn a great deal by actually "walking through" a day with someone—you get a front-row seat to their world of work. If it is possible for you to arrange this type of extended informational meeting, do so. It will be well worth the time.

While visiting any business organization, try to absorb as much as possible about the jobs employees perform. Observe the types of communication they are involved in, how they handle themselves in various situations, what is expected of them, how others respond to them, the tone and style of the organization, and the pace at which they conduct their duties. Paying attention to such details may tell you more about the job and the organization than the information you learn verbally.

You may discover as a result of networking or job shadowing that an occupation you thought you would enjoy isn't right for you after all. It may not seem like it at the time, but that realization is a blessing. It is better to learn this now than to spend years preparing for an occupation that turns out to be a bad fit.

If you find after an interview that you are not as interested in a field, it may be the result of one of two things.

1.  You may be learning the true nature of the work for the first time, and you may realize that it isn't right for you. If this is the case, regroup and take another look at the self-assessment and occupational research you did. See if there is anything in those two steps that led you down this cul-de-sac, and take steps to get back on track. You may have interpreted some of the results a bit rigidly, and now would be a good time to open yourself up to something else that interests you.

    Testing and probing are part of making a choice. Changing your mind (or your focus) is something many people do, sometimes more than once. It is a normal and necessary part of finding an occupation that's right for you.

2.  You may have talked to the "wrong" people. Try to interview at least three people in the field. Connecting with as many people as possible provides you with the broad view that you will need to consider all the aspects of an occupation. If you meet people who have nothing positive to say about their jobs, keep looking. Just because the job is not a good fit for them doesn't mean you won't love it.

## Elizabeth's Story

Elizabeth was beginning university and was unsure of her focus. She found in her self-assessment that she is interested in occupations in which she can use her strong skills in math and science, and that she enjoys tasks that involve some problem solving. As a result, Elizabeth thought she might like to pursue a career in engineering.

Engineering is a vast field, and Elizabeth felt that she needed to focus more. After looking at the NOC and *Job Futures* and conducting some research online, she decided that she needed more information about what different engineers do on their jobs. She decided to conduct information interviews with engineers specializing in a variety of areas of engineering.

Her existing network yielded two contacts specializing in different types of engineering. One was a friend of her mother who was an architect, the other a former neighbour who was an environmental engineer. Both were available to meet with her, so Elizabeth arranged to meet each of them at their place of work.

The architect worked at a firm that specialized in medical/health care facility design. This meeting showed Elizabeth how one person interacts with professionals from a variety of disciplines on a long-term project. The architect described the type of work and training she had been involved in that led to her current job. She also candidly described some of the obstacles she had had to overcome to achieve a position of responsibility.

In her second interview, Elizabeth met with the environmental engineer at a site that was being investigated for hazardous waste cleanup. Elizabeth was in no danger, but she did get to wear a hard hat and went with the engineer to meet the site manager. She enjoyed the atmosphere and found the work to be a great deal more complex than she had originally anticipated.

Elizabeth decided that it would be valuable to expand her network to an area related to manufacturing. She contacted a local automotive company and spoke with a supervisor in the design department. He referred her to an engineer in the department who was responsible for the redesign and improvement of a passenger-side air-bag system. Elizabeth was surprised that a young woman who had graduated from university just three years before was responsible for redesigning this system.

Elizabeth's meeting included a short tour of the plant's production area, where she was introduced to other engineers in the department. Elizabeth was most impressed with the respect that her new contact enjoyed among her colleagues and with how much she loved her work. The woman shared with her that she had found her academic work extremely difficult, but she was glad she had stuck with it because she enjoyed her professional work much more. At the end of the meeting, the engineer suggested that they keep in touch as Elizabeth progressed through school.

Elizabeth learned much from these meetings. She was in the process of deciding about the field in which she might spend most of her working life, so the meetings were instrumental in helping her form her perspective. She was now more certain that engineering would offer her the challenges she was seeking. As she began the preliminary academic work to prepare for her career, she resolved to look further into the possibilities offered at her school in the mechanical and industrial engineering fields.

**TAKE A CLOSER LOOK**

**5.1 Your "FOY Club"**

Think about your FOY Club, your circle of friends and acquaintances. Then look at the categories of people and jot down any names that come to mind. You may be surprised to learn how many people you can think of while doing this exercise. Be sure to include everyone who comes to mind, including people you might not have seen in years.

Family members

_____

_____

Classmates/roommates

_____

_____

Co-workers

_____

_____

Former co-workers

_____

_____

Social club members

_____

_____

Neighbours

_____

_____

Sports team members/competitors

_____

_____

Social friends

_____

_____

Fellow volunteers

_____

_____

Former girl/boyfriends

_____

_____

People from place of worship

_____

_____

Parents' friends and associates

_____

_____

People with the same hobby

_____

_____

Incidental acquaintances (e.g., bus stop companions)

_____

_____

## TAKE A CLOSER LOOK
### 5.2 Develop Contacts

Using any resource available to you (newspaper articles, directories, Yellow Pages, etc.), including your circle of friends and family, make a list of five companies or organizations in your area that might employ people in your field of interest.

**COMPANIES/ORGANIZATIONS PHONE NUMBERS**

1. _____

2. _____

3. _____

4. _____

5. _____

Write the name of the organization and the phone number at the top of a blank sheet of paper. Under it, place anything else that you think is important to remember about this company (e.g., type of product, number of employees) that you may have picked up from your research. Figure 5.1 illustrates a typical Occupation Information Data Sheet and the type of information that might be pertinent. If you don't have a great deal of information to put down, that's all right. That will be the goal of your research and information interview—to gather more information.

After determining the area within the organization in which the jobs you are interested in might be found (e.g., engineering, marketing, accounting, public relations, etc.), call the main phone number and ask for the name of the manager of that department. Most operators will provide you with that information; some may also give the extension or ask you if you want to be connected. For now, just get the person's name.

Some operators will explain that the company does not give out the information over the phone. If this happens, explain that you are taking a course and working on an assignment requiring you to contact a person in that field. Then your request may get forwarded to human resources. Since you are not seeking a position at this time, just information, you may be able to get some names or tips from the human resources personnel. If not, simply offer your thanks and move on to the next company.

Once you have the name of the person in the department you are interested in, add it to the other information on your data sheet. You are now ready to expand your list of contacts through information interviewing.

*Discuss with your group or class how your actual inquiries were received.*

### TAKE A CLOSER LOOK
### 5.3 Practise Your Telephone Style

Use this exercise to prepare your own practice script for making an appointment for an information interview. Constructing your own dialogue will help you to sharpen and tailor your responses so that you will feel comfortable when you make your calls.

**"Arranging the Meeting" Dialogue**

Operator:    Good morning, _____.

You:    Good morning. May I please speak to _____?

Operator:    One moment, please.

You:    Hello, Mr./Ms. _____. My name is _____ and I am taking a course at _____ here in _____. I am conducting research into occupations related to _____. I'm not looking for a job, just some information. I am wondering if you would have 15 or 20 minutes to chat with me at your convenience about your job and about the field in general?

Response:    I'm quite busy. I'm not really sure I can help you.

You:    I am trying to make some decisions regarding going into the _____ field of work and I want to learn more about the day-to-day work. I'm sure that any information you can share will be very valuable to me, and I promise I won't take more time than you can spare. Perhaps I could come out and chat with you next week some time? Say _____ perhaps?

Response:    Well, all right. _____ would be good. I can talk to you for a short time then.

You:    Thank you, Mr./Ms. _____. I look forward to meeting you.

How did the dialogue feel? Maybe a little stiff the first time, but you'll become more comfortable with it as you practice and use it. Now, try practising with someone and have them vary the responses to see how you might react under different circumstances. Role-play situations in which your contact is rude, rushed, distracted, resistant, evasive, or disorganized.

*Discuss your practice experiences with your group or with the class.*

**TAKE A CLOSER LOOK**

**5.4 Pulling It All Together**

List all the contacts you have made who have provided you with helpful information about the occupation you are exploring. Then note the information that you found to be most helpful. Also, note anything that you found of special interest during your meetings.

**CONTACT/ORGANIZATION** _____

Helpful information

_____

_____

Observations

_____

_____

**CONTACT/ORGANIZATION** _____

Helpful information

_____

_____

Observations

_____

_____

**CONTACT/ORGANIZATION** _____

Helpful information

_____

_____

Observations

_____

_____

Were you able to develop other contacts for future reference from referrals during your meetings? If so, list them here.

| NAME | ORGANIZATION | PHONE NUMBERS |
|---|---|---|
| _____ | _____ | _____ |
| _____ | _____ | _____ |
| _____ | _____ | _____ |

As a result of your meetings, have you begun to determine a possible occupation? If so, write it here.

_____

_____

If you are still undecided, have you narrowed your search to one or two possibilities? What are they?

_____

_____

Did you find from your meetings that the occupation you had an interest in is not a good fit for you?

_____

_____

If you answered yes to the previous question, are there related areas that interest you that you uncovered from networking, or will you need to look in another area?

_____

_____

Have any of your new contacts offered to act as a resource to you as you continue your career preparation?

_____

_____

_Discuss the results of your networking experience with your group or the class._

_____

## A Look Back

If you have followed the suggestions for doing this part of your career exploration, you will have developed a much better understanding of the occupation in which you have an interest. You have probed the boundaries of your existing network to identify people you might already know who would be a willing resource for you. You have learned more about the field that interests you and the type of work involved in that occupation. You have begun to expand your network into areas that are directly related to your future occupation, or you have found from your meetings that the work you thought you'd enjoy actually might not be right for you. You may even have initiated a professional association that could benefit you and your new network partner for many years.

Networking is a component of career development that is here to stay. If you have tried the approaches described here, you have already benefited from this process. Be prepared in the future for a call from someone like yourself who will be asking you to take some time to provide information and encouragement. Make sure you respond generously, just as your new friends have responded to you.

## Other Sources and Suggested Reading

*Canada Student Employment Guide* by the Student Employment Network
This book is a directory of major employers across Canada. Through interviews with human resource departments, the authors have described characteristics that employers deem important in selecting their employees.

*The Canadian Key Business Directory* by Dun & Bradstreet of Canada
This is a directory of Canadian businesses. It includes information such as business address, number of employees, line of business, and names of management contacts. One can search the directory by alphabetical listing, geographical location, or type of business.

*The Career Directory* by R. W. Yerema and K. Chow
This book lists Canadian employers that hire people with particular educational backgrounds. It provides a description of the company and contact information. Employers are listed according to educational requirements, industry, geographical region, and starting salary.

*A Foot in the Door: Networking Your Way into the Hidden Job Market* by Katharine Hansen
While this book is better suited for those who are ready to seek employment, it provides useful insight into the networking process.

*Information Interviewing: How to Tap Your Hidden Job Market* by Martha Stoodley
This is a good resource for anyone going through career transition. A guidebook for experienced careerists about ways to create career visibility, it offers insight to people just entering the job market into how networks can benefit all participants.

*Power Schmoozing: The New Etiquette for Social and Business Success*
by Terri Mandell
Knowing what to say after you get through the door is an incomparable tool. This book makes it easier to feel comfortable in situations you may be experiencing for the first time.

*What Color Is Your Parachute?* by Richard Nelson Bolles
Since its initial publication in 1970, this manual for career decision making has become an all-around resource for anyone contemplating a career move. While the methods Bolles proposes are not for everyone, the philosophy of investigating occupations in order to make an informed decision is presented in an interesting, "user-friendly" style.

## Web Sites and Internet Resources

**www.cdm.uwaterloo.ca**
The Career Services Centre at the University of Waterloo has developed a user-friendly Web site that addresses career decision making in six simple steps. The steps include self-assessment, research, decision making, networks and contacts, work, and life/work planning. The site includes clear, useful information offered in print and through video and audio clips.

**workinfonet.ca**
This Web site is a national partnership of career planning, learning, and employment information Web sites in each province and territory of Canada. It offers relevant information on jobs, education, training, occupations, labour markets, self-employment, workplace issues, finances, and more.

**www.jobboom.com/conseils/top100A.html**
Jobboom offers links to 100 Web sites relating to learning and employment. The sites are categorized according to eight basic topics, including "I need to choose a career," "What is the job market like?" and other relevant topics.

**www.peer.ca/mentorprograms.html**
This site is supported by the HRSDC Youth Initiatives Directorate. It provides information and lists mentoring programs and contacts.

# Chapter 6
# Trying an Occupation

## Gaining Experience, Education, and Training

*Actually, I'm an overnight success. But it took 20 years.*

MONTY HALL

Deciding on an occupation can be compared to buying a car. Both are major decisions that you have to live with for some time. We all use various methods to come to a final decision on what car to buy. Some consumers trust the auto advertisements. Others might read consumer ratings or automotive magazines to find out more. They might talk to people who own the kind of car they're interested in. Almost everyone looks over the cars at a showroom, checking stickers to compare prices. Usually, whether the car is new or used, they negotiate the car's price with the salesperson. Finally, after they've decided, signed the papers, and paid the money, the transaction is concluded.

"But wait," you say. "What about the test drive?" You're right. Few of us would be willing to purchase an automobile without first sitting in the driver's seat and driving the car ourselves. The test drive doesn't always guarantee that we will love the car, but it gives us a feel for the automobile that we cannot obtain from reading books and talking with people. Getting the feel of the car is one part of the information-gathering process we undertake before the final decision.

The process of career decision making is not unlike the process of selecting a car to purchase—with one important difference: Most career decision makers don't bother to "test drive" their occupational choice before they decide. Most of us are in too big a rush to jump into our professional lives and start building a career to stop and take the time to try one out.

The value of trying an occupation before committing to it cannot be overstated. Although the information you gather from your occupational research, networking, and your informational interviewing is very useful and important, having the chance to sample an occupation hands-on can tell you a great deal about the nature of work in the field and about your "fit" for the occupation you have chosen.

There are several ways to try an occupation. In this chapter, we examine a number of avenues to "test drive" occupations before you actually make a choice.

The possible ways of trying and experiencing occupations are volunteering, part-time employment, classroom study, co-operative education, and internship/practicum opportunities.

# Gaining Experience

## Volunteering

Opportunities to experience occupations are available through a number of community agencies and organizations. Many businesses and organizations welcome volunteers to work with them. Social service agencies, hospitals, government agencies, businesses, libraries, schools, and parks and recreation centres all are possible places where you might offer your energy and abilities in exchange for an introduction to the occupational field of your interest.

If you have an interest in health care, hospitals and long-term care facilities are eager for volunteers to interact with patients and health-care professionals in providing service. While you wouldn't be involved with the patients in the same way as a nurse or doctor is, you would be in the same setting and have a first-hand opportunity to witness the pace and atmosphere associated with the work.

If your skills or interests are in business areas, many agencies welcome accounting, marketing, and business majors who would like to try out their skills. You might even be able to take on more responsibility as a volunteer or practicum student than you would in the more formal hierarchical setting of the business world.

If your interest is in social work, education, business, health, or athletics, the YMCA is another community resource that you might want to explore as a volunteer opportunity. The YMCA depends on volunteers to help in programs and administration. Volunteers serve on boards, teach fitness classes, and help with fundraising, special events, youth and children's programs, and many other events and activities. The YMCA counts on more than 30 000 Canadians as volunteers.

The Volunteer Canada Web site (**www.volunteer.ca**) is dedicated to the promotion of volunteerism. It has volunteer centres across Canada that can assist you in making contact with a resource in your community where you can work as a volunteer. Also, most township and city halls provide information on volunteering opportunities in their communities. This information is often also listed on their Web sites.

Volunteering with community businesses, organizations, and resources is an ideal way not only to gain direct access to information to help you make a career decision, but also to gain learning and experience in your chosen field. Although you will not be paid for volunteer work, the rewards you gain through volunteerism can be substantial. For paid work experience, you might consider part-time employment or co-op education opportunities.

## Part-Time Employment

A part-time job that brings you into the setting related to your occupational choice is another excellent way to try an occupation. Many aspects of part-time work parallel volunteer experience. In both situations you are working in the setting in which your occupational work would take place and observing the type of work there. Part-time work also offers you the added benefit of income, which can be particularly important for enhancing your résumé.

One negative aspect of part-time work is the lack of flexibility typical of entry-level positions. For example, if you have been hired to file and deliver mail, then you will have little opportunity to experience aspects of the occupational field outside of those duties. You are employed not on your terms but on the terms of the employer, which are not geared to accommodate your individual need to understand a particular field or discipline on a broad level. Still, if your objective is to work in a particular field, getting in anywhere, even the mail room, is a great way to get your foot in the door and learn more about the occupation, business, or organization.

## Classroom Study

Classroom study may have already played a role in getting you this far in your career adventure. You may have already begun your post-secondary education, or may be considering training for an occupation. You probably already have a good understanding of how different fields of study relate to the world of work and how much or how little you might enjoy working in each of these fields.

Now you are ready to use classroom experiences to determine further what occupation might be a good fit for you. This is particularly true if the field that you are considering is a trade or technical field. Engineering, accounting, information systems, health care, and the skilled trades are all fields that require classroom experiences in which you are immersed in the data and language of the discipline. If you are considering a career in one of these fields, then your study in the classroom will quickly tell you whether you would enjoy working in the field. If you enjoy the course work, do well, and have much in common with your peers, then you may enjoy the occupation. On the other hand, if you are bored with the class's subject matter and are very different from the people who enjoy the class, it may be better that you consider examining other career options.

Of course, if you have a deep interest in a particular field, don't be put off if one or two classes are difficult. Almost everyone who has attended school to train for an occupation has had at least one or two classes that they did not enjoy. Some people even hated their academic work but love their chosen occupations, so keep an open mind and use a variety of experiences to make your decision. That is, in addition to classroom study, you might also consider gaining experience through co-op education or internship/practicum opportunities.

## Co-operative Education and Internship/Practicum Opportunities

The opportunity to participate in a co-operative education experience or internship/practicum is one of the best ways to try an occupation. These programs allow students to apply the theory they have learned in the classroom to the world of work and find out at the same time if their career choice is the right one for them.

"Co-op job" refers to a paid job in a field related to your education or training that allows you to obtain academic credit that will be applied toward your degree. While such credit may not be necessary to graduate, it does provide you with a work/learn experience that is otherwise unavailable.

A co-op education program differs from an "internship," or "practicum." Internship/practicum experiences are usually a required part of the education or training program necessary to qualify the student for graduation. Also, an internship or practicum does not include a salary, whereas co-op jobs are paid.

The benefits associated with co-op education and internship/practicum programs can be summarized in three statements:

◆ You experience how the academic learning to which you have been exposed relates to the world of work.

◆ You get a head start on your work experience by being exposed to the standards and expectations of the professional world; this establishes a platform from which to launch your own career.

◆ You have an opportunity to begin visualizing yourself as a professional by working as an associate and colleague with others who are established in the field.

In a co-op job, internship, or practicum, you enter the work environment as an extension of the learning environment. You earn credit toward your diploma or degree as is approved by the educational institution. Your work must meet certain standards related to your field of study or it will not be recognized by the college or university. That requirement ensures that your co-op job, internship, or practicum will offer you the opportunity to be involved in tasks and responsibilities that are substantial and integral to the work environment. Your time will be spent on meaningful work providing you with hands-on training and experience.

The easiest way to become involved in these work/learn education programs is to find out if your local college or university offers co-op and/or internship/practicum opportunities. Most institutions now offer some co-op programs and have some provision for granting credit for experiential learning through internships and practicum placements.

In addition to these experiential learning programs, Canada has begun to adopt comprehensive training programs that include a substantial commitment to the idea of workplace training. For example, most provinces now recognize prior work-related learning, called Prior Learning Assessment (or PLA), and many institutions are now giving course credit for PLA. This means that if students have acquired training on the job that meets the objectives of the learning required in a course, they can use this training to get credit toward their certificate, diploma, or degree.

Also, apprenticeship programs are available for many skilled trade occupations. Apprenticeship programs provide for hands-on practical training by the employer in the workplace and a minimal amount of classroom instruction at a college or approved training organization. To become an apprentice, you must find an employer who is willing to train. Such jobs are rarely advertised, and, instead, employers often rely on word of mouth to attract applicants. People who want to become apprentices usually apply directly to an employer, union, or local apprenticing committee.

# Finding Education and Training Programs

When considering an occupation, it is important that you also consider the education and/or training required. It is necessary to consider the length of training, cost, location, entrance requirements, course load, and credentials earned. For some people, these issues may not influence their career decisions; however, for most, these are important and influential factors.

Fortunately, this information can be easily accessed. There are a few good resources for researching education and training programs in Canada. They are the *Spectrum Publication Series*, the Association of Canadian Community Colleges (ACCC), the Association of Universities and Colleges of Canada (AUCC), and School Finder. For information on studying abroad, the Distance Studies Web site is a useful starting point.

The *Spectrum Publication Series* is a comprehensive guide detailing information on post-secondary education and training programs across Canada. The series is divided into three books, *Ontario Spectrum*, *Eastern Spectrum*, and *Western Spectrum*, each concentrating on that region of Canada. The *Spectrum* books are updated annually and include information on programs; the institutions that offer them; entrance requirements; full-time, part-time, and distance education; university and college transfer; career development; apprenticeship programs; and more. These guides are available at most public libraries, college and university libraries, and career resource centres.

The Association of Canadian Community Colleges (ACCC) hosts a Web site that maintains a database of programs offered by each of its 150 member colleges and institutes in Canada. You can access this database by selecting the "Colleges" menu and then "Training Programs Database." The database can be searched by key words, and then by province or territory, or language of study. Where the *Spectrum* publications offer information on colleges and universities, the ACCC database will only provide information on college programs and university transfer programs of institutions that are members of the ACCC.

Another similar database is found at the Association of Universities and Colleges of Canada (AUCC) Web site. This database can be accessed by clicking on "Canadian Universities" on the home page. It provides information on programs offered through universities or university-colleges in Canada that are members of the AUCC. The database lists the institutions that offer the programs, the languages they are offered in, the degree granted, and whether co-op programs are available. Also, it provides links to the institutions where you can then get further information.

The last resource that is also very useful for searching Canadian institutions is School Finder. **SchoolFinder.com** is a Web site providing a database of over 1400 universities, colleges, and career colleges in Canada, including admission requirements, costs, programs, and contact details. You can search by keyword for programs, schools, careers, and scholarships, and even take an e-tour of a university or college campus.

If your interest is to study abroad, some Canadian universities offer student exchange, study abroad, or study/work/travel programs. You can acquire information on these programs from individual institutions. If you are interested in acquiring your education or training in the United States, one Web site to explore is **distancestudies.com**. This site gives you access to a searchable database of more than 1000 programs at all academic levels at many colleges and universities across North America.

Institutions across Canada, and across the world, vary in terms of their programs, entrance requirements, course offerings, costs, and credentials earned. To ensure that you are enrolling in the education and training that will best serve your needs and those of your chosen career, it is best to take the time to thoroughly investigate all options available to you. You might find your program of interest at your local college, or it may be across the country, or even abroad. Nevertheless, choosing your education and/or training is an important step in ensuring your career success. Further ensure the long-term survival of your occupational choice by acquiring education, first-hand work experience, and transferable employability skills in your chosen field.

## Long-Term Survival

One of the most valuable lessons to be gained from work experience is exposure to the workplace. First-hand knowledge of the behaviours that can serve your long-term growth is a strong base on which you can build your career. In the workplace you will be able to observe how people in different disciplines interact together to achieve group goals, defuse tension, and resolve conflict. These are transferable skills that you can take with you from one work environment to another.

Your first exposure to the occupation you are considering may make you feel anxious and awkward, which are completely natural responses. You are transitioning to a new role and a new realization of who you are becoming. Use this opportunity wisely. Compare the styles of people in your work team. Note which behaviours contribute to the group's progress and which detract from the ability of the group to work effectively. Listen closely to the ideas and feelings expressed by the people with whom you are working. Ask questions that help you understand the relationships within the work environment.

It is easy to dismiss issues of style, work relationships, and group cohesiveness as irrelevant to your career decision-making process. However, the demands of the work environment go far beyond the mechanics of production and output. Your ability to identify and adapt to the complexities of interacting in a work setting will be at least as important as any theoretical knowledge you bring to your career. It is your chance to gain transferable employability skills and become "work wise" about the environment you are about to enter.

Your direct experience with the occupation you are considering can take you far beyond the obvious objectives you have set for yourself. It can be the foundation for your growth as a professional and the beginning of a new type of learning: learning that promotes understanding, creativity, communication, patience, prudence, courage, wisdom, caution, planning, decisiveness, tolerance, trust, enthusiasm, autonomy, confidence, vision, and leadership. Taken as a whole, it constitutes learning how to make your life and your career a success, and that lasts well beyond the workplace experience.

## Teri's Story

Teri had been working as a framer's assistant in the construction industry for the last two years. She enjoyed the work very much, but now she wanted to take on more challenges and earn a higher salary. Teri realized that the construction trade was booming and that labour market analysts were predicting a shortage of skilled tradespeople over the next few years. Her home town was already experiencing a shortage of skilled framers and carpenters to work in residential construction.

Teri decided to enquire about becoming a fully qualified certified carpenter. She searched the ACCC Web site database for construction programs. There were various carpentry programs offered at various institutions across the country. She explored each of them and came across an apprenticeship program offered at a college in the city where she lived.

The apprenticeship program combined classroom learning with on-the-job training. About 90% of the training was completed on site by an employer and the remaining 10% was classroom learning. The program could be completed in one year and would qualify her as a fully certified journeyperson.

Becoming a fully certified journeyperson appealed to Teri because it would allow her to take on more responsibility, do complex jobs, and even become self-employed. It would also mean an increase in salary. The training program also seemed perfect for her because she could continue to work and receive an income. In addition, the program was only one year long; she would be able to complete it in plenty of time to take advantage of the local construction boom. Finally, the program would also provide her with certification to work elsewhere in Canada in case she ever decided to move.

Once Teri had done her research and made her decision to apply for the carpenter apprenticeship program, she spoke to her employer about her plans. Her employer was very supportive of her decision because he was in desperate need of qualified framers and carpenters. Teri was an excellent employee and he did not want to lose her to another construction company, so they discussed the possibility of her completing her apprenticeship program with his company.

Teri contacted the college and met with an advisor to obtain more information about the program. Three months later, she was enrolled in the apprenticeship program, training with the framer she had previously been assisting, and was on her way to becoming a fully certified carpenter.

## TAKE A CLOSER LOOK

### 6.1 Sampling Occupations

Classroom study is one way to measure your interest in an occupation, especially when you think you may be more attracted by the image of a certain occupation than by the work itself. Taking a few classes might be enough to confirm your interest or to set you on a different path.

Check through a college or university catalogue and see if there are introductory classes with few prerequisites—you then have a chance to see what a particular discipline is like. Identify any classes that you think could help you learn more about a particular field.

**CLASSES**

_____

_____

_____

_____

If you haven't done so already, you may wish to schedule an appointment with a college or university advisor to learn about courses available to you.

*Discuss the results of your catalogue scan with your group or with the class.*

**TAKE A CLOSER LOOK**

### 6.2 Learning from Your Community

Enquire about volunteer work. Find out which organizations in your community would have opportunities for you to volunteer your time and talents. The information and insight you would gain from such an experience could help you make the right career decision now, rather than making a mistake later that could be costly in time and money. Note the agencies that would be interested in your contribution.

**AGENCIES INTERESTED IN VOLUNTEERS**

_____

_____

_____

_____

*Discuss the different types of organizations that offer opportunities with your group or with the class.*

**TAKE A CLOSER LOOK**

### 6.3 Acquiring Hands-On Experience

Brainstorm a list of entry-level positions that you could apply for that might give you some experience in the field you are interested in.

**JOBS IN AREA OF INTEREST**

_____

_____

_____

_____

*Discuss the results of your brainstorm with your group or with the class.*

## TAKE A CLOSER LOOK
### 6.4 Finding a Setting to Hone Your Skills

In order to learn more about co-op education, internship/practicum, or apprenticeship programs, find out if your local post-secondary institution offers these programs. Make an appointment with an advisor and discuss the opportunities available. You could also request assistance in contacting a typical employer or student of one of these programs to conduct an information interview. Using the information from the advisor as well as the resources available to you through the library (directories, newspapers, professional journals, Internet, and so on), make a list of agencies, organizations, or companies that offer co-op, internship/practicum, or apprenticeship opportunities.

| NAME | ORGANIZATION | PHONE NUMBER |
| --- | --- | --- |
| | | |
| | | |
| | | |
| | | |

If you are interested in one of these programs, find out what requirements you would have to meet to qualify.

## TAKE A CLOSER LOOK
### 6.5 Pulling It All Together

List one or two classes, volunteer settings, part-time jobs, co-op or internship/practicum opportunities that might offer you the chance to try an occupation.

**CLASSES**

_____

_____

**VOLUNTEER SETTINGS**

_____

_____

**PART-TIME JOBS**

_____

_____

**CO-OP JOBS/INTERNSHIPS/PRACTICUMS**

_____

_____

*Discuss the results of your survey of learning opportunities with your group or with the class.*

## A Look Back

This chapter explored ways to further investigate whether an occupation will offer you what you are seeking. "Test driving" an occupation might not guarantee you long-term satisfaction, but it will give you a feel for the nature of the work, the work setting, and the people with whom you would interact.

We examined different ways of trying an occupation.

◆ *Classroom study*: a chance to check out subject matter and meet other people who enjoy that subject to see if you have anything in common with them.

◆ *Community resources*: places to learn more about jobs and occupations first-hand and perhaps even perform work related to your field of interest.

◆ *Part-time employment*: earn a salary while you learn more about a work environment and related tasks; a good addition to any résumé.

◆ *Co-op, internship/practicum, and apprenticeship programs*: a superior way to transition to the world of work while learning more about your chosen field and earning credentials.

One final advantage to trying out an occupation is the opportunity to learn more about the skills, behaviours, and traits that might enhance your chances for survival in the workplace. These are employability skills that can mean the difference between success and failure.

## Other Sources and Suggested Reading

*Spectrum Publication Series: Ontario Spectrum, Eastern Spectrum,* and *Western Spectrum*
These guides provide information about post-secondary programs offered at institutions across Canada.

## Web Sites and Internet Resources

**www.volunteer.ca**
The Volunteer Canada Web site where you can learn about volunteerism and volunteer opportunities.

**www.accc.ca**
Web address for the Association of Canadian Community Colleges (ACCC) home page. For the database of programs offered by each of 150 member colleges and institutes in Canada, the address is **www.accc.ca/english/colleges/programs_database.cfm.**

**www.aucc.ca**
Home page of the Association of Universities and Colleges of Canada. To search its database of programs, the address is **http://oraweb.aucc.ca/showdcu.html.**

**www.schoolfinder.com**
This Web site provides a database of over 1400 universities, colleges, and career colleges in Canada and information about their programs.

**www.distancestudies.com**
This site gives you access to a searchable database of more than 1000 programs at all academic levels for institutions across North America.

**www.ymca.ca**
The YMCA Web site with links to local centres across Canada. This site also offers information on volunteer and job opportunities at local YMCAs.

# Chapter 7

# Decision Making and Goal Setting

## Putting It All Together

*The way to get started is to quit talking and begin doing.*

WALT DISNEY

Imagine yourself at the oceanside looking through the viewfinder of your camera at a sailboat gliding atop the waves. Your first glimpse is cloudy and blurred, but as you adjust the focus, you are able to see the boat more clearly. That process of focusing a camera is similar to what happens in this phase of your career adventure, that is, decision making and goal setting.

Up until this point, you have spent time gathering and interpreting information, some of it about you, some of it about the world of work. You have completed the necessary steps to make some choices about your career direction. Now it is time for you to focus in on just what your career choices are and to determine the best way to achieve your career goals.

"But," you say, "I've made dozens of decisions just to get to this point in my career exploration. Don't all those decisions count?" Of course they do. You have made many important choices. These decisions were part of your self-discovery and your exploration of the labour market. They set your direction up to this point by excluding options that didn't meet your needs and by including possibilities that kept you on your present course. Making these preliminary decisions has given you direction, stability, and momentum.

You are now ready to leave this phase of exploration and move to a new level of decision making, a level beyond information gathering. Decision making will help you to organize your thoughts and feelings as they evolve about what you have learned in your experience and research and to develop meaningful career goals. The key word here is "evolve." This process is an evolution, a refining. You will now strive to establish goals that are achievable and that will set you on a definite path and still allow you to be your own person.

That being said, in reality, you never stop examining and exploring. You have selected a direction, but you want to keep all avenues open as you learn more about your path. As physicist Richard Feynman said in Clark McKowen's *Thinking about Thinking,* "I can live with doubt and uncertainty and not knowing. I think it's much more interesting to live not knowing than to have answers which might be wrong."

You may change your mind many times before you find the occupation that fits you. That is part of the excitement and wonder of choosing. One can never know for sure that his or her decisions will lead to sure-fire success or a sense of satisfaction. Nevertheless, we do know that you can always change your mind. You are not required to live with unsatisfying choices.

# Decision-Making Styles

People approach career decisions in much the same way that they approach other decisions in their lives. Some people prefer to analyze data and think things through while others "go with their gut," relying on how they feel about the issues.

Some people use a *cognitive* approach to make decisions. These people always thoroughly contemplate any decision by researching and analyzing all the data. For example, when making a purchase, no matter how small, they always consult a consumer buying guide, and research the product, manufacturer, and retailer. Some cognitive decision makers will chart and graph every scintilla of information until all they know about a subject is down on paper. Only then can they make a choice. Another way that people who use this approach make decisions is to draw a line down the middle of a sheet of paper, write "pro" above one column and "con" above the other, and then analyze and examine all the advantages and disadvantages of each possible decision. These are all valid techniques for making decisions using the cognitive approach. People who are comfortable with this approach rely on reason and logic to determine their choices.

Other people prefer to make decisions based on feelings and intuition. Thus, this approach is referred to as the *intuitive* approach. People who prefer this approach will think about issues, but when all is said and done, their feelings guide their decisions. The "facts" take on a secondary role; the facts may produce the feelings, but the decisions are based on the feelings. Some might say that sensitivity to all the issues, implied and unspoken, actually enhances judgment since it factors in more than what's on paper. Therefore, this intuitive approach is just as useful as the cognitive approach.

Which approach—the cognitive or the intuitive—do you use? In order to assess which approach you tend to use as your decision-making style, look at how you typically make decisions. Do you research, analyze, and weigh the options before you decide, or do you typically respond to a decision by how you feel about the options? Does this approach work for you? Consider the decisions you have made in the past. Did your decisions yield the results that you had hoped? Were you satisfied with the outcomes? If your answer is yes, then you may have a style of decision making that works for you, whether it is cognitive or intuitive, or maybe a bit of both. Current research shows that people who use both— intuitive abilities in combination with cognitive analysis—make effective, wise career decisions. On the other hand, if you think that the results of your past decisions have been disappointing, you may want to try some of the alternative decision-making techniques presented in this section.

You already have an idea about your decision-making style from the personality exercises in Chapter 3. As you may recall, the third letter in Jung's four-letter code represents how you prefer to make decisions. People who prefer the "T" tend to prefer logical, structured approaches, and people who prefer "F" are those who prefer to focus on their feelings and intuition. Try to determine if one of these styles fits you better than the other. Is there a way you might incorporate both approaches in your decision making?

## Career Decision-Making Process

So far in your career adventure, you have taken the following steps:

♦ *Self-Assessment*—You started by looking at yourself—your motivations, life stage, values, interests, personality, and skills. From this base you began your career exploration, looking first at broad categories of occupations that interested you.

♦ *Occupation Research*—You expanded your knowledge through research into jobs and occupations to which you were initially drawn. You may have begun to do some actual decision making by discarding certain types of occupations and zeroing in on others that sounded right.

♦ *Networking*—You talked with people who were actually doing the work that interested you. This was your "reality check" to determine if your understanding of the job matched the real-world experience of others.

Now, the next step in your career decision-making process is to narrow your focus and set your goal. The first thing you must do is set priorities. This is critical to making your decision. Think about what issues will carry the most weight in your decision to follow a particular career path. Consider everything you have learned about yourself and the occupations you have examined. Think about what is most important to you in a job in order to evaluate whether one career path is better for you than another. What do you believe about yourself and your career needs?

If the differences between your needs and the occupations you are considering are dramatic, now is the time to address this and look at alternative career paths. One way of evaluating alternatives is to set up a checklist that compares your career priorities with each of the occupations you are considering. This point-by-point comparison helps you to see how a certain career choice might, or might not, meet your needs.

## Setting Goals

By this point, you have devoted a great deal of time and effort to your career exploration. You deserve to feel satisfied and excited about what you have done and where you are going. Part of the excitement comes from knowing that you are already on your way simply because you have made a choice (or perhaps a few choices). You may face obstacles ahead, but your enthusiasm for your goals will sustain you through the rough spots. You are now ready to set forth your goals.

A goal is defined as a destination or an end that one strives to attain. Goals channel our energy toward actions that are likely to get us what we want. They drive us. Think of goals in life as being similar to goals in sports. For example, in hockey, the energy of the players and all their actions are driven toward attaining a goal. The striving toward the goal is what directs their actions. If there were no goal net, the players would probably just skate aimlessly around the rink. The same is true for other aspects of life. Goals direct our actions, our decisions, our behaviour. Whether they are simple or extensive, goals keep us motivated and moving ahead with life.

Making a commitment to a stated (long-term) goal and then developing a plan that will allow you to move toward that goal on a step-by-step basis (using short-term goals) is one way to stay motivated and moving ahead. The first thing you need to do is establish your destination, the end result you want to attain. This becomes your long-term goal. Then, you need to analyze what smaller steps need to be taken in order to reach this goal. Each of the steps becomes a short-term goal. Figuring out how you will take each step becomes your plan for accomplishing each short-term goal, and these will eventually lead to the accomplishment of your long-term goal.

People are often quite familiar with setting long-term goals—"I will retire at age 55," "I will get into law school," "I will travel the world"—however, they fail to take the next step in the process, which is to plan how they will accomplish the small steps that lead to their bigger, long-term goal. Without this plan, the long-term goal becomes not a goal, but rather a wish. A goal requires a plan and action to be taken toward accomplishing it.

Exercise 7.2 at the end of the chapter offers you a way to start moving toward your goal by completing a goal commitment statement. Begin by completing this statement, and then post copies of it in places where you will regularly see it. Be as succinct and as clear as you can about this goal. Then, Exercise 7.3 helps you think about what you need to do to attain your goal. What will it take for you to achieve your stated long-term goal? Find out what stands between you and reaching the goal you have set out for yourself, and determine what you may need to do to keep your momentum going. Identify the individual tasks that you need to accomplish step by step in order to reach your long-term goal. It is important that you work out these steps because not only will this help you formulate your plan, it will also make your long-term goal seem more easily attained. You can focus on each one individually, and this is much less overwhelming than looking at that major goal in the distance.

A good strategy to use to establish your goals is SMART. In other words, make sure your goals are:

**S**pecific:    Be very specific as to exactly what you will do so there is no confusion. Be succinct and state the goal clearly and with conviction. Avoid saying things like "I will *try* to …."
Instead, say "I *will* …."

**M**easurable:    Your goal should be such that you can measure whether you have accomplished it or not. It feels good to see something completed and a job well done. State your goal so that it will be clear when it is accomplished. Rather than saying "I will do my best …" which is very difficult to measure—how will you know what is your best?—describe what the end result will look like so that when you accomplish it, it will be easily recognized. Pretend that someone else will be identifying the accomplishment. How will this person recognize when the goal has been met?

**A**cceptable: Your goal should be set by you rather than by someone else. You know best your strengths and weaknesses, and can use this information to maximize your chances of success. The goal must be something that you are committed to so that you will invest the time and effort needed to accomplish it.

**R**ealistic: Better to plan only a few things and be successful rather than to plan many things and be unsuccessful. Success breeds success! Don't plan to do things if you are unlikely to follow through. Start small, with what you can do, experience the joys of meeting your goal, and only then gradually increase what you ask of yourself.

**T**imely: Plan how long it will take to complete each of your goals. Give yourself realistic deadlines to work toward. Mark these deadlines on your calendar and refer to them often.

Taking many small steps toward the long-term goal is what actually gets you there. These short-term goals are the key to success. Your short-term goals become the benchmarks by which you will measure your progress, build your momentum, and keep your focus. As you progress with your short-term goals, plan points along the way when you step back, assess your progress, and fine-tune your direction. You might realize that you need to revise your plan, set different short-term goals, or even modify your long-term goal. This is okay. As in sports, it often takes different plays, different attempts, to achieve a goal.

## Consolidating Your Resources

Exercise 7.3 at the end of the chapter requires you to think in a concrete way about the resources you will need to accomplish your goal. The list includes a variety of items, both economic and personal. The people who will be involved in your journey are probably supportive and encouraging and will make an effort to help you on your way. In some cases, however, you may find that you are not getting the help you need—people don't understand or aren't concerned about whether you succeed or not. In such cases, stay focused on yourself and your goal. Concentrate on using your skills to work effectively within the system, and continue to reach out in a personal way to those people who can and will help you. Surviving and even flourishing in pursuit of your goal will require you to use all your energy and resources.

You may stumble upon some unanticipated obstacles in your path—people who are important to you may actively discourage you and express doubt about your choices. If people are uncomfortable with the career goal you have chosen, they may unwittingly make it much more difficult for you. For instance, if you announce that you are switching your major from pre-med to archaeology and that next semester you will be going on a dig in Zambia, don't be surprised if your plan is met with less than enthusiastic support from your tuition-paying parents. They may be wondering just what is going on and if you are in touch with reality. In fact, your decision may be quite reasonable, and you can present the data you have gathered through self-assessment and career exploration. In order to be supportive, people usually just need to know that you have made your decision carefully based on sound, thorough information.

If you find that even with convincing arguments the people in your life are still skeptical, consider their concerns and try to address them. However, sometimes in life we have to go out on the skinny limb because we can't live in ways that meet everyone else's needs and expectations. If this happens to you, make sure you have your own "cheering section" to keep you focused on your goals. Most important, be your own cheerleader—pat yourself on the back when things go well and give yourself a break when they seem to fall apart.

Career decision making is the heart of your career adventure. It requires courage, strength, and resolve. Now is the time to start developing the psychological "muscle" that will get you through the rough spots in life. Enjoy your chance to choose. You are exactly where you want to be.

# Dealing with Uncertainty

In the book *Bang the Drum Slowly* by Mark Harris, the baseball players play a card game called Tegwar to amuse themselves when on the road. Usually two players set up the game in the lobby of the hotel and start playing. As the game continues, passers-by stop to watch and ask questions about the game. Just when the observers think they understand the rules, the ball players introduce a new rule that turns the game around. Sometimes the onlookers join the game, pretending to follow every hand only to end up more confused than before. The rules of the game keep changing. That's because they are playing "Tegwar: The Exciting Game Without Any Rules."

Sometimes when you are experiencing the ups and downs that go with any career, you may feel like you are actually playing Tegwar and, in a sense, you are. You will sometimes have to make decisions without enough information or based on assumptions that you can't confirm. Checklists and goal setting help, but they can't eliminate all uncertainty and risk. Anxiety comes with uncertainty. If you are struggling with choosing, try to remain as flexible as possible. That is your best insurance against the unpredictability of the future.

Also, try to maintain a positive outlook. One way to maintain that positive outlook is through affirmations. Affirmations are statements you can use to give yourself a boost when you experience doubt and uncertainty. When you feel discouraged, try repeating some of these statements as a way to steady yourself during the rough spots.

"I make good decisions, and I am happy with the results."

"If I don't like the outcome, I am smart enough to know how to change things."

"I always achieve my goals."

"I'm gifted and energetic, and I believe in myself."

"Life is an adventure, and I am privileged to experience it."

Say these affirmations over and over as many times a day as you need. You will be surprised at how the use of affirmative statements refocuses your energy in a positive way. Exercise 7.5 will help you develop your own affirmations.

One final word: People often wonder if the day will come when they won't have doubts about themselves and the choices they make. They are disappointed when they find that even the most competent and respected professionals have moments when they question themselves and wonder if they can pull it off. If you are truly growing and challenging yourself, there may be times when self-doubt will cause you to hesitate. Your challenge is to keep trying, keep getting better. You might have fears but they needn't paralyze you. Facing your fears and doing your best is part of meeting the challenge to grow. You are working to achieve long-term goals. It's worth the risk.

## Charlie's Story

Charlie was confused about what he wanted as he tried to make a career decision. His parents were pressuring him to major in engineering, a field they believed would offer him a steady job after graduation. Charlie was interested in engineering and found that some aspects of the field matched his needs. But he wasn't sure if it was really what *he* wanted. Charlie loved to travel and thought that working in a hotel would be interesting and exciting.

Charlie went through the process of researching occupations. He networked, talked with several engineers, and thoroughly researched the occupation. As Charlie assessed his priorities and long-term goals, he found that doing interesting work in a friendly atmosphere was one of the things at the top of his list. Although he liked to work with data, he was more interested in travel and interacting with people.

Charlie laid out the two options he was considering on a checklist. The engineering option would offer various fields and a number of settings in which he could work. The other option that interested Charlie was to work in the hotel and hospitality industry. In comparing the options, Charlie found that, despite some of the advantages of a career in engineering, he clearly preferred a business career that would get him into hotel management.

Charlie recognized that gaining his parents' support was important to achieving his career goal. His plan of action was to compile information to assist his parents in seeing a balanced view of his choice. He discussed the pros and cons of each occupation with his parents and informed them of his goals. His father was concerned that Charlie pursue a "solid" career. Charlie was convinced that he could have a fulfilling, solid career in business, with a specialty in hotel management, and explained to his parents how he could make this happen. He also told his parents that he felt confident in pursuing his own goals and that he would be willing to accept the consequences of his decision. He was sure he could be successful in the field he preferred.

Given Charlie's feelings about the decision he was facing and the thoughtful answers he had for their questions, his parents acknowledged that it was indeed Charlie's decision. While they were still somewhat skeptical about his choice, they encouraged him to keep an open mind and offered their full support.

For his part, Charlie knew that to ensure his success he would have to inform his parents about his progress and future plans. He valued their support and was prepared to do whatever was necessary to maintain it. But he also felt strongly that if his parents decided not to stand behind him, he would still remain on his chosen path—the right path for Charlie—and would be able to move toward his goal on his own if necessary.

### TAKE A CLOSER LOOK
### 7.1 Occupation Options Checklist

This checklist gives you a chance to compare your career priorities with the occupations you are considering. The categories on the left represent some possible career priorities, needs, and preferences you may have identified through self-assessment and career exploration. The blanks at the end of the list are for priorities you may have identified as important that aren't mentioned in this list. As you review these priorities, rate the importance of each issue in terms of your career needs in the first Rate column. Use a number 10 to indicate items of highest priority and descending numbers to indicate items of lesser importance. The number 1 would thus indicate an item that is unimportant to you.

After you have rated each priority, use the first Relevant Information column to jot down any relevant information you obtained through career exploration about the occupation you are considering. For example, if you've identified a salary range of $30 000–$35 000 in your preferred geographical region, fill in that information. If you find you aren't sure how this occupation stacks up against the priorities you have set, you may need to return to the resources or contacts you used in prior chapters for that information. If you are currently considering more than one occupation, follow the same process, checking how your choices match your priorities and compare with each other.

| Career Priorities | Option 1: Occupation _____ | | Option 2: Occupation _____ | |
| --- | --- | --- | --- | --- |
| | Rate (1–10) | Relevant Information | Rate (1–10) | Relevant Information |
| Salary range | _____ | _____ | _____ | _____ |
| Availability of jobs | _____ | _____ | _____ | _____ |
| Opportunity for advancement | _____ | _____ | _____ | _____ |
| Interesting work | _____ | _____ | _____ | _____ |
| Good benefits | _____ | _____ | _____ | _____ |
| Pleasant work atmosphere | _____ | _____ | _____ | _____ |
| Location of job | _____ | _____ | _____ | _____ |
| Job stability | _____ | _____ | _____ | _____ |
| Value to community | _____ | _____ | _____ | _____ |

| Career Priorities | Rate (1–10) | Relevant Information | Rate (1–10) | Relevant Information |
|---|---|---|---|---|
| Variety of tasks/duties involved | _____ | _____ | _____ | _____ |
| Setting (indoor/outdoor, office, hospital, etc.) | _____ | _____ | _____ | _____ |
| Family friendly/flexibility | _____ | _____ | _____ | _____ |
| Other: | | | | |
| _____ | _____ | _____ | _____ | _____ |
| _____ | _____ | _____ | _____ | _____ |
| _____ | _____ | _____ | _____ | _____ |
| _____ | _____ | _____ | _____ | _____ |

After completing this process for your occupation option(s), does the information you have assembled confirm your thoughts and feelings about this occupation being a good choice for you?

_____

_____

What else could you do to ensure that the options you are considering are appropriate?

_____

_____

*Discuss the checklist exercise with your group or with the class.*

### TAKE A CLOSER LOOK
### 7.2 Your Long-Term Goal

State your career goal in a clear, specific way. To get started, fill in the Goal Commitment Statement.

**MY CAREER GOAL**

I, _____, will seek to enter the field
              (Name)

of _____, with the intent of becoming

a(n) _____. I intend to reach this goal
           (Occupation)

by _____. I will review my progress toward my goal every
    (Date)

_____ months and will be prepared to deal with the unexpected.
(Number of months)

Signed _____ Date _____

## TAKE A CLOSER LOOK
### 7.3 Fact Finding

The process of achieving your goal is already under way. To be successful, you will need to anticipate what resources are necessary to meet the challenges ahead. Using the information that you have developed from your self-assessment and career exploration, make a short list of the resources you will need to make your goal a reality. You may not be able to anticipate every obstacle you might encounter, but you will be much better prepared to overcome them if you gather together your resources now.

**FURTHER INFORMATION NEEDED (RESEARCHING, NETWORKING, ETC.):**

Do you need to talk to anyone or do more research about your career goal? Do you know where training is available?

_____

_____

**FURTHER TRAINING NEEDED (UNIVERSITY, COLLEGE, TECHNICAL, EXPERIENTIAL):**

Do you need to contact specific institutions that specialize in the field you want to enter? Will you need to relocate?

_____

_____

**ECONOMIC NEEDS (LIVING EXPENSES, TUITION, CARE OF DEPENDENTS):**

Will you need financial support to enter the occupational field? Are you eligible for financial aid? Will you have to take a paid job while preparing to enter the field?

_____

_____

**PERSONAL SUPPORT SYSTEM (FAMILY, FRIENDS, COLLEAGUES, ETC.):**

Are your family and friends aware of your career goals? Do they understand the reasons for your choices? Do they support your goals?

_____

_____

**CONTACTS NEEDED (ADVISORS, INSTRUCTORS, PLACEMENT PERSONNEL, ETC.):**

Whom do you need to talk with to find out how to be accepted into a program of study? Who can help you with financial aid? What about living arrangements? Do you know anyone who might help you get started in the occupation through entry-level work?

_____

_____

**SKILLS NEEDED (COMPUTER, TELEPHONE, VERBAL, WRITTEN, ETC.):**

What skills do you need to acquire to accomplish your goals? Do you need to grow beyond the comfortable behaviours that have worked up to now? Will you need to adapt your behaviour to fit in better in your new occupation?

_____

_____

**OTHER POSSIBLE RESOURCES (PLACES TO FIND EMPLOYMENT):**

Are there organizations in which you can find employment or volunteer work in areas related to this occupation?

_____

_____

Some of the resources you have listed may already be a part of your life. If not, obtaining the support you need to accomplish your goal will become part of your overall strategy, especially if you are considering a change that will take you into a different social and economic circle.

To complete your plan, note all the things you can think of that will move you toward accomplishing your goal. The list might include things such as arranging finances, changing housing location, talking with family and friends about your goal, or scheduling interviews with university or college administrators. The list may even include changes you would like to make in your own habits and behaviours that will make it easier to reach your goal. Come up with as many as you can think of and be as specific as possible. List them in the space below.

**STEPS TO THE GOAL**

1. _____

2. _____

3. _____

4. _____

5. _____

6. _____

(Add more as needed.)

Read the following statements. Complete the sentences with the information in the previous exercise. Here is an example:

"These are the things I can do within the next week to take me closer to my goal:"

◆ Discuss my plans with my family and identify any changes we might have to make to help me reach my goal.

◆ Make an appointment to meet with a financial aid advisor to discuss grants and aid.

"These are the things I can do within the next month to take me closer to my goal:"

◆ Register for classes to improve my English.

◆ Arrange for child care during class schedule.

"These are the things I can do within the next six months to take me closer to my goal:"

◆ Meet with a career counsellor to discuss opportunities for part-time employment in the field.

◆ Explore volunteer work in the field.

"These are the things I can do within the next year that will take me closer to my goal:"

◆ Join an organization that supports people in the field that I am interested in.

◆ Apply for entrance to a training program.

Now it is your turn.

"These are the things I can do within the next week to take me closer to my goal:"

_____

_____

"These are the things I can do within the next month to take me closer to my goal:"

_____

_____

"These are the things I can do within the next six months to take me closer to my goal:"

_____

_____

"These are the things I can do within the next year that will take me closer to my goal:"

_____

_____

*Discuss the results of the goal-setting exercise with your group or with the class.*

**TAKE A CLOSER LOOK**

**7.5 Positive Self-Talk**

Everyone has had negative experiences that cause self-doubt. But our faith in our ability to accomplish our goals can be reinforced through affirmations. Repeating affirming statements is simply an acknowledgment of what you may already believe but may have come to doubt because of bad experiences.

Think about a situation that might make you feel uncomfortable, hesitant, or even fearful. Maybe it's entering a classroom full of new faces or walking into a job interview. Whatever it might be, imagine yourself experiencing that same difficult situation in a way that you never have before—as your ideal self—confident, self-assured, at ease.

How do you look in this fantasy? Describe yourself as you might look and feel.

_____

_____

Pick a few words that describe how you are in your fantasy. Then develop an affirmation using those words to describe yourself in a positive, encouraging way.

_____

_____

Use the following space to come up with more affirmations to encourage and support yourself.

_____

_____

Repeat the affirmations, eyes closed, putting your trust in the words you have chosen. How do you feel now?

_____

_____

*Discuss your responses to your affirmations with your group or with the class.*

**TAKE A CLOSER LOOK**

**7.6 Pulling It All Together**

Read the following statements and answer them as honestly and realistically as you can. The most important issues for me in any job/occupation/career are:

_____

_____

The occupations that I listed on my Occupation Options Checklist (Exercise 7.1) were:

_____

_____

The most favourable options on my checklist were:

_____

_____

My career goal is:

_____

_____

My short-term goals are:

_____

_____

My realistic and achievable plan of action is:

_____

_____

*Discuss any reactions you have to this chapter with your group or the class.*

## A Look Back

This chapter has given you the tools you need to have a better, more focused view of where you are going. By now, you are able to set priorities and are aware of criteria for evaluating choices. You know how to complete a checklist that helps you compare your occupation options.

You have also been able to set long- and short-term goals. You have stated your goals with conviction and have developed a coherent plan of action that you can begin using right now to start on your new path. You have anticipated what lies ahead, and you are affirming your belief in your ability to achieve your goals.

Does this mean you are finished with your career decision making? While you may have made a choice that will lay the foundation for your career for some time to come, you will probably come back to some of these tools in the future. As you grow you will continue to be presented with choices regarding your career. Have faith in your ability to make the right decision. Stay flexible and keep a positive focus. These attitudes will be crucial in helping you reach your goals.

You have now completed Parts I and II of this book. As you recall, Part I included Chapters 1, 2, and 3 and focused on increasing your self-awareness. Chapters 4, 5, 6, and 7 made up Part II, which concentrated on the world of work. These chapters dealt with researching occupations, the labour market, and future trends; networking and establishing contacts; gaining experience, education, and training in a chosen occupation; and decision making and goal setting. Having completed each of these first two parts, you are now ready to move on to the final section of this book.

Part III includes Chapters 8, 9, 10, and 11. It focuses on the job search and the tools that are needed to get a job. You may not yet have made any concrete decision about your future occupation. This often takes time. Nevertheless, this final section of the book will provide you with the information you will need in order to acquire the skills necessary for competing in the job market and becoming employed once you are ready to begin working in your chosen occupation.

## Other Sources and Suggested Reading

*The Confident Decision Maker: How to Make the Right Business and Personal Decisions Every Time* by Roger Dawson
This author begins by identifying the qualities that make people good decision makers. From there the process is broken down and presented in a way that motivates the reader to try the techniques immediately. The book is an excellent guide for all types of decision making. Note the chapter on Intuitive Decision Making. The book is also available on audiocassette.

*Following Your Path* by Alexandra Collins Dickerman
This is a workbook that takes you on a journey of self-discovery to your intuitive side. The use of myths, symbols, and images highlights a fascinating examination of the power of your own intuition.

*How to Make Instant Decisions and Remain Happy & Sane* by Zelma Barinov
A book that limits the jargon and offers fresh techniques for coming to closure more quickly; it is easy to read with good use of the author's personal insight.

*Smart Choices: A Practical Guide to Making Better Decisions* by John S. Hammond, Ralph L. Keeney, and Howard Raiffa
This is an excellent resource for a systematic, step-by-step decision-making model.

## Web Sites and Internet Resources

**www.cdm.uwaterloo.ca/step3.asp**
The Career Services Centre at the University of Waterloo has developed a user-friendly Web site that addresses career decision making in six simple steps. The steps include self-assessment, research, decision making, networks and contacts, work, and life/work planning. The Step 3 Web page addresses decision making and goal setting.

**www.yorku.ca/cdc/lsp/tmonline/tm2.htm**
This Web page is one in a series offered by the Counselling and Development Centre at York University.

**www.coloradocollege.edu/CareerCenter/Services/DecisionModel.asp**
This site offers a brief, seven-step model on career decision making.

# Part III

# The Job Search

## Organizing Your Search

You are now prepared to take the next step in your career adventure: organizing your job search. This phase of your career development will provide the tools for actually entering the job market—your résumé, cover letter, interview preparation, and job-marketing skills.

Any formula for success includes being ready for opportunities when they arise. You have prepared for your decision by doing research on yourself and on occupations. You will continue to move toward your chosen occupation by gaining the technical and academic training you need to be a competent professional. It is time to focus on gaining the skills that will allow you to showcase your abilities when you are job hunting. This is an opportunity that might not happen for several years or it could happen next week. You will be ready for the challenge of competing in an increasingly crowded and complex job market.

Your next task is to organize information about yourself and your chosen occupation into a portfolio that markets you successfully. You are entitled to succeed. The way you use your information and training will make the difference in whether you stand out as a shining star or get lost in the crowd.

## Part III will include

## Objectives

**Chapter 8:** Developing Job Leads: Finding Where the Jobs Are

**Chapter 9:** Designing Your Résumé and Cover Letters: Communicating Your Skills and Abilities

**Chapter 10:** Job Interviews: Interviewing with Confidence

**Chapter 11:** Continuing the Adventure: Your Lifelong Journey

- ◆ To expand your network and access the "hidden job market."
- ◆ To research employers and job openings electronically.
- ◆ To tailor your cover letter and résumé to the job being sought.
- ◆ To know how to interview successfully.
- ◆ To develop skills for keeping and advancing your career.

# Chapter 8
# Developing Job Leads

## Finding Where the Jobs Are

*Try to find work in a field that interests you even if it means settling for less income than some other field. Working at something you are interested in is enjoyable; work in a field that doesn't really interest you can be soul-destroying no matter how much it pays.*

EDITH FOWKE

Part of the overall philosophy of your career adventure is the expectation that you have the greatest influence over the goals and outcomes that you choose to pursue. You have acted on this belief in each different portion of this book. The same philosophy is reflected in the final part of your adventure—finding the right job.

Finding a job can feel like a mystery where we play a detective with no clues. Earnestly we follow leads, but most result in dead ends of rejection and frustration. However, with persistence, preparation, and knowing where to look for clues, the mystery can be more easily solved.

Because job seekers using traditional search methods have ended up feeling helpless, frustrated, and rejected, over the years people have come up with new approaches to achieving their employment goals. In this chapter, we explore the methods and approaches that will give you control over your job search. The process won't remain a mystery. It is more like a guidebook that shows you how to move toward your goals. This is hard work, so be prepared to throw out any fixed notions of what success means when looking for a job.

## The Hidden Job Market

The most frustrating part of finding a job: You see an ad, you write a letter, you send a résumé, and wait ... and wait ... and wait. Without question, waiting is more discouraging to job seekers than any other single aspect of job seeking.

But you don't have to wait for someone to find a job for you. You can take responsibility yourself. If you want a job, you must find the employer, not the other way around. Too often, job seekers think that employers should look for them, either through newspaper ads or placement agencies. Those methods may work at times, but not often. You must be actively engaged in developing new leads and pursuing new possibilities in order to find employment.

You may have heard of the "hidden job market." The hidden job market refers to the process by which thousands of jobs are filled. The primary method used to fill jobs in the hidden job market is networking. You are already familiar with networking from the material in Chapter 5. The networking that employers use when filling a position is only slightly different.

Imagine you are Matteo, the manager of accounting in a small company. Everything is going well until your ace accounting associate, Josie, comes in and tells you that she is going back to school full-time and is giving you two weeks' notice. It's February and the April tax deadline is looming. You try to talk Josie into postponing her departure. She's firm, however, so you accept her decision. Josie tells you about her college schedule, which begins at the end of March, but you don't hear a word. Instead, you mentally scan your current staff to determine who might be able to pick up her workload. With difficulty, you acknowledge that the staff isn't up to absorbing her work, and you will have to hire someone new. Experienced accounting people are scarce this time of year. Slowly, you mentally return to the office, and you ask Josie if she knows anyone who might be able to take her place.

Bingo! That is how the hidden job market works. Now imagine that you are a good friend of Josie's—someone with comparable ability and dedication but unhappy in your current position. She knows you are available and so mentions your name and tells a little about you. It would be difficult to find a better way to be introduced to an employer. The trick is becoming "Josie's friend."

You may be surprised to know that you already are "Josie's friend." Somewhere in your existing network, there may be a Josie who is in a position to recommend you to her boss the next time a vacancy occurs. Your responsibility is to let Josie and everyone else in your network know that you are available for a job and that you have particular skills that their organization can use.

The process of alerting your network to your goals and availability is a great way to start your job search. It is an opportunity to practise your sales skills before you get to the interview. Here are some ways to get started.

## Alerting Your Network

For Chapter 5, you spent some time learning how to make contact with people to discuss jobs and occupations. Hopefully, you have made contacts. Those people are bona fide members of your network now. You are a member of their network as well and, as such, you can rely on one another for information or assistance when necessary.

At this point in your job search, it is important that all the people in your existing network are aware that you are seeking employment. Not just any job, though. Uncle John down at the automotive plant might know about an opening that is coming up in maintenance. That doesn't mean that you are qualified or interested in it. Uncle John also may know someone in design at the same plant. If design is an area in which you have an interest, it is up to you to let Uncle John know that he can help you.

Contacting some people in your network may feel easier than contacting others. Friends and family members are usually easy to contact because they are accessible and often happy to assist you. So start with those calls first as they are also important ones. Make your intentions clear to everyone you contact. Don't take for granted that they will automatically understand what you want from them.

When calling someone in your network, have a statement prepared that declares your request in a straightforward manner. First, let them know you are looking for a job and you need their assistance. Then, describe your skills and the job you are seeking. And most importantly, let them know what they could do for you that would help. It might not always be obvious, so be as specific as you can.

The following are some examples you can use for each of these steps:

1.  You are looking for a job:
    ◆   "I'll be graduating in June and I'm starting to look for a job."
    ◆   "I've decided to make some changes, and my career is one of the things I'm thinking of changing."
    ◆   "I'm eager for a chance to do something that's related to my training so I'm looking for a new job."

2.  Why the person might be in a position to help:
    ◆   "You work in the field I'm interested in and probably hear about things before anyone else."
    ◆   "I enjoyed working with you at the plant and thought you might know what's happening in the field."
    ◆   "You were a big help to me before, and I am hoping that you might be in a position to help me again."

3.  What skills you bring to the job:
    ◆   "I have a good background in engineering with special skills in the use of AutoCAD."
    ◆   "I've written ad copy for a number of local firms and have had some experience in public relations."

4.  What the person can do for you:
    ◆   "Can I use your name as a reference?"
    ◆   "Have you heard of any jobs that might be available at your company? Do you know someone specific I could contact about a job? Could I use your name when I contact that person?"

Just as you did in Chapter 5, compile a comprehensive list of people who could help you. Then get on the phone and let them know you need them to be your eyes and ears in your job hunt. The most valuable help you can receive is information about a possible opening and whom you might contact. Any help at all can be a welcome advantage over your competition.

## Accepting Support

For some job seekers, asking for help from the people in their network causes great anxiety and discomfort. Sometimes asking someone you know for assistance is more difficult than asking a stranger.

You learned in Chapter 5 that using the telephone to contact people can result in obtaining valuable information about occupations and organizations. The process of networking for a job is similar. You are not asking for a job. You are recruiting the people in your network to provide you with support through information, referrals, and clues to leads. Most people will be open to helping with this. When the time comes, you will provide the same support to someone else, whether it is the person who helped you or someone new. Anyone who provides information to someone that results in a job offer will likely have a favour returned to them at some time in the future. The network continually renews itself through everyone's efforts. Now it's your opportunity to become a part of a network that could be a continuing asset in your career for many years.

# Job Search

You are ready to throw yourself into a full pledged job search. You have informed all your initial contacts and may have been able to generate some leads from that effort. In what other ways can you market yourself and find job leads?

The most important aspect of marketing yourself is constantly being on the lookout for an opportunity to sell your skills. Every person you encounter during this time is a potential source of information and referral. Let everyone you meet, even through a chance encounter, know what you are looking for. Every time you leave your home is an opportunity to extend your network a bit further.

The newspaper can be a good source for finding job leads; however, you need to go beyond the want ads. Read the paper from front to back looking for any information that could lead you to your future employment. An article that mentions a company's new contract, a promotion, or the expansion of an organization can be a clue that the company will soon need to hire. This becomes an opportune time to make contact and submit an application.

Also, go back to the resources you accessed in Chapter 4. Look at the directories in the library that detail information about companies in your field of interest. As you will recall, these directories offer job seekers information about companies that provide a host of employment opportunities. Local resources such as the Chamber of Commerce and the Yellow Pages can also be valuable in your exploration of the job market. Specialized publications such as *The Career Directory* and the *Canada Student Employment Guide* focus on a wide range of information about companies and sources for leads.

## Want Ads, Job Banks, and Career Fairs

Many people use the want ads as their primary source for finding a job. It is estimated that up to 90% of job seekers apply to these ads even though they only represent about 10% to 20% of the jobs available. Using these traditional methods of finding employment is an adequate start; however, you should also include any other avenues you can.

At first glance, the ads can seem to offer a wealth of possibilities. However, there will be many people applying for these positions, and you have no way of knowing with whom you are competing. Also, with most ads, you have no way of knowing who will read your résumé. This is especially true when the ad asks that you send your résumé to a box number. Be wary about applying to ads that are vague about who will be receiving your résumé. At the very least, the ad should include the name of the business or organization. Using what you know about researching businesses and organizations, this will at least provide you with a starting point for checking out their legitimacy. You may also be able to acquire a phone number and the name of a contact person with whom you can follow up.

Sometimes ads that seem to describe you to a T will be the ones you enthusiastically write to but never hear from. Other times, jobs that seem like a long shot will be the ones for which the employers are dying to interview you. Do try everything.

Job banks may be useful if they are available where you live. HRSDC offers job banks at each of its offices. The jobs are also posted online at **jb-ge.hrdc-drhc.gc.ca.** Here you can search not only jobs in your local area but also those available in other parts of Canada. The site allows you to search by occupation, to search all jobs posted in the previous 48 hours, or to search specifically for jobs for students. There are also links to tools for building a résumé and for getting e-mails regarding new job postings.

Organizations such as hospitals, government agencies, public utilities, school boards, and colleges and universities frequently offer recorded message lines or information on their human resources Web sites that list positions that are available and how to apply. Some private businesses and organizations also do the same.

Many colleges and universities also offer career services offices. Using these services may be something you should consider as part of your search strategy. There are companies that rely heavily on university and college career services offices for referrals and résumés. Register for services and discuss the particulars of your search with the professionals there. Become familiar with the referral system and take full advantage of whatever information is available. The advisors are not in a position to "place" you in a job. However, take their advice and support seriously, and remember that you are responsible for your own success.

A more recent development is the rise of the career fair as a job-seeking tool. These events are typically focused on a particular career emphasis such as occupations in health care or information technology, for example. A career fair is essentially a sales pitch from employers with immediate openings seeking potential employees with hard-to-find skills. During the career fair, organization representatives meet and greet job seekers and present the organization's opportunities. They often screen candidates for possible consideration and, in some cases, may schedule interviews on the spot. If you are planning to attend a career fair, dress as you would for an interview. Bring several copies of your résumé for distribution and be prepared to answer a few cursory questions as part of the screening process. Smile warmly, shake hands firmly, and try to stay fresh through the repetitious ritual of meeting each human resources professional.

At some point you may consider working with a placement agency. If you decide to pursue this avenue, do so with your eyes wide open. The people with placement agencies generally work on a contingency basis. That is, they find people for jobs, not jobs for people, and they are paid only if they deliver. Your value to them is related to how much money they can make placing you in a job. An interview with an agency person will probably be congenial since the person never knows when an employer might call and need exactly the skills you have. Don't be disappointed if you don't hear from agencies. They will call you only if an employer has called them first. If they make the placement and charge their fee, your worth could be as much as 30% more than if you had called the employer yourself. You might be better off forgoing the services of a placement agency and marketing yourself directly to the employer.

## Internet Resources

Today it may be easier than ever to market yourself directly to employers, thanks to the networks that link computer users around the world. Depending on the career you wish to establish, the type of job you are seeking, and the geographical parameters you set for your job search, the use of Internet resources may be invaluable for you.

The key issue that may determine the extent of your use of electronic resources is access to the Internet. If you do not have a home computer with Internet access, visit your local public library or your college or university library. Libraries usually provide free Internet access. Also, librarians are very skilled at searching the Internet and will be able to help you scrutinize Web sites and reach reliable and useful resources.

With the number of career and employment Web sites currently available for review, you will probably have no trouble finding Internet sources. The real problem will be conducting your search wisely so as to avoid wading through information that is useless.

As described in Chapter 4, using Internet search engines and directories can be a quick way to find Web sites with the information you need. While there may be technical differences in what the various search engines cover, the process is similar for each. The key factor is narrowing your search to yield productive information. There are two approaches that can serve your needs.

1. *Search for specific sites*: Whether you are researching employers or seeking job postings, you can find specific sites that are dedicated to single subject areas. This requires that you choose key words that adequately narrow your search. The best approach is to take a few minutes and review the suggestions offered by the search engines themselves to help you narrow your search. Sometimes something as simple as phrasing ("all X not XY") will limit your search to more useful sources.

2. *Search for sites with links*: There are sites that offer links to other sources that can be equally valuable even though your original search might not have located them. This allows you to go to one site and then skip back and forth between your original site and the related sites offered by links. The downside of this type of search is, again, you end up with much more than you need or can use.

Many Canadian companies and professional associations have their own Web sites where they post job openings. These sites can easily be accessed by searching under the company name. However, if you are not sure of the company name or if you wish to avoid the one-by-one process of searching each employer's site individually, there are Web sites that provide links to employers' Web pages. For example, the Job Bus Canada Web site provides links to hundreds of Canadian employers' Web sites. Job Bus Canada has sorted the various Web sites into categories such as advertising, communications, tourism and hospitality, publishing and translation, and more. By searching the specified category, you will be able to link to various employers in that field. Job Bus Canada also allows you to perform quick searches using key words, and it provides a link to Web sites that offer job postings. These include Campus Work Link, Monster.ca, Canadajobs.com, and about 60 others.

There are many resources available to you through the Internet that allow you access to electronic "help wanted" ads quickly and conveniently. Using conventional methods, you would need to search through dozens of newspapers from all over the country to achieve this. Furthermore, many of these sites also allow you to download your résumé either to companies or to résumé distribution services as a way of advertising your availability and/or responding to openings. If you think this service may be of use to you, you must do some research. There may be résumé distribution networks and resources available specifically for individuals in your field. A good source of reference for electronic distribution will be the professional organization affiliated with the discipline to which you belong.

New ways of applying the world of computer information systems to the field of job search are constantly and quickly evolving. Some career services offices now offer employers interactive online services that allow human resources professionals to access résumés. Computer-assisted interviewing is also becoming more common. The potential for the development of new systems to assist both employers and job seekers seems unlimited. Your challenge is to keep informed about the latest in information technology innovations so you can take advantage of every job search tool available to you.

Nevertheless, computer resources, searching jobs online, and distributing your résumé electronically are not a complete substitute for a conventional job search. While these resources offer you as the job seeker access to a far greater number of employers than you would be able to reach using conventional methods, they also offer employers access to a greater number of applicants. This could potentially increase the competition for a job, which could be a disadvantage. Furthermore, while increasing the number of applicants might appeal to some employers, it might discourage others from posting positions online. Many employers do not have the time, resources, or maybe even the skills necessary to adequately screen hundreds of applicants. For this reason, they may prefer other means for advertising and hiring. Therefore, it is worthwhile for you to exhaust all job search methods available to you, including the Internet, job banks, want ads, and career fairs. You may find that you will be most successful in finding employment by marketing yourself and accessing the hidden job market through networking.

# Expanding Your Network

Now that you have activated your network, you can begin to expand it to include those people and organizations that might be in a position to hire you. Some of the people you contact might have been leads you obtained through others in your network. Others might be people of whom you are aware from newspaper articles, directories, Chamber of Commerce publications, or the Yellow Pages. All leads have two things in common: They are in a position to assist you, and they do not know you.

Your challenge is to reach out to each of these people to enlist them into your network. There are two basic ways to accomplish this. The first is by letter or e-mail by which you attempt to persuade the person to contact you to discuss possible employment opportunities. This method can be productive, but people typically get responses from only 1% to 2% of those contacted. That means you must send out 100 letters or e-mails to get one or two calls. To boost the possibility of results, you can include a line at the end letting the person know that you will be contacting him or her on a particular date at a particular time to follow up. You might get a few more interviews this way, so be sure to follow up with the phone call as promised and not squander that lead.

Perhaps a more productive method is to make contact by telephone. Think back to the example of Matteo, the desperate accounting supervisor. Suppose Josie tells him that she doesn't know anyone who can help him. Just as she leaves his office, the phone rings. You are calling to tell him that you are graduating soon. You are skilled in corporate accounting and tax work and would like to schedule an appointment with him. Not only might Matteo be willing to give you an interview, he'll probably also consider you an exceptional candidate based on your skills, initiative, and self-confidence. You might be surprised to know that obtaining a job this way happens regularly to people who use these methods. This approach can be successful for you if you know who to call and what to say.

## Who to Call

First, in order to be successful it is important to know who to call. It may not always be the best route to contact the human resources department. The people there may not necessarily know details about relevant job vacancies. Just as you did in connection with Chapter 5, contact the person who works in the field that you wish to enter. It is best to contact the person who will be doing the hiring directly. Usually, this is not done by personnel in the human resources department. Rather, the human resources personnel will collect the applications and pass them on to the people who will be screening, interviewing, and hiring. These people will have more information about current or future job availability. They might also be more eager to meet you. If you do well in the interview, you will then meet the human resources personnel whose responsibility it will be to help you fill out the paperwork necessary to hire you.

Smaller businesses and organizations might not have a human resources department. In this case, research the business just as you would with a larger corporation. Find out who does the hiring: Does the owner hire or are there managers who are responsible for hiring? Don't ignore small businesses as a viable means of employment. More and more people are becoming self-employed and operating small businesses, and it has long been recognized that small businesses are responsible for providing most of the job growth in Canada. Working alongside a small business owner can also provide you with an opportunity to take on various roles and responsibilities, get close personal training, and learn about running a small business first hand. This could be a valuable learning experience if your goal is also to start your own small business one day.

The most difficult part of a telephone campaign is picking up the phone the first time. With each successive call it becomes easier. That brings us to the second factor for success. You must know what to say.

## What to Say

Just as in the networking process discussed in Chapter 5, approach potential leads and employers with forethought and preparation. Although a large percentage of these people may not have an immediate opening, they might have an interest in you. Attract their interest by telling them immediately what your skills and qualifications are and what you can do for their business. Convey your enthusiasm without being aggressive.

Ask if you could drop by for a brief chat about opportunities at their business or organization. Many of the people you contact by phone will tell you right away that they don't have anything available. That's okay. Then you can ask if you can submit a résumé to be kept on file in case anything comes up unexpectedly, or if you can contact them again in a month or so. If you call again in a month, they will likely remember you and may even appreciate your interest, persistence, and enthusiasm. At this point, they might be more inclined to meet with you. If not, you might ask if they are aware of anyone who is looking to hire. Even a telephone call that doesn't result in an interview can offer you useful information.

The most important part of contacting people for job leads is to mention your specific skills related to the field. If the people you contact have an opening, they will begin to probe your background and ask questions. That is when you will know there is a potential opportunity. Grab it and start your heavy-duty marketing right there. It could be the first step in the interview process.

Employers will frequently request a résumé or ask you to call back at another time. Sometimes this is to put people off, but other times it may be simply because they are busy even though they may be sincerely interested in you. In these cases, it is essential that you stay organized and follow up. Call again as they requested or follow up after you send your résumé and they have had time to review it. Offer any additional information and request a time to meet to discuss your qualifications in person. Even if the person doesn't offer you an interview, see if you can get feedback about your résumé or a referral to another source. Be polite, persistent, and flexible, and you will be gratified with the results.

You need to stay organized to keep up with when and where your interviews are, and who is awaiting your résumé, a follow-up call, or a thank-you letter. Use your index cards or your Occupation Information Data Sheets to keep your job search organized and to record each contact you have made and the results of your calls. To market yourself effectively, try to make at least 10 calls each day to people who might be in a position to hire you or give you useful information.

It may sound like you will spend a lot of time on the phone if you make 10 calls a day. In reality, if you apply yourself to the task, it should take no more than 45 minutes to an hour. One especially effective way to ensure that you actually make the calls is to work with a partner in job seeking. Make a commitment to meet with your partner every morning in a private place where you won't be interrupted. Take turns making calls until each of you has completed your 10 calls for the day. Monitor each other's calls, encouraging your partner when the calls are not going well and celebrating when you get results. By the end of the first week, you should be booked with interviews that will keep you busy. Don't stop making calls, however. Continue until you have a firm job offer in hand.

Anyone who is in sales will tell you that persistence is the greatest predictor of success. Your willingness to keep calling will have a greater impact on your success than any amount of luck. Make the 10 calls. There is an old saying: "If breaking a rock takes hitting it 10 times, you don't want to stop on the ninth time." Don't give up on the ninth call or the second or the fifth. Keep calling. There are bound to be disappointments. Don't dwell on the calls that end quickly. You're well prepared and will be successful as long as you keep trying.

# Being a Resource to Someone Else

Now that you have experienced what it feels like to pick up the phone and persuade someone to give you their time and consideration, you can hardly go back to the old assumptions about seeking employment. The techniques described here are becoming more accepted as part of an overall employment strategy. The chances are very good that at some time in the future you may get a call very much like the ones that you placed. If you are looking for someone to fill a spot in your organization, you might welcome the call. If not, please remember your own experience and greet your job seeker graciously and with encouragement. Making calls requires a high level of confidence and courage for job hunters. Your support will help them continue to pursue their goals.

# Tatsuro's Story

Tatsuro was nearing the end of his rope. He had been looking for a job ever since he graduated in June but had been unsuccessful. It was almost February now and he was still looking for a job. His family and friends were trying to be supportive, but he dreaded even telling them that he was sending out another résumé. The look of hope on their faces was almost worse than the disappointment that typically followed.

Tatsuro paid regular visits to the career services office at the college from which he had graduated. He decided maybe it was time to talk with an advisor at the college to find out what else he could do to get something going. He was beginning to feel like a failure.

The career services office set up an appointment for Tatsuro with Don, an advisor who was in charge of on-campus recruiting. Tatsuro was encouraged. Surely Don would know somebody who would offer him a job, a job that nobody else knew about so he would have a good shot at it.

Don was understanding about Tatsuro's frustration but he wasn't aware of any "secret" jobs. He reassured Tatsuro that he was not the only person who was having a hard time. Many graduates were struggling to get their careers started. Then he asked, "What have you done to find a job, Tatsuro?" Tatsuro replied, "The usual. You know, read the ads, filled out some applications, gone on a few interviews. Same as everybody else."

Don felt that Tatsuro had some excellent skills to market but was having difficulty distinguishing himself from the mass of available candidates. His primary obstacle was not that he didn't have anything to offer but that he wasn't marketing his skills effectively. Don encouraged Tatsuro to focus on one or two primary skills that set him apart from the competition. With Don's help, Tatsuro revised his résumé to highlight those skills better.

Don also pushed Tatsuro to take a more active role in finding a job. He suggested that Tatsuro register for a job-seeking partner, someone like Tatsuro, who was facing the same challenges and would act as a support person. In return, Tatsuro would do the same for his partner.

Later in the week, Tatsuro attended an orientation session that explained how to develop contacts using the Internet, what to say when calling, and how to organize a job search. He also met Ravinder, who had graduated in December and was just starting his search. Even though Ravinder was looking in a different field, they decided to work together at finding jobs. Ravinder thought he could learn from Tatsuro's experiences and Tatsuro thought Ravinder's energy would keep him motivated.

Tatsuro and Ravinder decided to meet every other day at Ravinder's place to make their phone calls. On the days that they didn't make calls, they went to the library or checked other resources to develop new contacts. They also practised their role-playing and monitored each other's calls. By the end of their second week, Ravinder had an interview and a referral set up. Tatsuro reworked his opening statement, this time emphasizing the special skills the employer might want. By the end of the third week, Tatsuro had two interviews scheduled.

Tatsuro didn't stop there, though. He continued to monitor jobs through the placement centre, called friends, neighbours, and relatives, and followed the want ads. By April, Tatsuro had made countless telephone calls, followed up numerous leads, posted his résumé on the Internet, interviewed with a dozen employers, and had finally accepted a position as a human resources trainee with a company in a city 40 kilometres away. His experience in taking charge of his search had found him employment in his chosen field. It had also made him more confident and self-assured.

### TAKE A CLOSER LOOK

**8.1** Enlist Your Network's Support

During your initial contact with those in your network, let them know in exact terms what you believe their roles are. Choose your words thoughtfully. Your statement should cover the following four issues:

1. The fact that you are looking for a job.
2. Why the person might be in a position to help.
3. What skills you bring to the job.
4. What the person can do for you.

Use the following space to develop a statement for someone you will contact in your network.

**NETWORKING STATEMENT**

_____

_____

_____

_____

This statement will change depending on the person with whom you are talking and what that person might be able to do for you. Work on perfecting your delivery in a calm, self-assured manner. Remember, your current network of friends, family, acquaintances, and work associates will be the easy ones. Take advantage of this type of networking contact to see what it feels like to "sell yourself" both in person and over the phone.

*Try the statement out with a partner in your group or the class and then discuss how it might feel to ask for someone's assistance.*

## TAKE A CLOSER LOOK
### 8.2 Generating Interviews

Fill in the blanks in the following dialogue to practise your telephone campaign:

Operator:   Good morning. This is _____.

You:   Good morning. Could you please give me the name of your _____ manager?

Operator:   Yes, that would be _____.

You:   May I speak with _____?

Manager:   _____ speaking.

You:   Good morning, Mr./Ms. _____. My name is _____. I am highly skilled in the areas of _____, and I am wondering if _____ _____.

Manager:   I'm sorry but we don't have anything right now.

You:   _____

Manager:   _____

You:   _____

Manager:   _____

You:   Thank you for your help. Goodbye.

*Try out your telephone role-play with your partner in your group or in the class. Practise it until you are sure of what you are going to say and then discuss the results with your group or the class.*

## TAKE A CLOSER LOOK
### 8.3 The Mini Job Search

Using the resources mentioned throughout this book—Yellow Pages, directories, professional organizations, Internet sources, newspapers, etc.—develop a list of 10 new contacts. Using the following information categories, make up a form or spreadsheet to track your job search.

COMPANY _____

ADDRESS _____

PHONE _____

E-MAIL _____

CONTACT PERSON _____

OUTCOME _____

FOLLOW-UP _____

If you are ready to start your job search, use the prior role-play exercise, develop the list, and try to arrange interviews. Work with a partner and conduct a mini job search using all the techniques to market yourself. Keep track of your results, your thoughts, and your experiences.

*Discuss with your group or the class how you developed this new list of contacts and your experience at your mini job search.*

---

## TAKE A CLOSER LOOK
### 8.4 Pulling It All Together

This exercise looks at your overall job-search strategy.

What are your top three skills that an employer would find most useful in the work setting?

1. _____

2. _____

3. _____

Does your statement to the people in your network highlight these skills? Are you clear about what you need from your contact?

_____ Yes                    _____ No

Does your statement to a potential employer focus on these top three skills?

_____ Yes                    _____ No

A referral can be valuable in your job search. Does your telephone inquiry mention your interest in other opportunities that might be available?

_____ Yes                    _____ No

What resources have proven to be most valuable in providing you with contacts?

_____ Current network     _____ Job banks        _____ Internet

_____ Directories         _____ Placement office  _____ Other

_____ Newspaper           _____ Telephone book

What system of organization works best for you?

_____ Index cards                    _____ Organizing calendars

_____ Occupation Information Data Sheet   _____ Forms

_____ Electronic organizer

*Have your calls generated any interviews? If not, what part of your approach needs work?*

---

## A Look Back

The responsibility you assume for your success is the most important aspect of your career development. The methods described in this chapter are your key to open any door—for referrals, networking support, Internet links, or interviews. The critical factor in using these methods successfully is knowing the people or resources to contact and knowing what to say. Emphasizing your skills and probing for referrals will create opportunities that result in job offers. Persistence in pursuing leads will have more impact on your future than relying on outside agencies and newspaper ads. This chapter has described ways to make your job search a comprehensive, all-out marketing campaign that will take you where you want to go.

## Other Sources and Suggested Reading

*Canada Student Employment Guide: The Definitive Tool for a Successful Job Search in Canada* by Student Employment Network
This book is a directory of major employers across Canada. Through interviews with human resources departments, the authors have described characteristics that employers deem important in selecting their employees.

*The Canadian Internet Job Search Guide: An Essential Guide to Finding a Job Using the Internet* by Kevin Makra
This book profiles over 400 different Web sites that address employment topics. The authors have reviewed the Web sites and listed the "best" employment sites. The sites are also listed by categories.

*The Complete Job-Search Handbook* by Howard Figler
Figler covers every aspect of the job search. His section on "The Prospect List" is especially noteworthy.

*Get That Interview! The Indispensable Guide for College Grads* by R. Theodore Moock, Jr.
A good resource if you are interested in getting the most out of every resource available: direct mail, Internet, networking, and college career centres.

*Where the Jobs Are: Career Survival for Canadians in the New Global Economy* by Colin Campbell
This book explores the worldwide job market for Canadians by identifying industries with the best long-term prospects and where the best job prospects are located, both locally and globally.

## Web Sites and Internet Resources

**www.kwantlen.ca/library/Internet/job.html**
The librarians at Kwantlen University College have created a very useful job search Web page. They have evaluated Web sites for their usefulness and reliability and have listed them in categories related to every step of the career-exploration process. There are sites listed for choosing a career, education and training, job search, labour market, self-employment, work and study outside of Canada, and sites specific to First Nations people, international students, and people with disabilities.

The following are some popular job search Web sites. Among other services, these sites allow users to search for jobs and post their résumés. Each one is slightly different and each posts different jobs.

**http://campus.workopolis.com**
**www.jobbus.com**
**monster.ca**
**www.workopolis.com**
**canadajobs.com**

# Chapter 9

# Designing Your Résumé and Cover Letters

## Communicating Your Skills and Abilities

*You miss 100% of the shots you never take.*

WAYNE GRETZKY

Consider the vision you have of the professional you would like to become. Your career is a route to realize that vision. However, in order to reach your career goals, you will need to effectively communicate your skills and abilities. Your résumé and its associated cover letters are the primary vehicles for introducing yourself to employers who can assist you in reaching your goals.

## Conveying Who You Are

A résumé is a business document created to help employers and job applicants talk about possible employment. It is expected to adhere to a standard of organization that is characteristic of most business documents. The trick is, however, to conform to those expectations and still present you as an individual. Your résumé should highlight the unique blend of skills and experiences that make you the ideal candidate for a position, while still respecting the conventions and expectations of the work world.

You control what information is included in your résumé. A well-crafted résumé emphasizes those aspects of your background that make you a serious competitor for a job. Because the labour market is a competitive place, there will be situations in which you compete against other well-qualified candidates. Designing a résumé that presents your abilities best will give you the necessary edge to be successful.

Various styles of résumés serve the needs of job seekers in different ways. Your challenge is to find a résumé style with which you feel comfortable. Ideally, it will allow you to describe your background in ways that suit the various opportunities available to you and also to convey your abilities competitively and honestly.

Once you decide which résumé style works best for you, then you can develop its content. The content must relay your background and qualifications while taking into account the needs of the specific employer.

Although you may develop a generic résumé, you will need to revise and adapt it each time you submit it. If you are applying for jobs within the same occupational field, it may not be necessary for you to make many changes to your résumé each time you apply for a job. However, it always makes a better impression if an employer sees that you have taken the time to tailor your résumé rather than mass-producing and distributing a generic résumé. By tailoring it to each specific job, you send a message that "I've prepared this just for you because this is the job I'm really going for."

# "Sure-Fire" Résumé

In any library or bookstore you will find a great number of manuals for preparing résumés. These manuals often advertise a set way to write résumés that "win" jobs—if you simply follow the formulas in the book. There are as many ways of writing résumés as there are résumé writers and, so far, the "sure-fire," guaranteed-to-get-you-a-job résumé does not exist.

There is only one résumé that will work best for you—the one you develop using information about your special combination of skills, abilities, training, education, experiences, and qualifications. Be conscious of the standard formats when developing your résumé, but know that any one style prescribed by a book can never take into account all of your needs for a particular situation.

The reason that résumé writing defies simplistic formulas is that résumé reading is highly subjective. If you show your résumé to 10 different people, some may think it is perfect, some will suggest minor changes, and others may suggest substantial revisions. Depending on the circumstances, any or all of them may be correct. People in charge of hiring apply their personal preferences and idiosyncrasies when evaluating résumés. Trying to predict how a particular employer will respond is nearly impossible.

The only logical way to create your résumé is to be able to identify and describe those aspects of your background that relate to the potential position and then select a style of résumé that showcases you and your abilities to your best advantage. The following section looks at different styles of résumés and what each style offers job seekers. You might try developing your résumé using one of these styles, or perhaps a combination of styles.

# Résumé Styles

Almost all résumé formats and variations can be categorized under one of three résumé styles: chronological, functional, or achievement/accomplishment.

## Chronological Résumé

The résumé style with which most people are familiar is the chronological résumé. This résumé focuses primarily on work experience and presents your background in reverse chronological order. This means that you list your most recent job position first and work backward from there. Generally speaking, it is usually suggested that the résumé only list jobs going back about 10 years. This is particularly true if one has had many jobs with much experience in the field. On the other hand, if you have been in the same position for 10 or more years, this might not work for you. Instead, you could also describe positions you held before that and/or emphasize the various duties and responsibilities you held while in the long-term job.

At the top of the résumé page is where you place your objective. This is where you list and describe the job for which you are applying, and all of the information that follows on the résumé should be relevant to your stated objective.

The chronological style is excellent if you are seeking employment in a field in which you have an established and a successful track record. Most employers prefer the chronological résumé style since the focus is on your work history, the factor they consider most relevant. The emphasis on work experience presents your background in a way that helps the employer visualize you in that position. The format shows a natural progression of increasing responsibility and growth. The chronological résumé in Figure 9.1 illustrates how this style enhances the candidate's appropriateness for the job.

Emphasizing your work experience may work well if you have a strong background in the field to which you are applying, but this technique is less effective if you don't have much prior experience. If you have little or no employment history or your employment has been primarily in one particular industry, it may be more difficult for an employer to see you as a serious professional in another field. You may have an excellent academic record, plenty of organizing experience from volunteer projects, and maybe even co-op experience; however, if you use a chronological résumé that highlights only your work at an unrelated occupation, you may project that you are unqualified for the new position you are applying for. With this type of résumé, you need to be careful that the information demonstrating your qualifications does not get buried under loads of irrelevant data.

Work experience unrelated to the job you currently seek is not totally irrelevant, however. Steady employment of any type speaks well of you as an applicant and, more importantly, identifies skills that could benefit future employers. The key is to learn to identify and describe those skills using the appropriate format. It is critical that your first presentation to a potential employer establish an image that matches the employer's needs and assumptions about the job needing to be filled. The goal of your résumé is to make the connection between yourself and the employer's vision of the skills needed to fill the job, as different as they might be from what you have done in the past. You will need to decide which style best accomplishes this, the chronological, functional, or achievement/accomplishment styles.

## Functional Résumé

The functional résumé highlights the skills and abilities of the job seeker rather than the settings in which the person obtained those skills. It allows you to describe those aspects of yourself that make you the ideal candidate for a job and takes the focus off of less relevant work experience, changes in jobs, or long periods out of work. Its focus is on describing you rather than your work history. This makes it an ideal résumé for the midlife career changer or someone with limited work experience in the field.

**The Chronological Résumé**

# Julia Moore

315 Cedar Street
Winnipeg, MB
R2L 101

(204) 658-9341
jmoore@netlink.net

**Objective**  To obtain a management position as an accounting professional.

**Qualifications Summary**  Accounting professional with broad range of experiences. Strong background in computer accounting applications

**Professional Experience**

1999 to present   Basic Printing, Inc., Winnipeg, MB

*Accounting Assistant*
Responsible for assisting controller in performance of accounting functions, including posting journal entries, general ledger, forecasting, and accounts payable/accounts receivable; some tax experience
- Specialized Skills: Microsoft Excel/Word, Windows, Accounting Software

1994 to 1999   Hawkins' Lithography, Winnipeg, MB

*Accounting Clerk*
Responsible for posting to general ledger and journal entries
Work with automated accounts system

**Education**  University of Manitoba, Winnipeg, MB
Graduated 2001, Bachelor of Commerce
Accounting Major (GPA: 3.6)

**Special Achievements**  1995 Recipient, "Leaders of Tomorrow" Scholarship
Dean's Honour List

**Extracurricular Activities**  Member, Accounting Club, 1996–2001
University of Manitoba Alumni Association

**Figure 9.1** The Chronological Résumé

The functional résumé may seem to be the perfect résumé format since it focuses on the skills relevant to the position you seek. While it is typically an excellent format for anyone trying to enter an occupation in which they have little experience, it is not the best style for the job seeker who has a strong work background. The functional style simply doesn't offer the proper forum to show the depth of skill and career maturity that come from extended or relevant work experience. In addition, a list of your skills isn't a helpful sales tool if you have nothing in your background to establish how you obtained those skills. Related academic study is helpful, but most employers are skeptical that it can completely take the place of hands-on experience for developing a high level of proficiency in any field.

Figure 9.2 shows a sample functional résumé.

### Achievement/Accomplishment Résumé

The achievement or accomplishment résumé, sometimes referred to as the combination résumé, uses many of the same elements of the previous styles with one important difference. It uses actual events from prior experiences and training as the method for conveying information about you. This type of résumé provides the employer with the basics of your training and work life and also substantiates your skill through outlining your past accomplishments. Figure 9.3 illustrates one style of the accomplishment résumé.

As noted in Figure 9.3, the achievements associated with the work Raj is performing support the image that he is attempting to convey—that of a motivated self-starter capable of making the sale.

Every employer is interested in two aspects of your background:

1. *What you can do.* This is the skills and abilities aspect. Effectively communicating this lets the employer know what you are capable of contributing to the job.

2. *What you have done.* This is the "prove it" aspect. You may have the skills and abilities, but that may not be enough. Citing your achievements enhances your credibility. It is the most powerful and understated way of backing up what you claim to be able to do.

The functional and chronological formats are good vehicles for describing your skills and history but do little to establish the dynamic image conveyed by the achievement résumé. This type of résumé is especially beneficial to people with extensive experiential background who are facing particular career obstacles, such as job displacement through downsizing.

Practise building an achievement résumé as it is a good way to quantify your accomplishments. Even if you choose to use a different form of résumé, this exercise will come in handy at your interviews where you will verbally discuss your skills and abilities. Everyone has accomplishments that can be quantified. In a later exercise you will have the opportunity to generate ideas for listing accomplishments and achievements.

# The Right Style for You

The style of résumé you choose is largely determined by the type of position for which you are applying. If the position is in a field in which you have a significant

The Functional Résumé

# David Muñoz

654 Walnut Drive
Vancouver, BC
V2Z 1W1

(604) 465-5729
dmunoz@telus.net

| | |
|---|---|
| **Summary** | Seasoned self-starter able to create opportunities and make the sale seeks a position in sales and marketing |
| **Skills and Abilities** | • Recognized abilities in all areas of market forecasting<br>• Knowledgeable in marketing aspects of product development<br>• Practised in developing sales leads and creating interest<br>• Well-developed organizational skills<br>• Able to make the sale; strong closer |
| **Education** | Kwantlen University College, Surrey, BC<br>Graduated 2004<br>Bachelor of Business Administration in Entrepreneurial Leadership<br>GPA: 3.4 |
| **Awards and Achievements** | President's List, 2001, 2002<br>Member, National Honour Society |
| **Work Experience** | The Ski Shop, Vancouver, BC<br>Retail Salesperson for sporting equipment, 2000 to present<br><br>Hale's Quick Stop Photos, Burnaby, BC<br>Customer service and sales for photo development outlet, 1998 to 2000 |
| **Extracurricular Activities** | Volunteer, United Way, Special Funds Committee Member<br>Western Youth Entrepreneur Program<br>(Vancouver, British Columbia) |

**Figure 9.2** The Functional Résumé

amount of experience, you may wish to use the chronological style. It will meet the employer's expectations and highlight your strengths in the field.

If you are trying to enter a new occupational field or looking for your first job, you may want to consider the functional style. This style shines a bright light where it belongs, on your ability to do the job, not on the places where you developed your ability. If you can identify events in your life that you feel are noteworthy and will make you an appealing candidate for a position, then the achievement résumé is probably the résumé style for you.

As we proceed through the various phases of developing a résumé, you will see how you can integrate elements of each format based on specific situations to give your résumé a customized look. You can custom design your résumé simply by shuffling the various components to suit the specific needs of the job you seek. It is a good idea to keep an updated copy of your résumé on your computer hard drive and on diskette so that you can quickly and easily revise your résumé when needed.

When deciding which style of résumé to use, ask yourself, "What are my strongest qualifications for the job?" Your answer, whether it relates to academic skill, technical training, or work experience, will help you determine which style will present you in the best light.

Once you have decided on a résumé style, begin to focus on developing the content for your résumé.

# Developing Content for Your Résumé

What information should you include in (or exclude from) your résumé? Remember, you want to create a picture with words, which lets the employer imagine you in the job for which you're applying. Think about the following two questions:

◆   What skills are needed to do the job for which I am applying?

◆   What experiences and training have I had that match those skills?

One other aspect to consider when writing your résumé is that human resources professionals at large companies may scan résumés and store them in computer files in an effort to control paper flow. When résumés are later retrieved, they are often called up according to certain key words; for example, if a company conducts a search based on the criteria of "engineering, mechanical, automotive," the first résumés to be retrieved will be those that meet all criteria, next, those that meet most but not all, and so on.

Key words that describe the parameters of the job to be filled may determine whose résumé is read and whose remains in database limbo. Thus, depending upon the type of job you seek and the companies to which you apply, you may need to prepare yourself for a job search on two levels—one for people and one for electronic resources. Until now, the goal has always been to get someone to read your résumé in order to get a shot at an interview. Now, at some firms your résumé won't even be read unless it is developed with a clear understanding of the position you want. That requires some thoughtful work on the content of your résumé.

If you are just beginning a new career, you probably will not have had any positions that relate directly to the job you're seeking. That's nothing to be

# RAJ SINGH

733 Elm Street
Toronto, ON
M5J 7E4

(416) 233-1562
rajsingh@aol.com

**OBJECTIVE**

To obtain a marketing position with an up-and-coming retailer

**SUMMARY OF QUALIFICATIONS**

Skilled sales/customer service professional able to anticipate and respond to customer needs; technical sales orientation

**ACCOMPLISHMENTS**

- Increased sales volume with two major grocery wholesalers by over 30%
- Received Outstanding Quarterly Sales Representative Award three times in one year
- Developed team approach to marketing product with local store managers

**EXPERIENCE**

**Charlie's Chocolate Factory**
Toronto, ON
Sales Representative, July 2000 to present

Responsible for service and expansion of major wholesale accounts in the Toronto area

Coordinate corporate promotions and advertising campaign through wholesalers

Negotiate ad rates and charges

Monitor use of displays, product samples, pricing, distribution, and warehouse inventory

**EDUCATION**

**Niagara College, Ontario**

Ontario College Advanced Diploma

in Business Administration—Marketing

Completed June 2000 with 3.0 GPA

**SPECIAL ACTIVITIES**

**Volunteer, Small Business Development Centre**

Toronto Office

Assisted small business owners in various development activities, including creating employee handbooks and developing and presenting training

**Figure 9.3** The Achievement/Accomplishment Résumé

discouraged about. Regardless of their setting, all jobs can be broken down into specific tasks. Focus on your experience and qualifications that most closely parallel the tasks and skills necessary for the job you seek. For example, perhaps you have an extensive background in retailing and customer service but would like to work in social services. By focusing on certain aspects of customer service, you can establish your qualifications for work in social services. Skills such as sensitivity to customer concerns, listening skills, and the ability to work under pressure contribute to your portfolio as a social services professional. Combine these skills with your academic background and you can begin to see that you have a strong foundation for a winning résumé.

The same process is equally effective for other disciplines. If your work experience has been in one area and you want to get started in another profession, focus on the skills that relate to your new job, regardless of their importance in your current role. It's what you are going to do with them that counts, not where you got them. If you already have paid experience in a field, you are halfway there. Use Exercise 9.1 at the end of the chapter as a way to find the parallels that will help you achieve your goal.

# Components of a Résumé

The six basic components of a résumé are the *identifiers*, the *summary or profile*, *skills, employment history or work experience, education or training,* and *related information*. Each of these components is examined in more detail in the following sections.

## Component 1: The Identifiers

The identifiers on your résumé are those parts that tell the employer your name and how you can be reached. While these are the most straightforward parts of the résumé, it is quite common for people to forget to include their phone numbers or to overlook a typographical error in their names. Be sure to carefully proofread your résumé to ensure there are no errors. Even the smallest items tell the employer much about your attention to detail and your ability to present yourself professionally.

A good rule to remember when seeking employment is that written responses are most often rejections but phone calls are usually invitations to an interview. That's why your correct phone number is critical. When you include the phone numbers where you can be reached, be sure that anyone answering the telephone at those places knows who you are and that a potential employer might be calling. Be sure that professionalism is maintained at all times. That is, avoid having loud background music when answering the phone or rude responses from anyone answering. It is worthwhile to have an answering machine or voice mail on your contact phones so that employers will not be frustrated by the inability to reach you. Be sure your outgoing voice message is clear, professional, and free of any "cute" devices, such as background music or funny sounds. If appropriate, you may also want to include your e-mail address and/or fax number on your résumé. Whether you give your home phone number, cell phone number, e-mail, or fax number, be sure you can be contacted. Check your messages regularly, and return calls promptly.

## Component 2: The Summary/Profile

The summary, or profile, component of a résumé is a statement about you, your background, and your strengths as they relate to the position you seek. It usually goes at the beginning of the résumé immediately following the identifiers. Some people still like to include the "objective" where they specify the position they are seeking. The summary/profile component evolved from the more traditional "objective." The use of a summary or profile statement accomplishes the same thing by focusing attention on your ability to do the job. You may choose to continue to include the objective or to eliminate it. However, the summary/profile should be included as it provides the employer with a useful synopsis of your skills and qualifications.

This component can be a valuable part of your résumé, but you must use it carefully. If your summary statement is vague or too general, you will not be providing useful information. Be sure that your statement is specific and memorable. For example, an all-purpose statement such as "A strong performer able to use my skills and abilities in any setting" is not very effective. People who begin their résumés with this type of statement would do better to exclude it altogether or to change it to a specific statement. An example of a more effective summary statement is, "Experienced customer service representative with excellent problem-solving and organizational skills with the ability to work in English and French."

A well-crafted summary or profile statement ideally should do three things:

1. Communicate that you are a thoughtful, mature individual with a clear idea of who you are and what you are able to do.

2. Briefly summarize your primary skills as they relate to the position, attract employers' interest in you as a potential employee, and encourage them to continue reading the rest of the résumé.

3. Assert your goals and commitment to growth.

Developing a summary or profile that accomplishes all of these things is not an easy task. Ideally, your profile, and your entire résumé, should be tailored for the specific job for which you are applying. That isn't always possible, however, especially if you are providing a résumé to be distributed by a third party such as an employment placement office. Nevertheless, in most cases, your résumé and its summary must correlate closely to the specific needs of the position in order to be competitive. For this reason, the summary is one of the components that might need to be slightly revised each time you submit your résumé. The requirements of the job you are applying for will determine how you frame your summary statement. Once you have fully developed the summary/profile, the rest of your résumé will fall into place.

## Component 3: Skills

Sometimes people with little paid experience find that résumé writing is just one long, discouraging exercise. They may have spent years preparing for their first job, but when they begin to summarize everything they've learned using conventional résumé formats, their background looks insignificant, hardly representative of their hard work and preparation. If this is true for you, then you will have better results emphasizing your skills over your paid experience.

A combination format that focuses on skills will allow you to flesh out your résumé using experiences from a variety of sources including part-time jobs, co-op and intern experiences, volunteer work, lab work, and/or classroom learning.

The skills component of your résumé is simply a series of statements that expand on the profile statement by describing in detail the abilities and qualifications that are suited to the position you seek. This section builds credibility for the statement with which you began the résumé. Here are a few examples.

"Knowledgeable in all aspects of tax compliance accounting"

"Strong written and verbal communication skills in both English and French"

"Skilled in Web design, HTML, and the use of JavaScript"

"Experienced in using scientific methods and observation"

"Able to read and implement architectural blueprints"

"Capable in full range of administrative and clerical skills"

As you develop a broader, deeper knowledge of your chosen field, you can expand this part of your résumé to reflect your increasing level of skill, citing specific buzzwords that not only identify you as a pro but also better flag your résumé for electronic search. These skills deserve to be highlighted in a special section. You have worked to acquire them so showcase them in a way that markets you effectively. Communicate them clearly and, like the summary, be specific. Don't assume that employers will take the time or the effort to "read between the lines" of your résumé. Instead, do the work for them; tell them clearly and specifically what qualifies you for the job.

## Component 4: Work Experience

Your employment history, or work experience, is a significant part of your résumé. Most employers will not consider someone a viable candidate without some knowledge of that person's employment background. If you have not already done so, it will benefit you to look for opportunities to acquire hands-on experience in your field. Part-time jobs, volunteer work, and co-op/internship positions are all fruitful areas for you to begin your experience and add to your résumé. When you detail your experience, mention where you worked, your job title, and how long you worked in that position. Remember, if you are competing for the chance to interview alongside people who have qualifications as strong as yours, strive to showcase your experience in a format that best highlights your capabilities.

Your prior employment can be divided into two aspects:

◆ *Your routine duties.* These were the responsibilities you were expected to fulfill on a daily basis. The particulars might be cut and dried and may sound at times like your job description.

◆ *Your accomplishments.* These are the high points of your work or academic life that serve as the basis of the achievement résumé. They usually reflect your unique combination of skills and abilities.

When you describe routine duties, try to use phrases and action words that convey a dynamic image. Words such as "designed," "managed," "organized," "supervised," "wrote," and "created" work better at establishing an active image than do words like "was responsible for" or "acted as." Figure 9.4 lists some of the

## Action Verbs

| | | | | | |
|---|---|---|---|---|---|
| activate | conceive | file | market | promote | revise |
| address | conceptualize | forecast | monitor | prove | schedule |
| administer | conduct | formulate | move | provide | select |
| allocate | contact | gather | negotiate | publicize | sell |
| approve | convert | generate | observe | purchase | service |
| arbitrate | coordinate | guide | obtain | question | set up |
| assemble | create | handle | operate | realize | shape |
| assess | cultivate | head | order | receive | ship |
| assist | decode | hire | organize | recommend | solve |
| attain | define | identify | originate | reconcile | speak |
| balance | design | illustrate | oversee | recruit | structure |
| bring about | dispense | implement | participate | refer | succeed |
| buy | display | improve | perform | refine | supervise |
| calculate | distribute | increase | persuade | regulate | supply |
| coach | edit | initiate | place | reorganize | test |
| collect | entertain | install | plan | repair | train |
| command | estimate | interview | prepare | report | update |
| communicate | evaluate | investigate | present | represent | upgrade |
| compile | examine | lead | process | research | validate |
| complete | explain | lecture | produce | resolve | verify |
| compute | facilitate | manage | program | review | write |

**Figure 9.4** Action Verbs

action verbs you might use in describing prior jobs and responsibilities. Keep in mind that you should use present tense for your current position and past tense (-ed) for prior jobs.

The task of a résumé is to get the employer's attention quickly and to keep it, so use short, concise statements, without pronouns and modifiers that may bog down your description. Succinct phrases do not need to be complete sentences. Accomplishments should include one brief statement highlighting the specific results you achieved.

In most cases, the experience component should include only jobs you have held within the last 10 years. Emphasize jobs and skills that are relevant to the job you're seeking. Mentioning relevant skills will ensure that your résumé is "grabbed" when the computer does a key word search if the employer is using an electronic database to store résumés. If a job you have held is not related to the field you're entering, omit or condense it. State only the basics, using one line to describe your duties. A statement such as, "Various customer-service-related duties" serves the purpose.

Look at the following example. The paragraph on experience is a concise overview of the person's responsibilities. The accomplishment statements tell the reader that the person was involved, responsible, and willing to go beyond what was expected to help the organization.

**Experience:**

Kremer's Supply, Inc., Halifax, Nova Scotia

Mail Clerk, December 1999 to present

Responsibilities include sorting and delivering mail to all personnel in company of over 150 employees; organizing and distributing packages and priority mail; arranging for overnight shipment of priority packages; delivering messages for executive personnel

**Accomplishments:**

- Supervised mail room duties when mail room manager was absent
- Reorganized mail sorting system resulting in approximate savings of $800 annually

The figure of $800 savings noted in the second accomplishment was developed by estimating the average amount of time saved on a weekly basis and multiplying it by the hourly rate of the employee. When extrapolated, the annual savings might be $800. Estimates and approximations are legitimate methods for calculating quantifiable results of an accomplishment.

## Component 5: Education/Training

When presenting your education, again, the key factor is whether the training you have had is relevant to the stated objective. Anything—university, college, seminars, workshops, on-the-job or private training—that is related to the objective is important to include in this component of your résumé. The format to present this information is quite flexible, and this example is only one of many possibilities:

**Education**

Certificate in Supervisory Development

University of Prince Edward Island, PEI

Completed June 2004

The basics of this component are the name of the institution from which you received your training, the location, the year you completed (or attended), and the type of training. You may also want to include your grade point average if applicable, but only if you have achieved a GPA of 3.0 or above; a lower GPA does not "show" well on a résumé. Some people also choose to offer a copy of their transcript or certificate, or to bring it to the interview.

If you have attended workshops or seminars related to your field, either on your own or through your job, include these under a subheading in this section of the résumé. You can choose to group these experiences either chronologically, providing dates, or under subject headings. A title such as "Additional Training" or "Seminar Training" suffices to indicate the education subcategory.

Some people have prior educational experiences or classes from one or two years of college that they want to include. Include only the information that you think will help you. For example, perhaps the time you spent involved in previous study explains a gap in your résumé. Note the institution, location, dates, and the type of study in which you engaged. A statement such as "Various

"...Hmmm... Under your favorite three activities: 'Hanging around Riverside Mall, hanging around Quail Run Mall and hanging around Chestnut Hill Mall.'"

business courses" offers enough pertinent information for the prospective employer.

If the training you received is not relevant to the goal of your job search, you risk hurting your chances of getting the job by including it. It is understandable that you would want to acknowledge your past efforts; however, sometimes unrelated information can detract from the vision you are trying to create. For example, if someone has been trained and worked as a truck driver but is now making a career change and seeking a job in risk management, inclusion of his or her prior training in truck driving school may not be helpful on the résumé. The history as a truck driver might be confusing and distracting to people who will be screening and hiring for the risk management job. Remember that it is not uncommon for there to be dozens or even hundreds of applications for a position. People who are screening résumés are typically looking for those that most closely fit the requirements of the position.

## Component 6: Related Information

The final component of your résumé is a section on related information. This section can include any information that doesn't fall under another component and further supports your appropriateness for the job. Included in this area would be:

◆ awards or scholarships you may have received

◆ extracurricular activities

◆ licences and certifications related to the field

◆ memberships or offices held in professional organizations

◆ published works

◆ community involvement

As in all the previous components, keep the focus on the skills, abilities, and experiences that directly relate to the employer's needs and to your objective. You might well be proud of your hobbies and outside activities, but employers' reactions might be considerably less enthusiastic, as you can see from the response of the employer in the cartoon.

# Appearance, Format, and Electronic Distribution

The overall appearance of your résumé is very important. First and foremost, the résumé must be easy to read and understand. Your résumé should be not only informative but also attractive and pleasing to the eye. Frame your résumé with margins wide enough to present the document as if it were a picture to be admired. It is best to use only one, or at most two, of the more traditional typefaces, such as Times New Roman or Courier. The use of upper case, underlining, italics, and boldface can add to a résumé's appeal. Use these functions systematically, yet conservatively. That is, if you underline job titles, for example, then don't also italicize them, and make sure that all job titles are in a similar style. Experiment with different highlights, and choose an attractive final format that emphasizes your qualifications. Be generous with white space—too much print is difficult to read and unappealing. Keep those screening your résumé interested by presenting the information in an eye-catching and welcoming style.

Generally, a résumé should be confined to one or two pages. Don't hesitate to use a two-page format if your details fill both pages in a balanced way. Details lend credibility to your résumé, and this may be especially appropriate if you have a strong experiential background. On the other hand, don't worry if you only come up with enough for one page. One strong page is better than two pages of "fluff." Aim for quality and not necessarily quantity.

Any word-processing software can be used to create your résumé. There are also résumé software packages available that allow you to use formatting tools to create a résumé and distribute it on the Internet. Some of the job search Web sites also offer these tools, tips, or examples of résumés. Your résumé can then be printed, e-mailed, or downloaded to a Web site database for distribution to possible employers.

Always use word processing to prepare your résumé and cover letter, don't even consider handwriting. If you do not have your own computer, use a friend's, the library's, or those available at quick print shops. Save your résumé so that you can easily revise it when necessary, and make a backup copy. Print your résumé on conservative white, ivory, buff, or light gray, high-quality bond paper and use a good quality laser printer for printing. Have it reproduced at a reputable copy shop on high-quality photocopiers so that the original résumé and its copies look identical. That is, one should not be able to tell that the résumés you send to employers are photocopies. Figure 9.5 provides a list of résumé writing do's and don'ts you can use as a reference.

Your résumé is a living document that should change as you grow and acquire new skills. Keep updating it, even while you are employed, because at all times it should be a current reflection of your skills, experiences, and accomplishments.

The next step is to write a persuasive cover letter.

## The Cover Letter

Once you have developed your résumé, the next step is to write its accompanying cover letter. The cover letter acts as your résumé's escort, and your résumé should never leave home without it. The cover letter is just as important as the résumé because it is what convinces the employer to read your résumé.

Just as it was previously suggested that you tailor your résumé to each job you apply for, you must also write a separate letter to each employer. This letter must convince the employer to review your résumé, interview you, and then discuss employment with you. A well-written cover letter follows a logical progression in each of its paragraphs:

Paragraph 1: Why I am writing to you (Introduction).

Paragraph 2: Who I am (Main Body).

Paragraph 3: What we have in common (Main Body).

Paragraph 4: We should get together (Conclusion).

## Résumé Do's and Don'ts

**Do:**

- Do gear your résumé to the job you are applying for and include all relevant experience and information.
- Do keep your résumé to a maximum of two pages.
- Do word process your résumé and use a laser printer. Photocopy onto good quality paper. Use black ink and the same type of paper for both your covering letter and résumé.
- Do make your résumé neat and orderly. Use point form and leave lots of white space.
- Do include as much information as you can, but keep it to the point and easy to read.
- Do send a cover letter with your résumé.

**Don't:**

- Don't use a title page, binders, or paper that is flashy or makes the résumé difficult to read.
- Don't overload your résumé. Keep it clear and concise.
- Don't make spelling or grammatical errors.
- Don't cross things out and hand write new information in. If you need to make changes, use a computer and reprint.
- Don't include the names of your references. Include a line such as "References available upon request" and bring your list of references to the interview.
- Don't include personal information such as marital status, social insurance number, or hobbies.
- Don't fold it into a small envelope. It is better to use a full-size 9 × 12 envelope. This will stand out from the other mail.

**Figure 9.5** Résumé Do's and Don'ts

If you follow this format and back it up with solid reasoning, you will increase your chance that the employer will clearly see your value as a serious candidate for the position. The cover letter in Figure 9.6 uses this traditional but effective approach. Each of the paragraphs in this letter contributes to the writer's goal of making a logical, persuasive presentation. In addition, the candidate takes every opportunity to refer to the attached résumé, further encouraging the employer to read on and consider him a serious candidate.

Tailoring a cover letter to the specifics of each job for which you apply is one way to ensure that you are doing everything you can to market yourself effectively. Every employer wants to believe that the job he or she is offering is the only one in which you are interested. Take advantage of this fact by paying careful attention to the job description. Address your letter to a specific person within the organization. If it becomes necessary for you to send your letter to a blind address, then use the salutation, "Dear Sir or Madam" rather than "To Whom It May Concern." (Never use just "Dear Sir"—it would rightly be interpreted as sexist.)

Again, cover letters are crucial. As with your résumé, consider having one or more people read/edit/proofread your cover letters. You may miss errors or awkward statements that others may catch. You will need a cover letter every time you send out your résumé, so take the time now to come up with a format that you can revise and fine-tune for specific jobs. Use the form provided in Exercise 9.6

**Sample Cover Letter**

1463 rue Drummond
Montreal, QC
H1N 1Y2

June 10, 2004

Ms. Rita Huss
The Vaughan Group, Inc.
45, boulevard Harwood
Montreal, QC
H3H 1H0

Dear Ms. Huss:

I am writing in response to your ad for the position of entry-level software designer, which appeared in the *Montreal Gazette* on June 5, 2004.

I am currently attending McGill University and will be graduating at the end of this month with a B.Sc. degree in software engineering. My recently completed internship with Affiliated Programmers has been an important part of my education, and that is why I am very interested in an opportunity to work with you and your staff at The Vaughan Group.

I am confident that I possess the combination of skills and training necessary to become a valuable asset to The Vaughan Group. As you can see from my enclosed résumé, I have dedicated myself to academic excellence with the long-term goal of working as a software professional. I feel that my background is ideally suited to the needs of your firm and that this position will offer me the challenges I am seeking.

I am eager to learn more about the advertised position at The Vaughan Group. I am available for an interview at your convenience and look forward to hearing from you in the near future.

Sincerely,

William R. Gooding

Enclosure

**Figure 9.6** Sample Cover Letter

**Ten Tips for Cover Letters**

◆ Do your homework about the company and the job you are applying for. The cover letter should be written specifically for the job you are applying for.

◆ Show that you know what the employer needs and can fill the need. Clearly emphasize one or two valuable skills that match the needs of the employer and make you qualified.

◆ Address the letter directly to the person who will be hiring. If you do not have that information, telephone the company and ask for it. Remember to ask for the correct spelling of the person's name and his or her title.

◆ Be sure there are no spelling or grammatical errors.

◆ Always use a word processor to write the letter. Print the letter on paper that is the same as what you used for your résumé. Never send a photocopied letter. Also, do not send one that is handwritten unless this is specifically requested.

◆ Keep the letter brief—just one page—and make it professional.

◆ Never mention salary.

◆ If you do not have much experience, attract the employer's attention through your qualifications and skills.

◆ Use a personal touch and mention something that will let them know that you have done your homework about the position and the company.

◆ If you qualify, and the organization you are applying to has an employment equity program, consider stating in your letter that you would like to be considered under the program.

**Figure 9.7** Ten Tips for Cover Letters

to write your own persuasive cover letter. Figure 9.7 has a list of tips to help you write a successful cover letter.

Once you begin sending out your résumé and cover letters, you can start to determine the weaknesses in your job search. If your résumé is reaching employers and yet you are not being invited to interviews, then you may need to fine-tune your letter or your résumé. If you are getting interviews but no offers, then you may want to evaluate your interview style and make the necessary adjustments as discussed in the next chapter. You will be able to see exactly where you need to focus your attention based on the real-world results of your efforts.

# Job Application Forms

Many organizations may ask you to complete an application form as part of the process of applying for a position. Your résumé allows you the freedom to decide what aspects of your background to highlight and what to exclude, but the application process doesn't give you quite as much latitude. Application forms are usually straightforward, fill-in-the-blank documents that would appear to dictate your responses. You may have little choice about the questions that are asked on a job application form. Although the forms usually ask for standard information, there are some questions that should not appear on an application form, and if they do, you should not feel obliged to answer them.

Your name, address, and telephone numbers are usually standard requirements on an application form. Sometimes application forms will also ask for your social insurance number. You will be asked to list prior positions, the organizations in which you have worked, the inclusive dates, and the responsibilities you held. Carry an index card with you that lists this information so you can be sure of the dates of your former employment. If you are asked to state your reason for leaving a job, always relate your departure to an opportunity for growth or improvement. Avoid mentioning causes such as you couldn't get along with an employer or supervisor.

It is possible that the application form may ask questions that are inappropriate and probe areas of your life that the Canadian *Human Rights Act* considers to be private. Questions asked by an employer must be restricted to those that are relevant to the job. That is, information related to race, national or ethnic origin, colour, religion, age, gender, sexual orientation, marital status, family status, disability, or conviction for which a pardon has been granted are private and protected by law. Furthermore, attempts to elicit private information to exclude you from a job are illegal. The only time it would not be illegal for an employer to collect this type of information is if it is to be used in adopting or carrying out a special program, such as an employment equity program. These programs are designed to eliminate or reduce discrimination and/or improve opportunities for employment for groups of individuals who have suffered disadvantages.

Despite laws that prohibit private questions, you may find that some employers continue to include them as part of the application process. Your answers may make the difference between an opportunity for an interview and no response. If full candour is going to jeopardize your chance at the job, then you must make a decision. Never answer dishonestly, but if you feel that being straightforward with an employer will decrease your chance of getting a job, then leave that question blank. It may not be the answer that the employer wants to see, but if your background makes you a strong candidate for the job, there is still a good chance that you will get an interview. Once you are in the interview, you have an opportunity to market your qualifications for the job. As it is illegal for an employer to ask private questions on an application form, the Canadian *Human Rights Act* also prevents employers from asking these questions at an interview and from discriminating when hiring.

The most difficult decisions about disclosure must be made by people who have a disability and also by those who have had encounters with the criminal justice system. Despite laws that protect people with disabilities, many employers are still not ready to leave their biases behind when evaluating people for employment. Employers may incorrectly assume that any physical, cognitive, or emotional disability may represent increased costs. For this reason, if you have a disability but it is not apparent, do not indicate your disability on the application form. You are being hired for your ability to do the job. Anything else is irrelevant. If your disability is apparent, then when you get to the interview, emphasize your skills, accomplishments, and ability to do the job. If you require some accommodations that would help you to meet the demands of the job, go to the interview prepared with information regarding those accommodations and, if relevant, their estimated costs. Many job accommodations do not cost much and are simple to put in place. If this is the case for you, make sure the employer knows it. On the other hand, if the accommodations you require are expensive, you may want to investigate incentive programs offered to employers, which may assist with the costs, and relay this information to the employers.

Use your own judgment, instinct, and past experiences to decide when and how to discuss your disability with an employer. Some people want to wait until the interview; others might want to do it sooner. For example, if the organization you are applying to has an employment equity program, you might want to state in your application that you would like to be considered under the guidelines of this program. If you are going to do this, be sure the organization has a strong commitment to the program. It is really up to you to decide when and how to discuss your disability with an employer. You only need to share information that is appropriate and relevant to your ability to perform the job.

Having a criminal record can pose another obstacle to employment. In Canada, no one may access another person's criminal record without the consent of that person. In other words, if employers wish to access criminal record information, they must inform the individual of the kind of criminal record information being sought, and they must obtain the person's consent.

In addition, under the *Young Offenders Act*, youth records are not public information, and therefore, no documentation should be made available to the public that could tie a youth with his or her criminal record. Nevertheless, some employers get around this by asking youths to provide proof of no record or to make the request to access their own criminal records. If this is the case, people can either agree to provide the record or refuse and withdraw the application for employment. Employers who proceed in this way are breaching the *Young Offenders Act* and putting youth in a difficult position.

Employers should only ask criminal-record-related questions if they impact the job directly. For example, many application forms ask if you are bondable. Some positions require that you be bondable, a term that refers to a type of insurance policy on employees that vouches for their performance. Unless you have had a criminal conviction, you should not have any trouble being bonded. Answer these questions simply and honestly.

All job applicants must be prepared to answer questions regarding past employment. Most applications ask the reason for leaving past employment. Write something positive such as "left to pursue other opportunities." Avoid responding negatively or even saying something like "left for personal reasons" as this can leave questions about your attitude or reliability. Similarly, if the application form asks for expected salary, answer "open to negotiation," or write the salary range you have researched for this type of work.

Almost all application forms will also ask for references. Employers should really not be contacting your references until they are prepared to offer you the job. It is your decision as to whether you submit your references' names and contact numbers on the form or bring this information to the interview. Either way, make sure that the people whose names you provide know you are using them as a reference and will speak favourably of you. Generally speaking, you should be willing to provide three references. They should not be immediate family members but rather former employers, instructors, coaches, or anyone else who has observed your work and can speak about the type of worker you are.

One final note about completing application forms. Some employers will prefer you complete an application form instead of submitting a résumé. If this

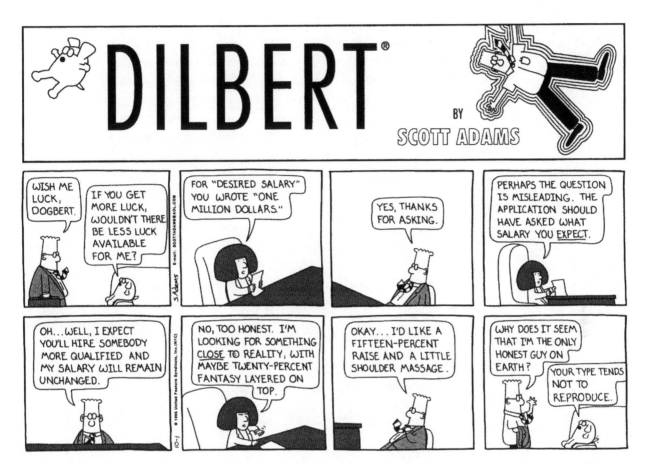

DILBERT reprinted by permission of Universal Feature Syndicate, Inc.

is the case, if possible, request that your cover letter and résumé be attached to the application form. However, if you do this, never leave any parts of the application form blank and then state "see résumé." Remember that employers have requested the application form for a reason and asking them to flip back and forth between your résumé and the form may only irritate them and probably eliminate your chance for an interview. Instead, complete the application form in its entirety, and if a question does not apply to you, write "N/A."

## Rosalind's Story

Rosalind had been looking for a job for over four months and was getting discouraged. She had attended a few interviews but was disappointed that she wasn't getting positive results. Even when considering other factors like experience and grades, she knew something wasn't working.

Rosalind took her résumé to the college services centre and met with Yolanda, an advisor there. Yolanda reviewed Rosalind's résumé and immediately saw what might have been causing her difficulty. Rosalind's résumé was completely factual and honest, yet it did little to convey the real talent and hard work that she had demonstrated in the past or was capable of in the future.

Rosalind didn't realize that there was more than one way to design a résumé and that there might be a style that could more effectively communicate her skills and experiences. With Yolanda's help, she was able to articulate the qualities she possessed that would benefit potential employers. She designed her résumé more effectively to bring out the skills and achievements that she and her advisor thought would be most marketable. She highlighted her degree differently and left out things that didn't relate directly to her profile. Rosalind's new résumé made her feel

## Rosalind Banks

542 Lawrence Street
Toronto, ON
M1G 5Z2

Phone: (416) 446-6639

### Objective

Seeking a position in which I can use my skills to benefit myself and the organization.

### Education

Seneca College, Toronto, ON
Ontario College Diploma, Graduated 2003

### Experience

Tool Room Monitor, June 1999 to present
Heritage Tools, Inc., Toronto, ON
   Monitor use of tools by employees, maintain orderly system for tool use, display tools to be rented or purchased.

Retail Selector, June 1995 to September 1998 (Part-time/summer)
Sears Distribution Centre, Toronto, ON
   Took catalogue orders and pulled items from inventory for delivery to customer.

### Personal

Birth date:  May 23, 1978            Marital Status:  Single
Birthplace:  St. John's, NF          Health:          Excellent
Hobbies:     Softball, jogging, fitness, art

### References

Available upon request.

more competitive, and just writing it helped her focus her thoughts for interviews.

As Rosalind resumed her job search, she continued to fine-tune and improve her new résumé each time she applied for a job. After a few more weeks of looking and a couple more interviews, Rosalind landed a job in a major department store as a Visual Merchandising Coordinator.

Here are two different versions of Rosalind's résumé. The first is her original résumé and the second is the new and improved résumé.

---

# Rosalind J. Banks

rjayb@hotmail.com

542 Lawrence Street, Toronto, ON  M1G 5Z2                                    (416) 446-6639

**PROFILE**
Very knowledgeable in all aspects of visual merchandising with experience in purchasing. Reliable and creative team player able to take initiative and direction.

**SKILLS AND ABILITIES**
- Knowledgeable in all aspects of visual merchandising including
  - Lighting
  - Photography
  - Display Practices
  - Computer Design and Drafting
  - Trade Shows and Advertising
- Capable of operating the following software:
  - Microsoft Excel, Microsoft Word, AutoCad

**EDUCATION**
Seneca College, Toronto, ON
Graduated 2003, Ontario College Diploma in Visual Merchandising Arts
GPA: 3.1
Other Training:    Introduction to Computer Graphics, September 1999
                   AutoCad, January 2000

**RELATED EXPERIENCE**
Heritage Tools, Inc., Toronto, ON
Associate, June 1999 to present

Manage and control distribution and retrieval of tools used in manufacturing company with annual sales over $5M

Display of new tools and demonstrations to public on use and features

Company representative at local road shows

*Major Accomplishment:*
- Developed and implemented improved method for displaying tools resulting in approximate increase in rental revenue of $2500

**OTHER FACTS**
- Organized and coordinated college fundraiser to benefit Children's Medical Centre—net contribution $6580
- Displayed artwork at local exhibition and won prize for use of colour and shape

## TAKE A CLOSER LOOK
### 9.1 Finding Parallel Skills

In this exercise, summarize your prior experiences and skills that match those required in the job or occupation you are seeking. By now you have done the homework necessary to know which skills are important in the occupation to which you aspire. See if you can match your experiences (including jobs, internships, volunteer work, workshops, courses, training, etc.) and the skills acquired through them to the skills needed in your future occupation.

| SKILLS REQUIRED IN THE OCCUPATION YOU WANT | RELATED SKILLS YOU'VE DEVELOPED IN PRIOR JOBS AND OTHER EXPERIENCES |
|---|---|
| _____ | _____ |
| _____ | _____ |
| _____ | _____ |
| _____ | _____ |
| _____ | _____ |
| _____ | _____ |
| _____ | _____ |

Keep in mind that even the most routine and basic jobs offer the opportunity to use and master skills that can become the building blocks for other positions. Try to find the parallel skills that intersect with job titles and categories. These skills will help you determine what to include in your résumé. As you develop the components of your résumé, reinforce your qualifications by including experiences and examples that reflect your skills as they relate to the position you want.

*Discuss the results of this exercise with your group or the class.*

## TAKE A CLOSER LOOK
### 9.2 A Practice Summary Statement

Your work on your summary or profile statement will continue throughout your career as you grow, develop your skills, and seek new goals. To get started, try the fill-in-the-blanks format below.

"A(n) _____(a)_____ background in _____(b)_____ with ability in _____(c)_____ and _____(d)_____ ."

Doesn't look like much at this point? That's okay. Try to provide the specifics related to your career goal, interests, and specialized experiences that fit the situation. Here's an example of a summary that might work using this format:

"A broad background in human resources development with ability to develop and implement programs."

Or:

"Specialized experience in elementary/preschool education with emphasis on special needs populations."

Each blank has a purpose. Blank (a) gives you the chance to present a positive description of your experience. Blank (b) offers the category of experience that your background falls under: accounting, education, business, engineering, management, health care, and so on. Blanks (c) and (d) allow you to focus on skills and specifics that spotlight your greatest strengths.

Now develop your own summary or profile using the parts of the format that you think work best for you. Review the following list of words to help you fill in the blanks.

## BLANK (A)

| | | | |
|---|---|---|---|
| strong | broad | proven | extensive |
| effective | advanced | outstanding | demonstrated |

## BLANK (B)

| | | | |
|---|---|---|---|
| administration | accounting | sales | education |
| social services | research | management | programming |
| marketing | customer service | graphics | engineering |
| business | library services | food service | retailing |

## BLANKS (C) AND (D)

(These terms should be related directly to the job or field in which you are applying.)

| | | | |
|---|---|---|---|
| implementing | initiating | troubleshooting | administering |
| organizing | problem solving | coding/ | team building |
| tax/cost | design/layout | debugging | developing |
| accounting | developing | acute/critical | leads/closing |
| programming/ | counselling/ | care | Java/Web design |
| systems analysis | referral | | |

If the suggested model seems like too much, don't worry. Just take what you need to get started. Here are some more examples:

- "Recognized performer, able to provide full range of accounting support services."
- "Chronic and long-term care specialist, familiar with needs of geriatric clients."
- "Public relations expertise with specialized skills in copywriting and marketing development."

Any of these models or your own statement are fine as long as they set the right tone for the employer by briefly expressing your unique combination of strengths and interests.

*Discuss the results of this exercise with your group or the class.*

**TAKE A CLOSER LOOK**

### 9.3 Highlighting Your Skills

When developing your skill statements, keep in mind the exercises in Chapter 3 devoted to skills and abilities. Remember to focus on those parts of your skill portfolio that are relevant to the position you seek. Use the phrases below to start developing a few statements that concisely communicate your greatest strengths.

"Knowledgeable in all areas devoted to _____ ."

"Comprehensive background in _____ ."

"Able to _____ ."

"Exceptional skills in _____ ."

"Experienced in _____ ."

"Knowledgeable in use of the following (software, machines, and so on)

_____ ."

Continue to develop statements that highlight your relevant skills. Focus on skills that are as specific as possible to the job for which you are applying. The more detail you can include, the better—you can include as many as five or six statements in this special section, more if you have strong credentials in a particular area.

*Discuss the results of this exercise with your group or with the class.*

**TAKE A CLOSER LOOK**

### 9.4 Showcasing Your Work Experience

To describe your work experience, focus first on your routine duties and then on the accomplishments that resulted from applying your skills. Remember to emphasize the skills that relate to the job for which you are applying.

**EXPERIENCE:**

Company name, city, province or territory:

_____

Title:

_____

Dates of employment:

_____

Duties:

_____

_____

Accomplishments:

_____

_____

If you are having trouble coming up with accomplishments, answer these questions:

Have you ever supervised anyone?

Have you ever worked as part of a team on a specific project?

Did you ever see a problem and suggest a solution that was adopted? Did it save time or money?

Did you ever improve an existing system or situation? Did the improvement save or increase funds?

Did you sell anything? Did you meet your goals? Did you exceed your goals?

Did you receive awards for your work, as an individual or part of a team?

Did the workload increase while you were on a job? Did you handle the increase successfully?

Develop a concise description of your experience at all the recent and relevant positions you have had.

**JOB A**

_____

_____

**JOB B**

_____

_____

**JOB C**

_____

_____

Review the information you have compiled about your experiences and see if it reflects your current job goal and the skills that might be needed. If you see something that may detract from your relevant skills or aren't sure if the information applies, leave it out. Be brief and focused.

_Discuss the results of this exercise with your group or with the class._

The related information component of the résumé gives you the opportunity to broaden your image for an employer; however, choose carefully when providing these details. Fill in the categories that might be helpful in presenting yourself.

**PROFESSIONAL MEMBERSHIP/OFFICES:**

_____

_____

_____

**AWARDS/SCHOLARSHIPS:**

_____

_____

_____

**EXTRACURRICULAR ACTIVITIES:**

_____

_____

_____

**PUBLISHED WORK:**

_____

_____

_____

**VOLUNTEER/COMMUNITY WORK:**

_____

_____

_____

**OTHER:**

_____

_____

_____

If you have devoted a substantial amount of time to volunteer or community work that is related to your objective, you may want to include it under your experience component instead. Remember that no matter how committed you may be to a cause, you may scare off an employer who has a great job opening if you broadcast your political or social position in your résumé. Be careful! Keep the focus on your skills and ability to do the job.

**TAKE A CLOSER LOOK**

**9.6 Writing a Persuasive Cover Letter**

Complete the form letter using the approach described in this chapter. Refer to Sample Résumés and Cover Letters for another example of a persuasive cover letter.

| | |
|---|---|
| _____ | Your Address |
| _____ | City and Province or Territory |
| _____ | Postal Code |
| _____ | Date |
| _____ | Name of Contact Person |
| _____ | Title |
| _____ | Company Name |
| _____ | Address |
| _____ | City, Province |
| _____ | Postal Code |

Dear Mr./Ms: _____ (Salutation)

Paragraph 1: Why I am writing (Introduction).

_____

_____


Paragraph 2: Who I am (Main Body).

_____

_____

_____


Paragraph 3: What we have in common (Main Body).

_____

_____

_____

Paragraph 4: We should get together (Conclusion).

_____

_____

Sincerely,

_____
(Signature here)

Typed name

Enclosure

If it is a little awkward at first to write about yourself, that's okay. You'll get used to it. You aren't expected to be original or creative in cover letters. So feel free to get ideas from books or manuals with phrases that you think capture what you are trying to say. Just be sure that your letters don't sound "canned." If you use ideas from manuals, alter the language.

_Discuss your reactions to all of the exercises with your group or with the class._

### TAKE A CLOSER LOOK
### 9.7 A Practice Application

Complete this sample application, deciding how to deal with any questionable entries.

**APPLICATION FOR EMPLOYMENT**

Name _____

Address _____

Phone Number(s) _____

Marital Status _____ Single _____ Married _____ Divorced

Spouse's Name _____

Spouse's Employment _____

Spouse's Salary _____

Children _____ Yes _____ No

Names/Ages _____

Date of Birth _____ Citizenship _____

Sex _____ Height _____ Weight _____ Disabilities _____

Recent Hospitalizations _____

Person to Contact in an Emergency _____

Have You Ever Received or Applied for Employment Insurance? _____

If so, when? _____

Have You Ever Received or Applied for Workers' Compensation Benefits? _____

If so, when? _____

Have You Ever Been Convicted of a Crime? _____

Do You Have a History of Mental Illness? _____

**EDUCATION**

High School _____

University, College, or Vocational Training _____

Other Training _____

**EMPLOYMENT HISTORY**

Employer _____

Job Title/Dates of Employment _____

Job Duties _____

_____

Reason for Leaving _____

Employer _____

Job Title/Dates of Employment _____

Job Duties _____

_____

Reason for Leaving _____

Employer _____

Job Title/Dates of Employment _____

Job Duties _____

_____

Reason for Leaving _____

**REFERENCES**

Name _____    Phone _____

Address _____

Name _____    Phone _____

Address _____

Name _____    Phone _____

Address _____

I, the undersigned, submit this application for employment. If at any time the information included in this application is found to be false or untrue, it shall be considered grounds for immediate dismissal with no recourse.

Signed _____    Date _____

*How did you respond to the questionable inquiries on this application? Discuss your responses with your group or with the class.*

### TAKE A CLOSER LOOK
### 9.8 Pulling It All Together

Now that you have had a chance to work on the individual components that compose a résumé, try pulling the components together to develop a solid integrated document.

**IDENTIFIERS**            _____

_____

_____

_____

**SUMMARY/PROFILE**

_____

_____

_____

**SKILLS**

_____

_____

_____

_____

**EXPERIENCE**

Company/City _____

Title/Dates _____

Duties _____

_____

_____

Accomplishments _____

_____

Company/City _____

Title/Dates _____

Duties _____

_____

_____

Accomplishments _____

_____

Education _____

College/University _____

Date of Graduation/Degree Awarded _____

Major Area of Study/Emphasis _____    GPA [if over 3.0] _____

Other Training _____

Related Information _____

Memberships/Awards/Scholarships/Licences/Volunteer Work, etc.

_____

_____

_____

Based on your career goal and the unique combination of skills and abilities that you possess, decide whether a chronological, functional, or achievement résumé will work best for you.

*Chronological:* Showcases work experience and continued growth in one field

*Functional:* Showcases skills; ideal for career changers, new job seekers

*Achievement:* Showcases accomplishments as they relate to expected job skills

You may already have a good idea of how to lay out your résumé. If not, use scissors to cut out the different components of the résumé you have developed. Shuffle the components around, remove those that don't work, and see how different combinations sound and flow. This should help you decide which format and layout will work best for you. Try formatting your résumé on the computer.

*Discuss the results of your "shuffling" with your group or with the class.*

# A Look Back

To review, you have learned that the résumé is a unique document in which you determine what information to provide and how to present it. You can conform to the conventions of typical hiring practices and still present an image of competence and self-assurance.

You should now be able to decide which résumé style will work best for you in different job-seeking situations and how to present the information you include. You also should be comfortable designing a document that will change and evolve as you progress in your career, a document that is as appealing as it is informative. You also are able to take advantage of a variety of conventional and electronic means to circulate your résumé.

You are now ready to write cover letters that do more than "cover" your résumé. Your letters should be developed using facts that persuade the employer to act on your résumé and offer you an interview. You are now prepared to distribute your résumé, as well as respond to inquiries on applications that could be awkward or ambiguous.

Finally, go over this checklist before you send out your résumé:

_____ Is my résumé completely free of errors in spelling, punctuation, usage, and grammar?

_____ Does my résumé have enough attractive white space?

_____ Is my use of type styles simple and appealing?

_____ Is my résumé one to two pages of solid information?

_____ If I have two pages, is the information meaningful or "filler"?

_____ Does my résumé flow and have a logical layout?

_____ Do I use short phrases and action words?

_____ Is the information focused only on the skills needed for the job, excluding irrelevant or meaningless facts?

_____ Have I enclosed a personalized cover letter?

## Other Sources and Suggested Reading

*The Damn Good Resume Guide* by Yana Parker
> This classic résumé-writing manual published by the same company that produces *What Color Is Your Parachute?* has been rewritten and is now easier to follow. Still a useful, all-around guide to writing your résumé.

*Dynamite Cover Letters and Dynamite Resumes* by Ronald L. Krannich and Caryl Rae Krannich
> These authors offer their philosophy on writing job-seeking documents that get employers' attention.

*Effective Phrases for Performance Appraisals* by James E. Neal, Jr.
> Although this book is really designed to assist managers in writing performance appraisals, it is equally helpful if you are looking for phrases that express your abilities.

## Web Sites and Internet Resources

**www.cdm.uwaterloo.ca**
The University of Waterloo Career Services offers an excellent Career Development eManual. It is organized into six steps of the career decision-making and job search process and is informative and user friendly. Included is information on writing résumés and cover letters.

**www.edu.gov.on.ca/eng/career/cover-le.html**
The Ontario Ministry of Education and Ministry of Training, Colleges and Universities has created a Web site with links to various Internet resources including career exploration and job search skills.

**www.jobhuntersbible.com**
This site is designed as a supplement to Dick Bolles' book, *What Color is Your Parachute?* (2004 edition). It includes ways to use the Internet in your job search and how to find the best sites to create and post your résumé.

**jobsearch.about.com/library/blresume.htm**
This is the Job Searching in Canada Web site with tips and examples of how to write résumés and cover letters.

**www1.umn.edu/ohr/ecep/resume**
The Resume Tutor developed by the University of Minnesota offers an interactive workbook designed to make résumé writing more fun.

**http://laws.justice.gc.ca/en/H-6/31147.html**
Canadian *Human Rights Act*

**www.johnhoward.ca**
The John Howard Society of Canada is a non-profit community organization providing programs for offenders and their families, ex-offenders, young persons, and the public.

**www.johnhoward.ab.ca/serv.htm**
The John Howard Society of Alberta Web site includes information about understanding criminal records and the *Young Offenders Act*. It also has information regarding employers and disclosure of information.

# Chapter 10

# Job Interviews

## Interviewing with Confidence

*Competition is natural and a great force for bringing out peak performances, not just for the winner but for everyone competing ... All those who enter a competition, and try hard to do their best, are winners. The losers are those who never enter the race.*

NANCY GREENE

Probably the most intimidating aspect of anyone's career development is interviewing for jobs. A job interview presents a unique challenge to most job hunters because they usually have little control over the circumstances of the interview. The interviewer decides where and when the interview will take place, what questions will be asked, and who will be offered the job. For this reason then, a job interview can feel like a test one needs to pass in order to get the job.

Contrary to popular belief, your challenge in an interview is not to please the interviewer. A positive dialogue with the interviewer is only one of the goals in interviewing. The real challenge is in preparing yourself and performing during the interview so that your capabilities are clear to the interviewer. All of the work you've done comes to a head at this point. That is, you know about the prospective job through your library research and network interviews, you are familiar with the field, and you have gained the technical and academic background you need to compete effectively. The only thing remaining is preparing yourself for the scrutiny that comes with the job interview.

## Preparing Yourself for an Interview

Preparing for a job interview involves a rather complex set of dynamics, which can be broken down into specific tasks. These are as follows:

◆ *Developing and sharpening your style.* One of the most significant parts of interviewing well is projecting a sense of personal power and confidence. This is accomplished through carefully assessing your appearance, poise, and presentation—everything from what you wear to the way you speak and move.

◆ *Conveying your skills as they relate to the job.* All the poise in the world will not make up for a lack of substance and competence. To be credible, you must convey the knowledge you have gained about the job, and the occupation, through education, experience, company research, and so on. You must operate from a solid base of knowledge and information.

◆ *Understanding the rituals of the interview.* Everything about you is magnified and amplified during the interview process. You will be expected to respond in certain ways to the process of interviewing. If you display a lack of understanding of what is expected, your judgment may be called into question. It is important for you to seriously consider the behaviours you exhibit at the interview and realize that they take on a much greater significance in an interview than they might in any other situation.

These tasks and the related dynamics of interviewing will be discussed in more detail throughout this chapter.

# The Dynamics of Interviewing

There are basically four different dynamics of interviewing that influence how successful an interview is. These are *exchange of information, sales presentation, social occasion,* and *theatrical performance.* These dynamics are flexible and change throughout the interview.

## Exchange of Information

The first and most important dynamic of the interview is that it is an exchange of information. Gone is the time when one would go to an interview and willingly accept anything that was offered. Nowadays, interviewing for a job can be compared to dating in that you certainly wouldn't want to marry every person you date and you definitely wouldn't want every job for which you interview. Your task is not only to relay information about yourself, but also to learn as much as you can about the job, the organization, the people, and the work, in order to see if it is a match for you. That means you must use your powers of observation, communication, and sensitivity during the interview, just as the interviewers use theirs. The interview is a time for you, too, to ask questions that you need answered to make the decision about whether to accept the job if it is offered. Everything you learn about the interviewer and the organization will help you determine whether the job will be a good fit for you.

## A Sales Presentation

This is the dynamic of interviewing with which you are probably most familiar. Part of interviewing well is promoting yourself and your skills to the interviewer. An interview is, in some respects, a sales presentation. As in any sales presentation, you will be showcasing information about yourself that makes you a strong candidate for the position and de-emphasizing those aspects of your background that conflict with the employer's assumptions. It is important to be "fast on your feet," reinforcing your strengths and enthusiasm, in order to encourage the employer to offer you the job. To do that, you have to know what the employer needs and draw attention to the ways you can meet those needs.

You will need to come prepared to the interview with information for your "sales presentation," information you will use to substantiate your claims about your qualifications. That is, you might want to bring copies of your certificate or a transcript listing courses that you have taken related to the job. You must also bring a typed list of names, titles, and phone numbers of people who will act as your references. Be sure that your references will speak favourably of your work ethic and your abilities. In addition, it is useful to bring two or three extra copies of your résumé, including one for yourself and some for any others who are present at the interview. It is handy to have your résumé to refer to and will help you and the interviewers to stay on track as you elaborate in depth about your experiences. Coming prepared with extra copies of your résumé will also demonstrate preparedness and forethought.

## A Social Occasion

Even though an interview is usually businesslike, sometimes even formal, it is also a social occasion. That is, people who are likable usually get job offers, and people who are not usually don't. Interviewers need to assess whether you will "fit in" with their present team; you can make them feel comfortable by being cordial and friendly during the interview. This is not easy for everyone, especially in a stressful situation such as a job interview. Take advantage of your assets when you interview. Without question, the ability to smile and respond openly is a key factor.

## A Theatrical Performance

The fourth dynamic in the interview is that it is indeed a theatrical performance. You are being observed by an audience of one, or maybe more: the interviewers. They will observe and interpret your actions, body language, and what you say. For example, think about how you might answer the interviewers' probable first question, "How are you today?" In all likelihood, you will answer with the expected response, "Fine, thanks." If you have a headache or nervous stomach, you will probably keep that to yourself and act as though you feel fine. Most often, job seekers work at appearing relaxed and confident. It helps to look confident and comfortable during an interview, but nervousness is actually not the worst trait you can display. Nervousness can even be interpreted favourably. It shows the employer that you care about the outcome of the interview and that your behaviour is authentic and genuine. Above all, you will be trying your best to act the role of competent professional.

Interviewing well by taking into consideration these four dynamics is a complex and difficult task. You may communicate well with the employer but feel that you did not sell yourself well, or you may convey the attitude of a professional but be unable to connect with the interviewer. Since you have limited control over most of the externals that dominate an interview—the time, the location, the person interviewing you, and the tone of the interview— interviewing is always a challenge. Nevertheless, it may help to remember that others interviewing for the job face these same challenges and may be less prepared than you. Furthermore, many employers also feel challenged by interviews because very few have ever received formal training in interviewing. They often feel anxious, overwhelmed, and inadequately prepared for conducting interviews. As you bear the responsibility of finding the "right" job, they bear the responsibility of hiring the "right" person. For these reasons, you may assist the process by taking control of some very important aspects of the interview.

# Aspects of the Interview You Can Control

Many of the factors that affect the circumstances of the interview may be outside your control, but they don't necessarily determine the outcome. The variables you can control have a much greater influence on the outcome of the interview than many of the external factors that you cannot control. Knowing what you can do to influence the interview will help you feel more comfortable with interviewing as a whole and help you focus your energy productively. Your appearance, answers, body language, tone, and questions are all aspects that you can control and that have a great effect on the outcome of the interview.

## Appearance

Your appearance is one variable over which you have influence and control. The way you dress, your haircut or style, makeup, and accessories all contribute to, or detract from, the image you project. The image you want to confirm in the employer's mind is that of a competent, credible professional. To do that, you need to dress the part. Dressing the part can also influence how you behave. If you look the part, you will find it easier to convey a professional demeanour.

Conventional wisdom has emphasized that the first five minutes of the interview are the most critical to success. Some say that interviewers decide within the first five minutes whether or not to hire you and then spend the rest of the interview confirming their decision. Therefore, the first impression created by the image you project can have a substantial effect on everything that follows.

Although some organizations have adopted casual dress in the workplace, interviewing still requires your most polished appearance. While traditionally the standard uniform for interviewees has been the business suit both for men and women, it is now acceptable to vary from this somewhat. A good measure for dressing correctly for an interview is to consider how people in the occupation or organization dress, and then to dress just a notch more formally. For example, if you are interviewing for work in a legal or financial office that typically dresses in business suits, you might consider wearing a dark suit, light-coloured shirt or blouse, and dress shoes.

On the other hand, if you were to wear a suit to an interview for work in landscaping, it might be more difficult for the employer to visualize you shovelling or pushing a lawn mower. Also, you might convey the image that you don't know what will be expected of you on the job. For this type of job, or one in construction, for instance, clean, dark jeans or khakis, cotton shirt or blouse with a collar, and dark, casual shoes might be more appropriate

Knowing the culture of the occupation you are entering is another way to give you insight into the expectations your interviewer may have for how you should present yourself. Will you be working independently, expected to take initiative and produce on your own? Or will you be working closely with other team members, expected to take direction from a manager or team leader? The more autonomous your role, the more latitude you may be given in the way you present yourself.

## Questions and Answers

At every interview you will be expected to answer questions in detail. Although you cannot control what you're asked, you can control your answers. Part of your preparation must include anticipation of the different types of questions you might be asked and thinking in advance about how you will answer them.

Many of the questions will be about your skills. *Skills questions* such as, "What can you do?" relate to technical or academic knowledge and skill. These questions can cause you unnecessary anxiety. Because they tend to deal with how much you know, you might feel that the interviewer will find a weakness in your knowledge, thereby eliminating you from the competition. Actually, skills questions are some of the easiest to answer and are a great way for you to showcase what you can do.

Employers will not interview you if you don't have the background they are seeking, so the chances are good that you will know how to answer questions about your skills. If you don't know the answer, don't try to cover up by saying just anything. Instead, say "I'm not familiar with that particular issue, but I have had some experience with _____ ." Let the employer know that even if you don't know the answer to a particular question, you do feel secure about your background. Some studies indicate that many employers rate answers to skills questions as secondary in determining the acceptability of a candidate. The more important factor is attitude.

Questions about attitude are another type of question that you can expect. *Attitude questions* are the questions employers might ask to see how you feel about overtime, weekend or shift work, working with a diverse group of co-workers, and so on. Answer these questions honestly, in a straightforward, sincere manner that accommodates the employer's needs. Sometimes questions like these can alert you to an employer's hidden agenda, or an issue with which the company might be struggling. For example, questions about overtime might mean that the company is chronically understaffed and manages its employee shortage by expecting people to pick up the extra workload. Listen carefully and see if you can detect what is implied by the question. In most cases, you should respond positively to the interviewer. Signs of lack of commitment or bias will be viewed negatively, as most employers are looking for "can-do" employees.

Some interviewers will use *scenario questions*. These questions typically describe a situation and then ask you to provide your ideas on how you would handle it. Sometimes employers might be looking for specific answers, while other times they might just be looking at how you make decisions and solve problems. These are difficult questions to prepare for, so use your best judgment and be thoughtful and creative. The more knowledgeable you are about the occupation and the field of work, the more prepared you will be to answer these questions.

Occasionally, just as on applications forms, employers may ask questions that are considered inappropriate or even illegal. Experienced interviewers will know better than to ask these types of questions. However, if you are asked a question that is personal in nature and seems unrelated to the job, it is your decision whether to answer or not. You have a right to privacy, so disclose only information you believe to be pertinent to the job. If possible, try to deflect these questions with a "non-answer" or by asking why such information is needed. For example, if an interviewer asks how many children you have, you might ask how that relates to the job. If you are asked if you plan on having any more children, you might simply state that you are happy with the size of your family. These types of questions give you much information about the employer you would be working for; information that might be a warning about whether you would be comfortable working in that organization.

Recently, a new type of interview has become more popular. It is called *behaviour-based interviewing*. This approach focuses on the skills required by the position and asks you to respond very specifically to events from your experience that reflect those skills. The circumstances of the event, how the skills were used, and the resolution are all part of exploring how you have actually performed in similar situations. The approach for this type of interview is based in the belief that past behaviour is the best predictor of future behaviour. Even if your interviewer doesn't use this approach, preparing for these types of questions offers distinct advantages. Being able to showcase situations from your experience in which you have demonstrated a high level of skill is a powerful way of responding in an interview.

Use the information about these events in your past experiences to respond factually to questions about specific skills and abilities. You don't need to wait for the interviewer to ask for examples from your past; relay this information as part of your answer. For example, if the interviewer asks how you are at meeting deadlines, rather than just saying, "I am very good at working with deadlines," you might also add something that gives an example of when you had to work with a deadline. In this case, you might say something like, "I am very good at meeting deadlines. For instance, when I was a student I had to manage deadlines

DILBERT reprinted by permission of Universal Feature Syndicate, Inc.

## Six Types of Interview Questions

There are six basic types of questions, and most interviews will include questions of each type. They are:

1. **Open-Ended Questions:** Usually short, unstructured questions that get the interviewee to talk. Keep your answers organized, structured, and relevant to the position you are interviewing for.

   *Example*: "Tell me about yourself."

2. **Closed-Ended Questions:** Usually can be answered by a yes or no. Try to elaborate on your answer.

   *Example*: "Can you use a computer?"

3. **Probes:** These are questions that the interviewer will use to challenge something you have said or get you to elaborate. Be confident and positive.

   *Example*: "Do you really believe that you could manage the department all on your own?"

4. **Loaded Questions:** These questions give hints of the answer the interviewer would like to hear. Listen carefully and ask for clarification before you answer if you are not quite sure what they mean.

   *Example*: "You wouldn't mind working after 5 p.m. sometimes, would you?"

5. **Traps:** Some interviewers use loaded questions that encourage you to divulge negative information. Be aware of them and answer with confidence. Give only information that will not hurt your chances at getting the job.

   *Example*: "What do you see might be your weakness in doing this job?"

6. **Scenario or Hypothetical Questions**: These are the "What would you do if ..." questions that give the employer an idea of how you would solve a problem. Make a quick plan of your answer, relating it to the job, and if you can, give examples of when you have successfully handled something similar in the past.

   *Example*: "What would you do if a customer was agitated and upset about a mistake that was made?"

The best strategy when answering questions in an interview is: *Think about your answer. Then speak.* Do it always in that order. It is more than all right to take your time before you answer. It demonstrates to the interviewer that you think about things rather than acting too spontaneously.

**Figure 10.1** Six Basic Types of Questions Asked by Interviewers

for assignments; sometimes I had many at one time. I always handed all my assignments in on time. I managed the deadlines by ..." and then describe your strategy. It is very effective to answer questions by giving examples from your past experiences because it gives proof that you really can do what you claim.

Figure 10.1 describes six basic types of questions commonly asked at interviews. Then, Exercise 10.3 at the end of the chapter lists some examples of these different types of questions. Practise answering these interview questions and get feedback on your answers. Focus on your communication skills and your ability to articulate your thoughts in a way that can be clearly understood. Be yourself and answer questions genuinely and honestly.

## Body Language

Surprising as it may seem, one variable that you may have difficulty controlling is your body language. While you might be very conscious of what you tell an employer verbally, you might find it a challenge to monitor the information you communicate nonverbally. Body language consists of the nonverbal habits and behaviours that we use to communicate our thoughts and feelings. We constantly communicate with our bodies, and sometimes this body language speaks louder than our words. An employer can learn so much about you, both positive and negative, by observing your body language. For example, tapping your foot, bouncing your leg, or playing with your hair is often unconscious behaviour that can communicate your anxiety about the interview. Be aware that your nonverbal behaviour can tell employers more than you might want them to know.

Your goal, therefore, is to manage your nonverbal communication to support the overall positive impression you are striving to convey. Convince the interviewer that you are confident and at ease, eager to respond openly and sincerely. The best way to create this image is to focus on the ways you can connect with the person(s) interviewing you. As the interviewer greets you, step forward with your hand extended and a warm smile on your face. Shake hands firmly, make eye contact, and greet the interviewer with a pleasant "Happy to meet you, Mr./Ms. _____ ." Make sure you say the interviewer's name, as this establishes the appropriate tone of a business meeting. However, don't call the interviewer by his or her first name unless invited to.

When you get to the interviewer's office, wait to sit until after the interviewer takes his or her seat. Maintain your warm demeanour while you get comfortable. Try to relax and observe the room. You might chat about the weather or perhaps an item in the interviewer's office that sparks your interest, but keep small talk to a minimum. Casual conversation is a good way to start, but the interviewer will want to move along.

When seated, keep both feet on the floor or crossed at the ankles. Sit up straight and relax your hands in your lap, or if you are seated at a table, place them comfortably on the table. Try not to appear rigid or stiff. Continue making good eye contact as this communicates attentiveness, interest, and respect. When you are talking, be expressive and enthusiastic, have a pleasant look on your face, smile easily, and use gestures that are appropriate to what you are saying.

Vary your tone of voice when you convey your ideas, rather than speaking in monotone. Also, try to avoid saying "ums" to fill in silences. These vocalized pauses and other habitual behaviours such as twirling your hair or bouncing your leg can be extremely distracting and conflict with the image of the professional you are trying to portray.

## The Interview's Tone

If you begin to feel more comfortable, you will better be able to communicate your enthusiasm about the job opportunity. Be comfortable, but always maintain a professional attitude even if your interviewer behaves quite informally.

It seems that formal, high-stress interviews are becoming much less common today because interviewers have found that putting candidates under stress can be counterproductive. The goal of the interviewer is to help you feel comfortable so you will reveal as much of yourself as is necessary to determine whether you are a viable candidate for the position. If you feel stressed and intimidated, you will be less likely to be yourself, and this is counterproductive to the interviewer. Therefore, friendly behaviour by the interviewer can encourage you to show your true self much more easily. Nevertheless, be careful to distinguish friendliness from friendship. The interviewer is not your friend but rather is working to qualify people for further consideration. Anything that might make you a risk, even trying to strike up a friendship, could disqualify you as a professional. Stay focused on your goals, your skills, and what you can do for the organization.

## Asking Questions

Gathering information about a job also requires you to formulate questions to ask your interviewer. Many of your questions about a position and the organization may already be addressed during the interview. If not, be prepared to bring them up at an appropriate point.

Typically, the questions you are most interested in are the very ones to avoid in an interview—those questions about salary and benefits. The interviewer is focused on how you meet the organization's needs and wants to believe that is your focus as well, although you are both aware that this is a job for which you will be paid. Save the money and benefits questions for a later date, when you are offered the job. It would be appropriate to enquire about and discuss salary then, before you accept the position. Instead, the questions you ask at the interview should focus on the nature of the work to be performed, the work team, the company, the industry, and future growth.

The best questions tell the employer that you have done your research on the company and the industry. Use the resources discussed in Chapter 4 to learn about the businesses or organizations you will be interviewing with. Another thing you might do is to call the company and ask the receptionist if you can pick up a brochure or an annual report if available. Most companies are happy to accommodate such requests. An added benefit is that you get the opportunity to "dry run" your visit to the company. Being well prepared for the interview is a strong statement of your willingness to go the extra mile to reach your goals, a definite plus with any employer.

Always leave an interview with a clear understanding of the next steps in the process. A necessary question for the end of the interview is what the next step will be, or when the hiring decision will be made. It is useful for you to leave the interview with an indication of when you may be contacted. Knowing this information will free you to continue your job search rather than waiting by the telephone. This also gives you some indication of when you should be calling to follow up after the interview. Remember, too, to offer your list of references before you leave the interview. Figure 10.2 provides a list of questions it would be appropriate to ask at an interview.

Interview etiquette also requires that you follow up immediately after the interview by sending a thank-you note to show your appreciation for the opportunity to be interviewed. This reinforces your professionalism and interest in the job, and brings the interview to an appropriate close. If you have not heard from the interviewer in a reasonable amount of time, be sure to follow up with a phone call. Even if you believe that the interview was a complete success, don't sit and wait for the phone to ring, just keep on schedule with your job search until you receive a firm job offer.

### Questions to Ask an Employer at the Interview

Toward the end of an interview, you will probably be asked if you have any questions. It is always good to ask two or three questions. This is another opportunity to show the employer that you are a serious candidate for the job and that you are interested in learning more about the job and the company. However, you must respect the employer's time; avoid asking too many questions or questions that would take a long time to answer, especially if you notice that he or she is ready to end the interview. Remember that you are still making an impression and want the interview to end well.

Below is a list of examples of questions that you could ask at an interview.

- Could you tell me a little more about the duties of the position?
- May I have a copy of the job description?
- Could you tell me more about your company?
- What are the opportunities for advancement with the company?
- Do you provide orientation for your new employees?
- Is there a probationary period for new employees?
- Could I have a tour of the office/factory/plant/building?
- Are there opportunities for professional growth in this position?
- Are there training opportunities in this position?
- Could you tell me about the team of people with whom I would be working?
- What skill would you say is critical to the performance of this job?
- How could I best prepare myself if I were to be selected for the position?
- What is the next step in the process? May I follow up with you?

And most important,

- When do you expect to make your decision?

**Figure 10.2** Questions to Ask an Employer at the Interview

# Electronic Interviewing

Given technology's impact on career planning, it is no surprise that it is also changing the boundaries of interviewing and job screening. A relatively new trend is teleconference interviewing. Teleconferencing allows the candidate and the interviewer to speak face to face although they are in different locations. It is cost effective in that it allows an interviewer to screen candidates without incurring the inconvenience and expense of travel. Although this practice is sometimes adopted for initial screening interviews, it usually does not take the place of final selection interviews. However, it is often used by companies that have locations in various parts of Canada or the world, or who are hiring to start up a new location in another region.

If you learn that your interview is to be conducted by teleconference, don't panic. Here are a few suggestions that will help you prepare for this new form of interviewing.

1.  Request a brief telephone conversation prior to the interview. Use this telephone call to establish rapport with the interviewer and to learn about the process or determine the technical requirements for the interview.

2.  Arrive at the interview site early and familiarize yourself with the teleconferencing equipment and set-up. Most of these types of interviews are conducted at third-party settings such as career services offices or employment agencies. See if you can spend a few minutes looking over the equipment and familiarizing yourself with it. That will allow you to feel comfortable and keep distractions to a minimum during the interview.

3.  Teleconference interviewing is the same as interviewing in person ... but different. Video cameras tend to mute our behaviours, so communicating enthusiasm through tone of voice and nonverbal communication is tricky. Speak slowly and clearly, but don't overdo it. Look at the camera and try to appear animated, but don't go overboard. You are not actually on TV so there's no need to put on a show. With some systems, there may be a gap between transmission times so wait until the interviewer is finished speaking before you respond.

## Keep Your Focus

Keeping your focus can be a challenge. You may understand the individual dynamics of interviewing well, but juggling all the different variables can be overwhelming. Set your goals before you go into the interview and stay focused on them. Try not to be consumed by anxiety or nerves. You must be an attractive candidate to have gone this far, so be proud of yourself. You are exactly where you want to be—one step away from your goal.

One way to keep your focus is by visualizing beforehand how you would like to see yourself perform in the interview. World-class athletes use visualization to inspire performances that win them championships. You can do the same. Exercise 10.6 at the end of the chapter will show you how visualizing helps you feel ready for the interview. Then simply imitate the images you create of yourself doing well.

## Interview Goals

As you prepare for the interview, you may feel like a programmed robot. "Sit straight. Feet on the floor. Smile. Shake. Answer. Question. Leave." You may feel that trying to integrate all the suggestions here is going to have you spinning like a top. The intent of this chapter is to offer you methods of communicating that have been proven to be successful. Ultimately, to be genuine and sincere, you must be yourself. If you want to strengthen your interview skills, set some goals that you want to achieve for each interview you schedule. Assess the variables and choose one or two areas in which you want to improve your performance.

Integrate these improvements into your presentation until they become spontaneous and you no longer have to think about them.

Although the overall goal is for you to find the right job, the primary goal of each interview is to get a job offer. Sometimes people agonize over an interview for a job they're not sure they want. If you go into an interview with any doubts, you will convey them to the employer, and this could eliminate you from consideration. Then, if you find out halfway through the interview that it is your dream job, it may be too late to make a comeback. Therefore, it is best to go to the interview with the goal of getting the offer. Let the employer tell you about the job and then make your decision about whether it is right for you or not.

The interview process is just as much an opportunity to see if the job is right for you as it is to see if you are right for the job. This decision needs to be made by you as well as by the employer. One way to judge whether the job is right for you is to examine your responses to the questions. For every question the interviewer asks you, there are two answers ... the one you want to give and the one he or she wants to hear. If the job is a good fit for you, the distance between these two answers will be small to negligible. If you find, however, that the answers are very different from one another, then this may be a clear sign that the job may not be the right one for you. Don't be disappointed—be glad you found out sooner rather than later. It will save you time and heartache if you simply withdraw yourself as a candidate or turn the job offer down.

Finally, you may need to be prepared to respond quickly to a job offer. The shortage of skilled employees has quickened the pace of hiring, so you may find yourself being asked to make a decision with little time to reflect. Go into the interview prepared. Set your goals, understand the issues that are most important to you, and use the interview to answer the questions you have about the job and the organization. If everything looks fine, you can say "yes" knowing that you've done your research and you are making an informed decision. Figure 10.3 summarizes the things you can do to prepare for an interview.

# Coping with Rejection

Unfortunately, one of the realities of searching for a job is dealing with rejection. With every application and subsequent interview, it is natural for us to raise our hopes and begin to plan for a future employed in the occupation we seek. But the reality is that there are usually many experiences of rejection before we obtain our goal.

Even with careful preparation and planning, it can often take up to a year or more to find the right job. Submitting application after application and going to interview after interview without receiving a job offer can be very discouraging. You can easily begin to take the rejection personally and to wonder what you are doing wrong. However, keep in mind that there are many factors involved in today's labour market that are also influencing your job search. That is, not getting the job may not necessarily be a reflection of you and your inability to do the job, but rather a reflection of the economy, unemployment rates, and the competition available for jobs. Stay positive and never take it personally.

When competing for jobs, it is always best to try and remain as objective as possible. Look objectively at your job search and examine why it might be that it has not been successful. Review the job search process we have examined

## Preparing for the Interview

Here are some suggestions for what you can do to prepare for an interview.

◆ Be prepared to attend an interview on short notice.

◆ Once you have been granted an interview, contact your references and let them know that you will be giving their names as references at the interview. Then prepare a typed list of three references to give to the employer at the interview.

◆ Prepare two or three extra copies of your résumé to take to the interview. There may be more than one person interviewing you, or the interviewer may not have your résumé on hand. This will reinforce your preparedness and forethought.

◆ Do some research before your interview. Learn as much as you can about the company and the job you have applied for.

◆ Think of questions and answers that are likely to come up in the interview and practise your responses.

◆ Plan what you will wear for the interview to form a good first impression.

◆ If you are not familiar with the area where your interview will be held, get directions and visit there beforehand. Plan your route, parking, etc. Be sure you know how long it will take to get there so that you are not late.

◆ Get a good night's sleep the night before.

◆ Be honest about your skills and abilities and be positive at all times.

◆ Be precise and to the point. Your answers should be concise; try not to talk too much, or too little.

◆ Smile and try to be at ease. This will help the interviewer to feel more comfortable with you.

◆ If you are not sure about the meaning of a question, ask the interviewer to clarify.

◆ Always avoid sarcasm, criticisms, or negative remarks.

◆ At the end of the interview, inquire as to when a decision will be made or what the next step will be.

**Figure 10.3** Preparing for the Interview

throughout the last few chapters of this book, and see if there are any aspects of your search that you could improve on. Consider whether you could revise and improve your résumé and cover letters, get additional training or volunteer work experience to add to your credentials, polish your interviewing skills, establish further contacts for your network, or even reassess your goals. Sometimes applying for lower-level, perhaps entry-level, positions or relocating for a short time to another city or town where there may be more opportunities can be a good move toward getting your foot in the door. Remember that finding the right job requires patience, stamina, and a positive outlook. Your persistence will pay off.

# Maya's Story

Maya was a highly competent student who had completed her training and all her courses at the top of the class. However, now that it was time to find work, she was failing miserably in her job interviews. She was getting the interviews, but she was so nervous about them that one time she even began hyperventilating during the interview. Maya realized she had to get a handle on this fear if she wanted to get a job.

Maya went to the library and borrowed two books to help her better understand how interviews work. She also borrowed a videotape about interviewing so she could develop a model to emulate. Maya read through one of the books on interviewing and watched the video but felt overwhelmed by what she was expected to do. How could she possibly display the kind of behaviour shown in the video and described in the book? It might be easy for some people but she doubted she could do it, and she didn't even want to try. She secretly hoped that employers would be able to see she was smart and hardworking just by looking at her academic record and her résumé, and that they would not need to interview her.

However, Maya was smart enough to know that this was unlikely. So she picked up the second book she had borrowed from the library. This book made suggestions for managing her anxiety. One of the suggestions was to set a goal before going to the interview. This goal could be something as simple as wearing a good suit and polished shoes. The book also suggested approaching each interview as an opportunity to improve one's interview skills rather than worrying about getting job offers.

Maya decided to try this at her next interview. She decided that her first goal was to manage her body language. Even if she didn't get the job, she was going to work on sitting straight, smiling, and maintaining eye contact throughout the interview. As she arrived at the interview, she began to sweat profusely. When the interviewer approached, Maya swallowed hard, rubbed her palms on her jacket, smiled, and shook hands. Most of the interview was a blur to Maya, but she got through it.

Four more interviews followed over the next month. Each one was difficult, calling on her to find courage. But she did it, and even more than that, she tried what the book had suggested. For each interview she worked on one thing. First it was her body language, next her answers to questions, then the questions she asked, and so on. She only worked on a new goal when she felt competent in her previous one.

By the end of the four weeks, Maya's hands were no longer sweaty, and her voice no longer shaky, as she spoke during the interviews. She smiled more and maintained eye contact, and felt more prepared for the questions that were commonly asked of her. She even had second interviews scheduled with two different companies. Maya wasn't sure whether either one would produce a job offer, but she felt more confident and at ease because now she regarded interviews as an opportunity for learning and improving her skills.

**TAKE A CLOSER LOOK**

**10.1** Mirror, Mirror on the Wall ...

Before your interview, appraise yourself in the mirror, from head to toe. Remember, you are trying to convey confidence and professional poise. Go through the following checklist and assess how you look.

_____ Is my clothing appropriate for a professional business meeting?

_____ Is it in keeping with the typical business dress of the profession that I am seeking to enter?

_____ Are my accessories (jewellery, footwear, makeup, fragrance) minimal and appropriate?

_____ Is my hairstyle conventional and neat?

_____ Does my appearance fit the culture of the job for which I am interviewing?

Some people may wonder if it is worth buying clothes just to accommodate the employer's expectations. It is worth the investment to buy one outfit you will use for interviews. Dressing well for an interview boosts your confidence and creates a favourable impression.

**TAKE A CLOSER LOOK**

**10.2** Telling, Not Bragging

Identify five to ten experiences or events in which you demonstrated exceptional skill with good results. These should be accomplishments that required you to use skills related to the position for which you are applying—a valuable way to "show off" your expertise.

Describe the events using a model that divides the experience into four components:

Event:    Describe the challenge you or your team (in work or school) faced in factual terms. Make sure the event was one that showcased a skill relevant to the position.

Skill:    Use details to create a picture for the employer that allows them to "see" you using the skill that they are seeking.

Solution: Relate the resolution of the situation, highlighting your role.

Results:  Make sure you include the results of your highlighted event. Nothing is as impressive as getting concrete, positive results.

Event 1:

_____

_____

_____

_____

Event 2:

_____

_____

_____

_not applicable_

Event 3:

_____

_____

_____

Event 4:

_____

_____

_____

Event 5:

_____

_____

_____

*Use additional sheets if you have more than five events to describe.*

### TAKE A CLOSER LOOK
### 10.3 Sample Interview Questions

There are some questions that seem to be quite standard in most interviews. Look over the following list of questions and think of how you might respond. Be aware of any hidden agenda in the questions. Role-play an interview with a partner and practise answering these questions. Get feedback on your answers.

*Tell me about yourself.*
Keep your answer focused on your skills and your interest in the field. Stay away from family and personal information.

*What are your strengths and weaknesses?*
You can take advantage of the strengths question to reinforce your suitability for the job, especially in the skill area, but be careful of the weakness part. Don't tell anything that is damaging to your image as a dedicated worker. For example, one favourite is "I find that sometimes I can't say 'no' to an opportunity to do something if it needs to be done." Avoid answers such as "I don't get along with people" or "Sometimes I'm late." The interview may continue but you will probably be out of the running. Also, think your answers through completely so that you avoid the dilemma depicted earlier in the "Dilbert" cartoon.

*What brings out your best?*
A suggested answer to this is something like, "A challenge." Go on to describe what that means to you.

*Under what conditions do you work best? Or, How do you work under pressure?*

Some people like to answer that they "work best under pressure." Unless the job you are applying for is naturally a high-pressure job, you might want to consider how you would answer this question. Would this answer lead an employer to think that you need someone constantly pressuring you in order for you to get things accomplished?

*Why should I hire you?*

There is only one answer to this: "Because I can be an asset to this organization." Tell how.

*Why do you want to work here?*

Try to say something that indicates you are looking for a place where you can use your skills to good advantage.

*What did you like the best in your last job?*

Focus on the similarities to the job you're seeking.

*What did you like the least in your last job?*

Provide an answer that reinforces your interest in facing challenges that might have been absent in your last job. However, never speak negatively about past jobs or employers.

*Where do you see yourself in five years? Ten years?*

This is a goals question, so project forward a few years and emphasize your commitment to growth and becoming a better employee. Be careful though. You don't want to sound as if you have your sights set on taking over the company or the interviewer's job.

*Discuss your experience in the role-playing dialogue with your group or the class.*

---

## TAKE A CLOSER LOOK
### 10.4 How Am I Acting?

Ask yourself these questions as a way of becoming sensitive to how you are communicating nonverbally through your body language.

_____ Do I look comfortable and friendly when smiling?

_____ Is my handshake firm without being too strong?

_____ When seated, are my feet crossed at the ankles or next to each other flat on the floor?

_____ Is my posture correct without being stiff?

_____ Are my hands folded in a relaxed manner in my lap?

_____ Am I comfortable gesturing appropriately when my remarks call for it?

_____ Can I refrain from fidgeting?

_____ Can I look at my interviewer in a confident manner, making appropriate amounts of eye contact?

_____ Is my speech clear and verbal tone pleasant?

*Discuss the challenge of monitoring your body language with your group or with the class.*

---

### 10.5 Prepare Your Questions

The best candidates are ready with meaningful questions, so take advantage of this opportunity to practise creating and asking some. Consider the sample questions given previously in Figure 10.2 and develop some of your own. Usually two or three questions are enough, so be sure to ask only what is pertinent as what you ask will tell much about you. Remember to save your questions about salary, vacation, or benefits until a later time.

---------------------------------------------------------------

---------------------------------------------------------------

---------------------------------------------------------------

### 10.6 Visualize Your Success

Diligently working through this exercise will help you feel relaxed, uplifted, and totally prepared for your interview.

Take 30 minutes each day for a week before your interview and imagine yourself going through the entire interview experience. Close your eyes and see yourself driving to the interview. You are calm and have been preparing for this meeting for a long time. You are obviously better prepared than any other candidate for this job.

You are shaking hands with the interviewer. You are smiling, happy to be there. Your handshake confirms your confident, open approach to the world. The interviewer likes you and wants you to do well. You answer questions thoughtfully, taking whatever time you need to feel comfortable. Your interviewer thinks your answers are excellent. You are poised and comfortable and ask questions that are impressive. Your interviewer closes the session, expressing regret that there isn't more time to explore your views on the position and the company. You are also disappointed that there isn't more time to share your thoughts but are pleased to have had the chance to meet your interviewer regardless of the outcome.

You leave the interview and return home to immediately write a thank-you note, reinforcing the ideas discussed in the interview and expressing appreciation for the opportunity to meet the interviewer.

How does that feel?

*Discuss with your group or the class how the visualization exercise worked for you.*

TAKE A CLOSER LOOK

### 10.7 Pulling It All Together

Before you go to each interview, check this list to make sure you are prepared.

_____ Does my appearance (dress, shoes, hair, and accessories) present the image that is appropriate for a business meeting for the field in which I seek employment?

_____ Have I thought through the answers to the typical questions encountered in an interview?

_____ Have I sat down and written about my skills and accomplishments that are related to the position for which I am interviewing?

_____ Have I thought about how I will respond to questions about attitude?

_____ Have I assessed my nonverbal behaviour or asked someone to observe and critique my body language so that it conveys a professional image?

_____ Do I have a list of relevant questions for my interviewer?

_____ Have I contacted my references and informed them that I will be providing their names to the employer?

_____ Do I have a copy of my typed list of contacts for references, including their names, titles, and phone numbers?

_____ Have I practised my interview visualization exercise?

_____ Am I excited and happy to be meeting my interviewer?

_____ Have I set my goals and do I know what I want to accomplish in the interview?

# A Look Back

This chapter has introduced you to the complex ritual of interviewing and your role in making it a productive and positive experience. It is part meeting to exchange information, part sales presentation, part friendly visit, part performance.

The interview can seem at times like a mystery over which you have no control. However, the variables you can control are those that have the greatest influence on the outcome. Your appearance is a variable over which you exert complete control and which you can use to your advantage. The answers to questions, whether about skills, attitude, or scenarios, are also under your control. Your body language can be an important part of communicating with the employer and demonstrating a positive image. The tone of the interview, though generally set by the interviewer, can offer you the opportunity to establish yourself as a professional yet likable individual. Finally, you can use the questions you ask the interviewer to support your image as a strong candidate for the position and lead the interviewer to recognize your most important skills.

You should be able to set goals when approaching the interview, with the primary goal of getting the job offer. Then prepare yourself fully by visualizing the kind of interview in which you achieve every goal and receive the recognition you deserve.

## Other Sources and Suggested Reading

*Can You Start Monday?* by Cheryl A. Cage, Scott Hareland, and Pam Ryan
   One of the best aspects of this book is the authors' emphasis on telling "stories" that characterize your skills during the interview.

*Creative Visualization* by Shakti Gawain
   This book focuses on tapping the power of the mind to energize growth and achievement. Regardless of your philosophical perspective, the techniques and exercises described here are useful and effective.

*Interview for Success: A Practical Guide to Increasing Job Interviews, Offers, and Salaries* by Caryl Rae Krannich and Ronald L. Krannich
   Preparation, etiquette, and effective listening are covered as well as negotiating salary.

*Job Interviews for Dummies* by Joyce Lain Kennedy
   Comparing the interview to a performance, Kennedy provides an upbeat take on interviewing successfully.

## Web Sites and Internet Resources

**www.cdm.uwaterloo.ca**
Again, the University of Waterloo's Career Development eManual is an excellent resource with information and guidelines for effective interviewing.

**www.links2work.on.ca**
This site is funded by the Government of Canada and offers links to useful Web sites on a variety of employment information including interviews and job offers, employers' perspectives, and job retention. It also includes a work sheet to be used for evaluating your job offers.

# Chapter 11
# Continuing the Adventure

## Your Lifelong Journey

*To be a Canadian is to be given the chance to benefit from this country's tremendous opportunities, to fulfill one's dreams... Some talent, hard work, motivation, a positive outlook on life and people, and a bit of luck are a magical combination.*

THE HONOURABLE CLAIRE L'HEUREUX-DUBÉ

Your career adventure has led you to many places but it is far from over. You have only begun to explore the surface of what your career will mean in your life. You will continue to grow and learn, going beyond the superficial aspects of work and success toward a deep understanding of what is meaningful and important to you.

Now is a good time to prepare for any obstacles and frustrations you may encounter. And you can be sure that there will be many, whatever path you choose to take. It is important to prepare yourself consciously for what might lie ahead.

## Transitioning to a New Occupation

Even once you have found employment, your career adventure is not over. The first few months in your new occupation will be a time of transition and change, filled with new learning, new demands, and new people. These changes can be overwhelming, so plan and prepare for them. Keep your life well rounded with focus not only on your new work but also on your health and spirit. Give yourself time for leisure, family, friends, and relaxation. To ensure your success in your new occupation, you will need to adapt to this new position and integrate it into your life.

The first few months at any new job are a time for feeling your way around and establishing your place, your role, and your professionalism. There are a few key pointers that, if applied, will help establish your professionalism and ease the transition to any new work environment. They are as follows.

## Ten Tips for Establishing Your Professionalism

1. Arrive on time to work and avoid bolting out the door at the day's end.

2. Stay focused on your task and don't distract your co-workers.

3. Accept change, suggestions, and feedback willingly and work hard at learning new things.

4. Avoid gossip and office politics.

5. Demonstrate that you can work without supervision.

6. Make sure your work is done on time and is complete.

7. Do not procrastinate. Plan your work and stick to your plan.

8. Work hard at communicating effectively with co-workers, supervisors, and clients.

9. Find out who the best workers are and learn from them.

10. Seek opportunities for growth. Commit to lifelong learning.

## Understanding Your Employer's Expectations

One of the tasks of new employment is to understand the employer's expectations. During the first few months, learn the policies, procedures, long-range objectives, and goals of the company or organization you are working for. Listen carefully, watch and observe, and when necessary, ask questions so that you can orient yourself to the new environment and learn what is expected of you. By having a clear understanding of what is expected, you will then be able to focus your energy on meeting those expectations rather than second-guessing and working toward faulty assumptions.

Although employers will each have their own expectations, there are some expectations that are common among most. As with almost every other aspect of our society, we have seen employers' expectations affected by the increasingly competitive global economy. Employees are now expected to become "partners" with their employers in learning how to do business better and how to respond to changes in the economy. For instance, more and more businesses are referring to their employees as "associates," and some are encouraging them to buy shares in the company and share in the profits. Undoubtedly, the expectation is that by doing this, employees will become more motivated, personally invested in their work, and, therefore, more productive. Employers are also increasingly hiring people on a contract basis. That is, rather than becoming employees of a company or organization, people are self-employed contractors hired to do a specific job for a specific amount of time. As we discussed in Chapters 3 and 4, the days of working for the same employer until retirement are disappearing.

These are just a few examples of the ways in which the global economy has influenced employers' expectations. However, given the changes in the world of work, we can infer some principles required for staying employed and taking charge of your career success. They are:

1. *Take initiative.* Self-starters will survive. You must constantly be on the lookout for new ways to apply your gifts and talents in the new economy.

This requires thinking creatively, actively promoting yourself and/or your services, and being actively involved in how your career progresses.

2.  *Be a contributor.* Demonstrate teamwork and work for the good of all. If your company is a winner, then you will be, too.

3.  *Seek new challenges.* Push yourself by taking on a new project or idea. Take responsibility for your career and what you accomplish each day.

4.  *Commit to lifelong learning.* Find opportunities to learn and grow. You must keep learning to keep earning.

5.  *Stay balanced.* Remember that work is just one aspect of your life. Be sure to pay attention to all facets of your life. Having an overall balanced life is what leads to fulfillment.

6.  *Develop resiliency.* Develop your ability to bounce back from setbacks, sudden changes, uncertainty, and the unexpected along your career adventure. You will likely experience many changes and transitions, so learn to be comfortable with this.

There are indications that most workers now accept responsibility for their own career and its success. They've internalized the reality of the workplace of the future and taken steps to secure their futures on their own. That usually translates to moving on when salary or opportunity no longer appeal. Companies are now trying to instill loyalty in their most valued employees through bonuses for longevity, profit sharing, and more autonomy in their positions. As our culture becomes more information focused, relying on the "brain power" of its workers, employees with the right skills will become the value centres of their organizations.

# Defining Career Success

As a whole, our society tends to define career success rather narrowly. If you have a job that provides you with regular promotions, salary increases, good fringe benefits, and greater and greater responsibility, then most would say you have been successful. Nevertheless, this narrow definition is changing. People are beginning to define career success much more loosely as they take on more innovative ways of working and incorporating their careers into their lives.

Careers are no longer straightforward choices. Making career decisions requires you to know what's ahead before you venture down a career path. Yet, predicting the future has always been a tricky endeavour. It can be frustrating or exciting, depending on how you approach the task.

The best way to plan for career success is to experience growth one step at a time. Use the research techniques you've learned. Actively seek the information you need to make a decision. Plan your steps to your goal. Have faith in your ability to handle the obstacles. And then work, work, work to make your goal a reality.

See the value in any work you do, regardless of the visibility or recognition associated with the job. Pay attention to the details of your work, and perform your job to the best of your abilities. You may have many more capabilities than the job gives you a chance to use; accept the fact that you will have to earn the right to move into a more rewarding position. Keep your mind and your eyes open, and eventually you will see a job that represents the next step in your career growth. It may be one that you've always wanted or it could be something brand new. Then plan for how you will get to that next step.

# Building Your Career: A Work in Progress

Building your career is always a work in progress, a lifetime adventure that must be taken step by step. This adventure may even involve some rough terrain, detours, and forks in the road. It is impossible for you to anticipate what you may encounter as your career progresses. It is almost as difficult to project the ways in which you will grow and change over the years. Locking yourself into a career path or goal that doesn't let you breathe and blossom could be a mistake. Give yourself room to grow, stay flexible, and move forward through the career that offers you what you need to have a happy and meaningful life.

Does this mean that you will automatically take any promotion offered? Or that your path will always be straight up—with no excursions on interesting side streets? Who knows? You will make those decisions when you get there. What you must do is stay in touch with the voice that guides you today, the one you have been in touch with throughout your career adventure. That inner voice will tell you which path is best when the time comes. If you are fortunate, you may find a career that offers you the opportunity to consistently challenge yourself, build your skills, and continually grow. This "flow," when everything seems to fit and fall in place, is the path to lasting career satisfaction.

Your career adventure began in this book with self-discovery and self-awareness. Self-discovery and awareness, along with evolution and learning, will continue to be a driving force in your career success. Your career is a work "in progress" that will mirror your growth and change, a vehicle to give you profound knowledge of yourself and the world. If you value your talents and the way you use them, your career will offer you satisfaction and meaning. Most important, you must pay attention to the brilliance that lies at your core and find a way to reveal that quality. This is part of the challenge of the career adventure. You are ready for the adventure to continue. If you are fortunate, it will never end!

# Appendix

# Sample Résumés and Cover Letters

## Chronological Résumé

# Yoko Sito

587 Sandalwood Road                                                (403) 567-2433
Calgary, AB  TIJ OH8                                              ysito@netzone.net

**PROFILE**          Experienced nursing professional; specialized training in an acute care setting

**EDUCATION**        Keyano College, Fort McMurray, AB
                     Bachelor of Science/Nursing
                     Graduated 2001

**EXPERIENCE**       Northern Lights Regional Health Service, Fort McMurray, AB
                     Med-Surg Nurse, June 2001 to present
                     Responsible for full range of patient care for five to seven patients; focus on
                     primary care

**CLINICAL**         Northern Lights Regional Health Service, Fort McMurray, AB
**EXPERIENCE**       Student Nurse, September 2000 to June 2001

**COMMUNITY**        South Central Free Clinic, Edmonton, AB
**EXPERIENCE**       Volunteered on weekends through special program in conjunction
                     with the University of Alberta
                     Provided nursing services through clinical training in variety of departments

**REFERENCES**       Available upon request

# Functional/Achievement Résumé

# Marc Luc

marcluc96@aol.com

2367 Golden Lane
Yellowknife, NT  X1A 3T3

(867) 473-5898

**CAREER PROFILE**

Strong analytical, financial, and interpersonal skills; acknowledged performer and team leader

**SUMMARY OF ACCOMPLISHMENTS**

*Analytical and Financial*

Proven analytical and financial skills as indicated by the following accomplishments:

- Researched and initiated the use of cost accounting software that increased assignment efficiency by approximately 35% over the prior year
- As treasurer of a social organization, undertook management and accounting of all financial transactions

*Interpersonal*

Exceptional interpersonal and communications skills:

- Organized and monitored a successful United Appeal Executive Prospector Program at Ernst & Young, which resulted in pledges in excess of $27 000 during the 2004 campaign
- Received highly favourable commendation based on client comments regarding work on a particular auditing assignment
- Demonstrated effective leadership qualities and organizational skills in management of small business

*Work Experience*

Ernst & Young, Internship, August 2004 to December 2004
Self-Employed Contractor, 1994 to 2003

*Education*

Diploma in Business Administration—Accounting
The Northern Alberta Institute of Technology (NAIT)

*Honours*

Dean's Honour List

## Chronological/Achievement Résumé

# Dal Johal

502 BIRCH STREET
VICTORIA, BC  V9A 3M4

(250) 457-9045
DALJ@HOTMAIL.COM

### SUMMARY

Recognized specialist in assessing and responding to customer needs; aggressive self-starter

### WORK EXPERIENCE

1998–2004    Policyholder Services Representative (PSR)
Metropolitan Life/Casualty Insurance Companies

Provided support to policyholders, sales representatives, and other interested parties primarily through telephone communications; furnished information and answered inquiries on billing, coverage, and rating criteria

*Major Achievement:*

Revised PSR response form to facilitate communication between customer and PSR, resulting in annual savings of approximately $560

### EDUCATION/TRAINING

2004–PRESENT    Camosun College, Victoria, BC

Currently completing General Insurance Salesperson/Adjuster Level 1 Licence

OTHER TRAINING:    Policyholder Services Representative Training, 1998
Customer Service Seminar, 2000

# Sample Cover Letter

2242 Springmill Road
Halifax, NS
B3H 3C3

September 23, 2004

Mr. Ben Jang
Mark-It Labelling Company
635 Courtney Road
Halifax, NS
B3L 1B1

Dear Mr. Jang:

Ted Rose, an associate of yours at Mark-It, suggested I contact you concerning the possible expansion of your design engineering department.

As a recent graduate of Nova Scotia Community College, I am currently exploring opportunities in which my training can be utilized most fully. My college diploma is in graphic design with emphasis on print and electronic media. In addition, my internship with Monarch Marking gave me an excellent chance to gain hands-on experience in this field.

My conversation with Ted confirmed my favourable impressions of your company. Mark-It's leadership in the areas of design and publishing has set a recognized standard for excellence. My ability to work hard and earn my place on a team has always been my strongest attribute. I am convinced I could become a valued member of your design team and would welcome the opportunity to discuss further how we might work together.

My résumé is enclosed for your consideration. I am available at your convenience for a personal interview and look forward to hearing from you.

Sincerely,

*Deon Neal*

Deon Neal

Enclosure

# Cover Letter, Parallel Format

34 Narrows Trace
St. John's, NF
A1G 1A3


March 17, 2005


Ms. Joy Wong
Advertising Fresh
59 Arundel Drive
St. John's, NF  A1V 7Y6

Subject: Account Representative (as posted in *The Globe and Mail*, March 16, 2005)

Dear Ms. Wong:

| YOUR REQUIREMENTS | MY BACKGROUND |
|---|---|
| ■ Strong communication skills | Communications Diploma |
| ■ Full-service client orientation | Sales account manager, North Atlantic Student Newspaper |
| ■ Detail-oriented, well-organized | Worked full-time while carrying full-time class load |
| ■ Good interpersonal skills | On good terms with all co-workers and clients |

As you can see from my enclosed résumé, my background is ideally suited for the account representative position you are seeking to fill. My current work setting is fast-paced and deadline oriented. It requires the skills of a juggler with the nerves and balance of a high-wire artist. I've been "walking the wire" for two years now and have loved every minute of it!

I'm ready to raise the wire to a new level. I believe I have the combination of dedication and aggressive creativity your organization seeks. I've enclosed my résumé for your consideration and look forward to hearing from you. Please don't hesitate to call if you have any questions.

Sincerely,

*Jean McKenzie*

Jean McKenzie


Enclosure

# References

## Chapter 1

Goleman, Daniel. 1997. *Emotional Intelligence*. New York: Bantam.

## Chapter 2

Bengis, Ingrid. 1993. Sunbeams. *The Sun*, April. Chapel Hill, NC.

Bolles, Richard Nelson. 2001. *What Color Is Your Parachute?* 2001 edition. Berkeley, CA: Ten Speed Press.

Brown, D., and L. Brooks. 1991. *Career Counseling Techniques*. Boston: Allyn & Bacon.

Combs, Patrick. 2000. *Major in Success: Make College Easier, Fire Up Your Dreams, and Get a Very Cool Job*. Berkeley, CA: Ten Speed Press.

*Dictionary of Occupational Titles*. 1991. Washington, DC.: U.S. Department of Labor.

Gordon, L. V. 1975. *The Measurement of Interpersonal Values*. Chicago: Science Research Associates.

Hall, Brian P. 1976. *The Development of Consciousness: A Confluent Theory of Values*. New York: Paulist Press.

Hart, Gordon M. 1978. *Values Clarification for Counselors*. Springfield, IL: Charles C. Thomas.

Maslow, Abraham. 1954. *Motivation and Personality*. New York: Harper & Row.

Maslow, Abraham. 1968. *Toward a Psychology of Being*. New York: Van Nostrand Reinhold.

McNeil, Elton B., and Zick Rubin. 1977. *The Psychology of Being Human*. New York: Harper & Row.

McWilliams, John-Roger, and Peter McWilliams. 1991. *Do It!* Los Angeles: Prelude Press.

Rokeach, M. 1973. *The Nature of Human Values*. New York: The Free Press.

Rokeach, M. 1979. *Understanding Human Values: Individual and Societal*. New York: The Free Press.

Ryckman, Richard M. 1978. *Theories of Personality*. New York: Van Nostrand Reinhold.

Sher, Barbara. 1996. *Live the Life You Love*. New York: Delacorte Press.

Zunker, Vernon G. 1986. *Using Assessment Results in Career Counseling*. Monterey, CA: Brooks/Cole.

## Chapter 3

Black, Sandra, and Lisa M. Lynch. 1996. *How to Compete: The Impact of Workplace Practices and Information Technology on Productivity*. Washington, DC: U.S. Department of Labor.

Bridges. 2004. *Choices*. Accessed September 29, 2004 at **www.bridges.com/canada/index.htm**.

Briggs, Isabel Myers. 1998. *Introduction to Type*. 6th ed. Palo Alto, CA: Consulting Psychologists Press, Inc.

Brown, Duane, and Linda Brooks. 1991. *Career Counseling Techniques*. Boston: Allyn & Bacon.

Career Cruising™. 2004. Accessed September 29, 2004 at **www.careercruising.com**.

Drapela, Victor J. 1987. *A Review of Personality Theories*. Springfield, IL: Charles C. Thomas.

Elksnin, L. K., and N. Elksnin. 2003. Fostering social-emotional learning in the classroom. *Education* 124 (1): 12+. Retrieved April 5, 2003 from Academic Search Premier Database.

Holland, John L. 1973. *Making Vocational Choices: A Theory of Careers*. Upper Saddle River, NJ: Prentice Hall.

Human Resources and Skills Development Canada. 2003. *Essential Skills and Workplace Literacy Initiative*. Accessed September 29, 2004 at **www15.hrdc-drhc.gc.ca**.

Jeffries, William C. 1991. *True to Type*. Norfolk, VA: Hampton Roads Publishing.

Jung, C. G. 1971. *Psychological Types*. Princeton, NJ: Princeton University Press.

Keirsey, David, and Marilyn Bates. 1984. *Please Understand Me*. Del Mar, CA: Prometheus.

Kroeger, Otto, with Janet M. Thuesen. 1988. *Type Talk*. New York: Dell Publishing.

Kroeger, Otto, with Janet M. Thuesen. 1992. *Type Talk at Work*. New York: Delacorte Press.

*Learning a Living: A Blueprint for High Performance. A SCANS Report for America 2000, Part I*. 1992. Washington, DC: U. S. Department of Labor.

Levy, Frank, and Richard J. Murnane. 1996. *Teaching the New Basic Skills: Principles for Educating Children to Thrive in a Changing Economy*. New York: The Free Press.

McIntosh, P. I. 2000. Life Career Development: Implications for School Counselors. *Education* 120 (4): 621–626. Retrieved March 31, 2004 from MasterFile Premier.

Maze, Marilyn, and Donald Mayall, with Michael J. Farr. 1991. *The Enhanced Guide for Occupational Exploration*. Indianapolis: JIST Works.

Moore, Roberta, Barbara A. Baker, and Arnold Packer. 1996. *College Success*. Upper Saddle River, NJ: Prentice Hall.

Sharp, Daryl. 1987. *Personality Types: Jung's Model of Typology*. Toronto: Inner City Books.

Slaski, M., and S. Cartwright. 2003. Emotional Intelligence Training and Its Implications for Stress, Health and Performance. *Stress and Health* 19: 233–239. Retrieved April 5, 2003 from Academic Search Premier Database.

Stewart, J. 1994. Counselling Individuals Who Experience Career Decision-Making Difficulties. *Guidance and Counselling* 9 (4): 11+. Retrieved March 31, 2004 from MasterFile Premier Database.

Tieger, Paul D., and Barbara Barron-Tieger. 1995. *Do What You Are: Discover the Perfect Career for You Through the Secrets of Personality Type*. New York: Little, Brown & Co.

# Chapter 4

Berkman, Robert. 2000. Internet Searching Is Not Always What It Seems. *The Chronicle of Higher Education*, July 28.

Calvert, Robert, Jr., Editor. 2000. Ready for Work in 2025? What to Anticipate. *Career Opportunities News*, October.

Coates, Joseph F., Jennifer Jarrett, and John B. Mahaffie. 1990. *Future Work*. San Francisco: Jossey-Bass.

Cosgrove, Holli R., Editor-In-Chief. 2000. *Encyclopedia of Careers and Vocational Guidance*. 11th ed. Chicago, IL: Ferguson Publishing.

*Dictionary of Occupational Titles*. 4th ed. 1991. Washington, DC: U.S. Department of Labor.

Dohm, Arlene. 2000. Gauging the Labor Force Effects of Retiring Baby-Boomers. *Monthly Labor Review*, July.

Feather, F. 1997. *Canada's Best Careers Guide*. Toronto, ON: Warwick Publishing.

Field, Shelly. 2000. *100 Best Careers for the 21st Century*. New York: Arco Publishing.

Fisher, Helen S. 1999. *American Salaries and Wages Survey*. 5th ed. Detroit, MI: The Gale Group.

Fleetwood, Chad, and Kristina Shelley. 2000. The Outlook for College Graduates, 1998–2008: A Balancing Act. *Occupational Outlook Quarterly*, Fall.

Futurework: Trends and Challenges for Work in the 21st Century. 2000. *Occupational Outlook Quarterly*, Summer.

Giangrande, Gregory. 1998. *Liberal Arts Advantage: How to Turn Your Degree Into a Great Job*. New York: Avon Books.

Hafner, Katie, and Michael Meyer. 1997. Help Really Wanted. *Newsweek*, December 8.

Human Resources and Skills Development Canada. 2004. *Job Futures Canada*. Ottawa: Minister of Public Works and Government Services Canada. Accessed September 29, 2004 at **www.emploiavenir.ca/en/home/shtml**.

Human Resources and Skills Development Canada. 2001. *National Occupational Classification*. Ottawa: Minister of Public Works and Government Services Canada. Accessed September 24 at **www23.hrdc-drhc.gc.ca**.

Kennedy, Shirley Duglin. 1998. *Best Bet Internet: Reference and Research When You Don't Have Time to Mess Around*. Chicago: American Library Association.

Kleiman, Carol. 1997. Employers Make Office A Great Place. *The Chicago Tribune*, September 21.

Korry, Elaine. 1997. Regaining Employee Loyalty. National Public Radio, December 11.

Kunde, Diana. 1997. Job Sharing Gives Clients, Employers Double Benefits. *Dallas Morning News*, September 21.

Lenox, Richard A., and Linda Mezydio Subich. 1994. The Relationship Between Self-Efficacy Beliefs and Inventoried Vocational Interests. *The Career Development Quarterly*, June.

Lewis, Diane E. 1997. Unwritten Pact Gets '90s Rewrite. *Boston Globe*, September 21.

Lieta, Carole. 1999. Evaluating Internet Resources: A Checklist. InFoPeople Project, Institute of Museum and Library Services. Accessed 1999 at **www.infopeople.org**.

Luzzo, Darrell Anthony, Dylan P. Funk, and Jason Strang. 1996. Attributional Retraining Increases Career Decision-Making Self-Efficacy. *The Career Development Quarterly*, June.

Maze, Marilyn, and Donald Mayall, with Michael J. Farr. 1995. *The Enhanced Guide for Occupational Exploration*. 2nd ed. Indianapolis: JIST Works.

Naisbitt, John. 1994. *Global Paradox*. New York: Morrow.

Naisbitt, John, and Patricia Aburdene. 1990. *Megatrends 2000: Ten New Directions for the 1990s*. New York: Morrow.

*Occupational Outlook Handbook*. 2000–2001 Edition. Washington, DC: U.S. Department of Labor.

O'Reilly, Elaine. 2001. *Making Career Sense of Labour Market Information*. 3rd ed. Accessed October 22, 2004 at **www.makingcareersense.org**.

*Peterson's 2001 Internships*. 21st ed. 2000. Princeton, NJ: Peterson.

Pottruck, David S., and Terry Pearce. 2000. *Clicks and Mortar: Passion Driven Growth in an Internet Driven World*. San Francisco: Jossey-Bass.

Rayman, Jack R. 1990. Computers and Career Counseling. In *Career Counseling: Contemporary Topics in Vocational Psychology*, edited by W. Bruce Walsh and Samuel Osipow. Hillsdale, NJ: Lawrence Erlbaum Associates.

Resnick, R. Linda, with Kerry H. Pechter. 1994. *A Big Splash In A Small Pond: Finding A Great Job In A Small Company*. New York: Fireside.

Samuelson, Robert J. 1992. The Value of College. *Newsweek*, August 31.

Thurow, Lester C. 1996. *The Future of Capitalism: How Today's Economic Forces Shape Tomorrow's World*. New York: Morrow.

Weise, Elizabeth. 2000. One Click Starts the Avalanche. *USA Today*, August 8.

Winefordner, David W. 1978. *Worker Trait Group Guide*. Charleston, WV: Appalachia Educational Laboratory.

Wright, John W. 2000. *The American Almanac of Jobs and Salaries*. New York: Avon Books.

# Chapter 5

Azrin, Nathan H., and Victoria A. Besalel. 1980. *Job Club Counselor's Manual*. Austin, TX: PRO-ED.

Bolles, Richard Nelson. 2001. *What Color Is Your Parachute?* 2001 Edition. Berkeley, CA: Ten Speed Press.

Dun & Bradstreet of Canada. 2004. *Canadian Key Business Directory*. Toronto, ON: Dun & Bradstreet of Canada.

Hansen, Katharine. 2000. *A Foot in the Door: Networking Your Way into the Hidden Job Market*. Berkeley, CA: Ten Speed Press.

Mandell, Terri. 1996. *Power Schmoozing: The New Etiquette for Social and Business Success*. New York: McGraw-Hill.

Stoodley, Martha. 1997. *Information Interviewing: How to Tap Your Hidden Job Market*. 2nd ed. Garrett Park, MD: Garrett Park Press.

Student Employment Network. 2004. *Canada Student Employment Guide*. Toronto, ON: Student Employment Network.

Yerema, R. W., and K. Chow. 2004. *The Career Directory*. Toronto, ON: Encore Pub. Corp.

# Chapter 6

Exploring. 1993. Boy Scouts of America. Brochure #34627.

Green, Marianne Ehrlich. 1998. *Internship Success.* Lincolnwood, IL: VGM Career Horizons.

Guidance Centre, University of Toronto. 2001. *Spectrum Publication Series: Ontario Spectrum, Eastern Spectrum, and Western Spectrum.* Toronto, ON: Guidance Centre, University of Toronto.

Nothdurft, William E. 1989. *SchoolWorks.* Washington, DC: The Brookings Institution.

*Peterson's 2000 Internships.* 21st ed. 2000. Princeton, NJ: Peterson.

Sweitzer, H. Frederick, and Mary A. King. 1998. *The Successful Internship: Transformation and Empowerment.* Pacific Grove, CA: Brooks/Cole Publishing.

# Chapter 7

Arnold, John D. 1978. *Make Up Your Mind!* New York: AMA-COM.

Barinov, Zelma. 1998. *How to Make Instant Decisions and Remain Happy & Sane.* Bala Cynwyd, PA: Access Press.

Carroll, John S., and Eric J. Johnson. 1990. *Decision Research.* Newbury Park, CA: Sage.

Dawson, Roger. 1995. *The Confident Decision Maker: How To Make the Right Business and Personal Decisions Every Time.* New York: William Morrow/Quill.

Dickerman, Alexandra Collins. 1992. *Following Your Path.* Los Angeles: Jeremy P. Tarcher.

Goza, Barbara K. 1993. Graffiti Needs Assessment. *Journal of Management Education* 17, no. 1, February: 99–106.

Hammond, John S., Ralph L. Keeney, and Howard Raiffa. 1998. *Smart Choices: A Practical Guide to Making Better Decisions.* Cambridge, MA: Harvard Business School Press.

Harris, Mark. 1956. *Bang the Drum Slowly.* Lincoln: University of Nebraska Press.

Kanchier, Carole. 1997. Using Intuition For Career Decision Making. *Counseling Today* 39, no. 8, February: 14–16.

Kaye, Harvey. 1992. *Decision Power.* Englewood Cliffs, NJ: Prentice Hall.

Lenox, Richard A., and Linda Mezydio Subich. 1994. The Relationship Between Self-Efficacy Beliefs and Inventoried Vocational Interests. *The Career Development Quarterly* 42, no. 4: 302–313.

Luzzo, Darrell Anthony, Dylan P. Funk, and Jason Strang. 1996. Attributional Retraining Increases Career Decision-Making Self-Efficacy. *The Career Development Quarterly* 44, no. 4, June: 378–386.

Martino, R. L., and Elinor Svendson Stein. 1969. *Decision Patterns.* Wayne, PA: MDI Publications.

McKowen, Clark. 1986. *Thinking About Thinking.* Los Altos, CA: William Kaufmann.

Miller-Tiedeman, Anna. 1988. *Lifecareer: The Quantum Leap into a Process Theory of Career.* Vista, CA: LIFECAREER Foundation.

# Chapter 8

Azrin, Nathan, and Victoria A. Besalel. 1980. *Job Club Counselor's Manual.* Austin, TX: PRO-ED.

Bolles, Richard Nelson. 2001. *What Color Is Your Parachute?* 2001 edition. Berkeley, CA: Ten Speed Press.

Branscum, Deborah. 1997. Life at High-Tech U. *Newsweek,* October 27.

Calvert, Robert, Jr. 1997. Why Pay for Something That's Free? *Career Opportunities News,* October. Chicago: Ferguson Publishing.

Campbell, Colin. 1997. *Where the Jobs Are: Career Survival for Canadians in the New Global Economy.* Toronto, ON: Macfarlane Walter & Ross.

Carmichael, Margot Lester, Michael Verne, and Nicky Rousseau. 1998. *Real Life Guide to Life After College: How to Hit the Ground Running After Graduation.* Chapel Hill, NC: Pipeline Press.

Consumer Reports Editors. 1997. That's Entertainment: WebTV. *Consumer Reports,* November.

Coxford, Lola M. 1995. *Resume Writing Made Easy.* Upper Saddle River, NJ: Prentice Hall.

Ehrenstein, Emily E. 2000. *The Adams Electronic Job Search Almanac 2001.* Boston: Adams Publishing.

Figler, Howard E. 1999. *The Complete Job-Search Handbook: All the Skills You Need to Get Any Job and Have a Good Time Doing It.* 3rd ed. New York: Henry Holt.

Gonyea, James C. 1995. *The On-Line Job Search Companion.* New York: McGraw-Hill.

Iwata, Edward. 1994. 1994 Job Hunters, Take Heart with Tips. Santa Ana, CA: *Orange County Register.*

*Job Hunter's Sourcebook.* 1991. Detroit: Gale Research.

*Job Seeker's Guide to Private and Public Companies.* 1992. Detroit: Gale Research.

Kennedy, Joyce Lain, and Thomas J. Morrow. 1994. *Electronic Job Search Revolution.* New York: John Wiley & Sons, Inc.

Kennedy, Joyce Lain, and Thomas J. Morrow. 1995. *Hook Up, Get Hired! The Internet Job Search Revolution.* New York: John Wiley & Sons Inc.

Kramer, Marc. 1997. *Power Networking: Using the Contacts You Don't Even Know You Have to Succeed in the Job You Want.* Lincolnwood, IL: VGM Career Horizons.

Krueger, Brian D. 1998. *College Grad Job Hunter: Insider Techniques and Tactics for Finding a Top-Paying Entry Level Job.* 4th ed. Milwaukee: Quantum Leap Publishing.

Makra, Kevin. 2004. *The Canadian Internet Job Search Guide: An Essential Guide to Finding a Job Using the Internet.* Toronto, ON: Sentor Media.

Moock, R. Theodore, Jr. 1996. *Get That Interview! The Indispensable Guide for College Grads.* New York: Barrons.

Mossberg, Walter S. 1997. Computers Are Still Too Complicated, But Changes Are Coming. *Wall Street Journal,* October 23.

Nemnich, Mary B., and Fred E. Jandt. 2000. *Cyberspace Job Search Kit.* 3rd ed. Indianapolis, IN: JIST Works.

Riley, Margaret, Frances Roehm, and Steve Oserman. 1996. *The Guide to Internet Job Searching.* Lincolnwood, IL: VGM Career Horizons.

Ringo, Tad and Editors. 1996. *World Wide Web Top 1000.* Indianapolis, IN: New Riders Publishing.

Student Employment Network. 2004. *Canada Student*

*Employment Guide: The Definitive Tool for a Successful Job Search in Canada.* Toronto, ON: Student Employment Network.

## Chapter 9

Besson, Taunee. 1999. *National Business Employment Weekly Cover Letters.* 3rd ed. New York: John Wiley & Sons, Inc.

Bolles, Richard Nelson. 2001. *What Color Is Your Parachute?* 2001 edition. Berkeley, CA: Ten Speed Press.

Jackson, Tom. 1996. *The New Perfect Resume.* New York: Doubleday/Main Street Books.

Kennedy, Joyce Lain, and Thomas J. Morrow. 1994. *Electronic Job Search Revolution.* New York: John Wiley & Sons, Inc.

Krannich, Ronald L., et al. 1999. *Dynamite Cover Letters: And Other Great Job Search Letters.* 4th ed. Woodbridge, VA: Impact Publications.

Krannich, Ronald L., and Caryl Rae Krannich. 1999. *Dynamite Resumes: 101 Great Examples and Tips for Success.* 4th ed. Woodbridge, VA: Impact Publications.

Levine, Donald, and Blythe Cozza. 1996. *Resume Magic: Master Resume Writer's Secrets Revealed.* Westbury, New York: Sharp Placement Professionals, Inc. Accessed 1996 at **www.liglobal.com/b_c/ career/res.shtml**.

Moniz-Lecce, S. 1998. *EmployAbility: Job Search Strategies for Students with Disabilities, a Facilitator's Manual.* Surrey, BC: Kwantlen University College.

Neal, James E. 1998. *Effective Phrases for Performance Appraisals.* 8th ed. Perrysburg, OH: Neal Publications.

Parker, Yana. 1996. *The Damn Good Resume Guide: A Crash Course In Resume Writing.* 3rd ed. Berkeley, CA: Ten Speed Press.

Resumail Network. 1996. *Resumail: Real People, Real Jobs, Real Fast.* (Software.) Irving, TX: Resumail Network.

Smith, Rebecca. 2000. *Electronic Resumes & Online Networking.* Hawthorne, NJ: Career Press.

Stromp, Steve. 1997. E-mail Resumes Require Special Format, Content. *The Dayton Daily News,* March 16.

## Chapter 10

*Adams Job Interview Almanac & CD-ROM.* 1997. Boston: Adams Publishing.

Bolles, Richard Nelson. 1994. *What Color Is Your Parachute?* 1994 edition. Berkeley, CA: Ten Speed Press.

Cage, Cheryl A., Scott Hareland, and Pam Ryan. 1998. *Can You Start Monday? A 9-Step Job Search Guide.* Englewood, CO: Cage Consulting.

Calvert, Robert, Jr. 1997. Video Interviews Coming, So Get Ready For Them. *Career Opportunities News,* September. Chicago: Ferguson Publishing.

Gawain, Shakti. 1995. *Creative Visualization.* Mill Valley, CA: Whatever Publishing.

Jackson, Tom. 1978. *Guerrilla Tactics in the Job Market.* New York: Bantam.

Kennedy, Joyce Lain. 2000. *Job Interviews for Dummies.* 2nd ed. Foster City, CA: IDG Books Worldwide.

Krannich, Caryl Rae, and Ronald L. Krannich. 1998. *Interview for Success: A Practical Guide to Increasing Job Interviews, Offers, and Salaries.* 7th ed. Manassas Park, VA: Impact Publications.

Levenson, Lisa. 1995. High-Tech Job Searching. *The Chronicle of Higher Education,* July 14.

Madigan, Charles M. 1990. Attitudes of Bosses Hold America Back, Study of Work Finds. *Chicago Tribune,* July 15.

Questioning Applicants for Employment. 1985. Brochure, June. Columbus, OH: Ohio Civil Rights Commission.

Simmons, B. 2003. Wisdom for the new kid on the block. *The Toronto Star.* Retrieved August 27, 2004 from **www.workopolis.com/servlet/content/toronto star/20030521/newkid?section=TORSTAR**.

Stucker, Hal. 2000. Rethinking the Interview. *Impress.*

*Thomas Register of American Manufacturers: 2000.* 2000. New York: Thomas Publishing Company.

Career Services, University of Waterloo. 2002. *Career development e-manual.* Retrieved August 27, 2004 from **www.cdm.uwaterloo.ca/step_5_2.asp**.

Zielinski, Jennifer, Editor. 2000. *Dun and Bradstreet and Gale Industry Handbook.* Detroit, MI: The Gale Group.

## Chapter 11

Career Services, University of Waterloo. 2002. *Career development e-manual.* Retrieved August 27, 2004 from **www.cdm.uwaterloo.ca/step_5_2.asp**.

Csikszentmihalyi, Mihaly. 1990. *Flow: The Psychology of Optimal Experience.* New York: Harper & Row.

Hafner, Katie, and Michael Meyer. 1997. Help Really Wanted. *Newsweek,* December 8.

Holmstrom, David. 1993. The Voice of a Writer 'In Process' *The Christian Science Monitor,* October 20.

Kingsley, Charles. 1994. Sunbeams. *The Sun,* February. Chapel Hill, NC.

Kleiman, Carol. 1994. College Grads Get a Dose of Reality. *The Chicago Tribune,* January 24.

Kleiman, Carol. 1994. New Rules Key to Survival in the Workplace. *The Chicago Tribune,* March 21.

Korry, Elaine. 1997. Regaining Employee Loyalty. National Public Radio, December 11.

Romac & Associates. Undated. Survey: Employers Versus Employees: What the Other Half Thinks. Romac & Associates. Index.

Simmons, B. 2003. Wisdom for the new kid on the block. *The Toronto Star.* Retrieved August 27, 2004 from **www.workopolis.com/servlet/Content/torontosta r/20030521/newkid?section=TORSTAR**.

# Index